Living a Moral Life
Gifted and Growing

Second Edition

Louise Marie Prochaska, S.N.D.

General Editor: Loretta Pastva, S.N.D.

Your light must shine before others, that they may see your good deeds and glorify your heavenly Father.
—Matthew 5:16

Benziger Publishing Company
Mission Hills, California

Consultant
The Reverend Ronald A. Pachence, Ph.D.
Associate Professor Practical Theology
Director, Institute for Christian
Ministries, University of San Diego.

Nihil Obstat
The Reverend Paul J. Sciarrotta, S.T.L.
Censor Deputatus

Imprimatur
The Most Reverend Anthony M. Pilla, D.D., M.A.
Bishop of Cleveland
Given at Cleveland, Ohio, on 3 February 1991

The nihil obstat and imprimatur are official declarations that a book or pamphlet is free of doctrinal or moral error. No implication is contained therein that those who have granted the nihil obstat and imprimatur agree with the contents, opinions, or statements expressed.

Scripture passages are taken from *The New American Bible with Revised New Testament,* copyright © 1988 by the Confraternity of Christian Doctrine, Washington, D.C. All rights reserved.

Excerpts from *Vatican Council II, The Conciliar and Post Conciliar Documents,* Austin Flannery, O.P., ed., reprinted with permission of Costello Publishing Co., Inc., Northport, NY 11768.

Revision Editor
Joseph Thometz, MA

Send all inquiries to:
BENZIGER PUBLISHING COMPANY
15319 Chatsworth Street
P.O. Box 9609
Mission Hills, California 91346-9609

Second Edition

ISBN 0-02-655824-6 (Student's Edition)
ISBN 0-02-655825-4 (Teacher's Annotated Edition)

Printed in the United States of America.

3 4 5 6 7 8 9   99 98 97 96 95 94

Cover Art: *St. Joseph and Jesus in the Carpenter's Shop* by
   Georges de la Tour, (from the Lourve):
   Scala/Art Resource, N.Y.

Contents

Acknowledgments

The authors wish to thank Sister Mary Joell Overman, S.N.D., Superior General, Rome; Sister Rita Mary Harwood, S.N.D., Provincial Superior of the Sisters of Notre Dame, Chardon, Ohio; and Sister Margaret Mary McGovern, S.N.D., Assistant Superintendent, Education, Diocese of Cleveland, Eastern Region, who supported and encouraged the writing of the *Light of the World* series.

Humble gratitude is also due to all who in any way helped to create the *Light of the World* series: parents, teachers, co-workers, students, and friends. The following deserve special mention for their assistance in planning, organizing, testing, or critiquing the series: Notre Dame Sisters Mary Dolores Abood, Ann Baron, Karla Bognar, Mary Brady, Mary Catherine Caine, Virginia Marie Callen, Deborah Carlin, Naomi Cervenka, Reean Coyne, Mary Dowling, Patricia Mary Ferrara, Dorothy Fuchs, Kathleen Glavich, Margaret Mary Gorman, Jacquelyn Gusdane, Margaret Harig, Joanmarie Harks, Nathan Hess, Sally Huston, Christa Jacobs, Joanne Kepler, Owen Kleinhenz, Mary Jean Korejwo, Elizabeth Marie Kreager, Leanne Laney, William David Latiano, Aimee Levy, Ann McFadden, Inez McHugh, Louismarie Nudo, Donna Marie Paluf, Helen Mary Peter, Nancy Powell, Eileen Marie Quinlan, Patricia Rickard, Mark Daniel Roscoe, Kathleen Ruddy, Kathleen Scully, Dolores Stanko, Melannie Svoboda, Mary Louise Trivison, Donna Marie Wilhelm, Laura Wingert; Dr. Jean Alvarez, Ms. Mary Anderson; Ms. Meg Bracken; Sister Mary Kay Cmolik, O.F.M.; Mr. Robert Dilonardo, Rev. Mark DiNardo, Ms. Linda Ferrando, Mr. Michael Homza, Sister Kathleen King, H.H.M., Ms. Patricia Lange, Mr. James Marmion, Mr. Peter Meler, Rev. Herman P. Moman, Rev. Guy Noonan, T.O.R., Ms. Christine Smetana, and Ms. Karen Sorace.

The following high schools piloted materials: Bishop Ireton High School, Alexandria, Virginia; Clearwater Central Catholic High School, Clearwater, Florida; Elyria Catholic High School, Elyria, Ohio; Erieview Catholic High School, Cleveland, Ohio; John F. Kennedy High School, Warren, Ohio; Notre Dame Cathedral Latin High School, Chardon, Ohio; Regina High School, South Euclid, Ohio; St. Edward High School, Cleveland, Ohio; St. Matthias High School, Huntington Park, California.

The following parishes piloted the original Abridged Lessons: Corpus Christi, Cleveland, Ohio; St. Anselm, Chesterland, Ohio; St. John Nepomucene, Cleveland, Ohio; St. Thomas More, Paducah, Kentucky.

Special appreciation and thanks to Sister M. Dolores Stanko, S.N.D., for typing the final manuscripts of the series as well as for her many helpful suggestions and her insightful editorial assistance.

Deep appreciation to Mrs. Anita Johnson for research; to Sisters of Notre Dame Mary Regien Kingsbury, De Xavier Perusek, and Seton Schlather; to Robert Clair Smith for special services; and to typists Sisters Catherine Rennecker, S.N.D., Josetta Marie Livignano, S.N.D., and Ms. Charlaine Yomant.

Uniquely Gifted

Consider some of the gifts you have received from God—your parents, your friends, food, the earth, the power to think, dream and love. Which would you consider the greatest gift you have received? Without doubt, the greatest gift would be your own individual life and personality.

God's love is poured out in all creation, but it reaches its highest peak in each human person. Being the kind of creature you are—a human person—is a unique gift. It means, first of all, that regardless of how beautiful or awesome other creatures may be, humans alone are made in God's image. Without our lifting a finger, without our doing one single thing, this gift makes us of more value and dignity than a million stars. It also means that we alone of all creation possess the special gift of consciously knowing what our gifts are. This endows us with the unique capability of developing our gifts—or denying them—in response to God's love.

The ability to determine the kind of person you will be and the kind of actions you will do to make it possible for all people to grow into their best selves is a **response-ability.** The trouble is that sometimes responsibility is hard to accept. Yet everything depends on your response—the kind of person you will ultimately become, whether you will be happy or miserable, as well as the kind of world in which you will live.

Morality has to do with this unique response-ability of yours. It asks, "What does it mean to be human?" It draws up guidelines gleaned from your own human experience about what it means to be the kind of person you ought to be and the kind of actions you ought to do in order to develop your best self and to allow others to fulfill their potential.

But we all know that it isn't always easy to respond appropriately. We run into a thousand difficulties, and we sin. Yet, as God told Cain, "Sin is a demon lurking at the door, yet you can be his master" (Genesis 4:7).

Self Worth from a Higher Power

The situation of a girl named Lori illustrates the power of self-determination.

When she was six, Lori liked it when her father called her his little girl and let her sip his beer. But when she grew older, she realized that her father was an alcoholic. She worried what others thought of him and her. In school she felt lonely and scared, ashamed to bring friends to her home. Around the seventh grade, she began to sneak her father's beer. Then she tried his liquor. Soon she found that when she was drunk, all her troubles vanished—only to return after the hangover. By her freshman year, she was an alcoholic herself.

At her mother's urging, Lori reluctantly attended her first Alcoholics Anonymous meeting. However, it wasn't until her drinking resulted in a traffic accident that she seriously decided to do something about her life.

"I drink because it makes me look cool." What it really makes these teens look like is drunk!

In AA she was warmly supported by understanding and accepting friends, but it was only through prayer that she came gradually to accept herself as loved by God. She had to find out the hard way that God had believed in her all along, even when she was on a downslide. All she had to do was to respond to that love.

Lori is still not perfect, but now she's doing well in school, meeting new friends, and on her way to a healthy, wholesome life. Above all, she says, "I'm happy and I like myself." (*Young, Sober and Free* by Shelly Marshall, © 1983 by Hazelden Foundation, Center City, MN. Reprinted by permission.)

---

1. *Choose one or two sentences from Lori's story and write a short letter telling her what touched you in her story.*

2. *Central to the A.A. process is the act of giving yourself over to a Higher Power. When you have felt helpless and alone whom did you turn to for help? Why that person?*

Recognizing God's Gift

Often you cannot help how you feel about yourself and you don't always know why you may feel the way you do. But you can control what you know and believe about yourself. You can decide to trust, as Lori did, that God is in charge and has a plan for your life. Lori came to know, to understand, and to feel like a good person by trusting. Trust in God can help you recognize the clues to understand God's special plan for you. These clues are the unique gifts placed within you by the Creator. They hint at the mission you were created to fulfill. No matter what that mission may be, it always involves the growth of your own personal happiness and a call to leave the world a little better than you found it.

Talented and Gifted

Many people assume that only talented people are gifted, but that isn't true if you distinguish between talents and gifts. A talent is any power to make or to do something useful or

Making A Moral World

Take a few moments to think about the people who have been most influential in your life. You may want to list them in order of priority.

The fact is that no one is an island, as the poet John Donne wrote. All people belong to one another. We are born social beings. You are the person you are today largely because of the people in your life. You were shaped by them, not so much by their words, as by their actions—which, as everyone knows, speak louder than words. The people you admire and would like to imitate accepted their gifts and used them for others besides themselves. Imagine how different your life would be if your favorite persons had not exercised their gifts out of love for you. They regarded their talents as an invitation to serve you. Simply put, they loved you into becoming your best self by being their best selves. To grow into the kind of person who influences others for the better and makes the world a fitter place for everyone to live in, you only need to accept the invitation as they did.

beautiful. This may mean the ability to make a salad or to wash a car, to compose music or to design a building. Talents need to be developed through training and effort. Yet, talents in themselves do not make a person unique. The value of a person should not be dependent solely upon these talents. Rather, talents can complement the gifts which make a person unique.

A gift is a God-given capacity or grace (from the Greek "charis" meaning gift) you carry in yourself to help others. It is not given to you for yourself, but for the building up of the community of love. Gifts need no development or training, yet they enable you to fulfill your particular mission during your lifetime. All that is needed to put your gifts to good use is acceptance of what God has given you.

Often, your gifts will require the development of your talents to fulfill your mission. As one who might be blessed with the gift of teaching, you might want to enact this power by developing your writing and speaking talents, or by learning a second language. Your gifts can only be fully realized in the development of your personal talents. This is what is meant by becoming your true self.

In trying to distinguish between talents and gifts, the following comparisons will be helpful.

Talents	Gifts
Produce visible, material results.	Produce peace, love, and joy in others.
Enable us to make money.	Enable us to love others and be loved.
Give us joy first.	Give others joy first.
Need development, training, effort.	Need no development or training.
Use up energy and can cause fatigue.	Increase energy and give us a feeling of being alive.
Can be replaced by machines or other persons with the same talent.	Need no physical or mental power. Cannot be replaced.
Can be mistaken for a person's sole value in society.	Make a person unique and irreplaceable.

When you appreciate your talents, you can accomplish great things. But it all begins with recognizing your giftedness.

New Testament Gifts

Here are some gifts mentioned in the New Testament: preaching, teaching, encouraging, helping, hospitality, governing, showing mercy, exhibiting faith, healing, loving (1 Corinthians 12). These gifts are still with us today. They take the more familiar forms of caring for the elderly, easing fears, using humor in tense situations, showing respect, being patient, and having wisdom.

Personal fulfillment and the betterment of the world depend on your use of God's gifts. By realizing and utilizing the gifts within yourself, you enact the will of God on earth. Saint Paul explains that your gifts are necessary for the growth of Christ's Body, the Church. Consider his thoughts and how they apply to your own life.

Healing is a gift mentioned in the New Testament which is still practiced today.

---

3. *Read 1 Corinthians 12 to discover additional gifts of the Holy Spirit and the comparison Paul uses to show how necessary each person is in society.*

4. *Read 1 Corinthians 13 and look for the qualities of the most important gift.*

5. *Name five persons you know well; next to each name write one talent and one gift you recognize in that person.*

Discovering Your Gifts

Below are listed a few tips to help you discover your unique gifts. Read and apply them to your own life. Then write down the gifts you possess. Perhaps you will find that you have gifts you didn't know you had!

1. Recall times when you felt most relaxed with others and they with you—times when you felt alive from within. What were you doing at these times?
2. Recall compliments others have given you which are not related to your looks or accomplishments. Most likely they express a friend's gratitude for your gifts as he or she perceives them. Examples might include:

   ■ *"You're a really patient person."*

   ■ *"You're so good with kids."*

   ■ *"You have the guts to speak your mind."*

   ■ *"Thanks for just listening."*

3. Ask three people whom you admire what gifts they recognize in you.
4. Ask several children what they like about you.

Gifts and God's Plan

Your talents and gifts, because they were given to you freely by God, are signs of God's presence in your life. They enable you to do the things God is calling you to do. That is, God has given you what you need to live a moral life. You don't have to compare yourself with anyone else. You have the talents you have—no more and no less. You are not superior or inferior to anyone because of them.

You can be more respectful of yourself and more helpful toward others if you know your own special gifts. You will respect yourself more because you will be assured that you are able to do someone good even though, at times, you may be at a loss for words, feel frightened, or be unpopular. You can save yourself energy, too, by not trying to force your gifts on others.

Your gifts might still be a mystery to you, but you do have spiritual power: "As each one has received a gift, use it to serve one another as good stewards of God's varied grace...so that in all things God may be glorified through Jesus Christ" (1 Peter 4:10-11). Here, then, is an important moral duty—to use your gifts to help others so that God will be praised.

Since you have received these powers as gifts, you owe gratitude to God for them. Gratitude relieves you of the worry that you are somehow not deserving of them. Of course, no one is "worthy" of his or her gifts. They aren't given to anyone as a reward. There is no reason to worry about "paying God back." Is it wrong to be proud of your talents? That depends on what being proud means. When it means that you appreciate your talents and want to use them without being shy, you have the kind of pride Jesus had in being the true Son of God. This pride allows you to be relaxed and happy when someone compliments you. If being proud means being pushy, showing off, making others feel inferior, or always feeling like a failure unless you are "Number One," then pride is bad. It shows that you have not yet accepted your talents for what they are—the tools for fulfilling your mission in life.

Whatever your talents are, you can share them with others.

Summary

- Trust that God has gifted you for a unique mission in this world. Realize that your gifts and talents are the best indication of what that mission entails.

- Know that you are following God's will when what you say and do produces peace, joy, and love in others.

- Realize that it is your moral duty to use your gifts to help others so that God will be praised.

■ Review

1. What are the differences between talents and gifts? Use examples to illustrate the differences.

2. What are some clues for following God's plan? How do you know that you are following God's will?

3. What is the moral importance of your talents and gifts?

4. Is it wrong to be proud of your talents? Why or why not?

5. Words to Know: talents, gifts, *charis*.

■ In Your World

Tell someone you admire what gifts you recognize in him or her. How would you feel about doing this? How would you do it? Who would you pick? Why? What would this task accomplish?

■ Cases

Identify the gifts and talents of the following individuals. What might prevent them from fully utilizing their talents and gifts?

1. Marcia has always had to put extra effort into her math classes. However, in Spanish class, she noticed how quickly she picked up the grammar. With relative ease, she could speak this foreign language. On weekends, she and her friends volunteer their time to work with disabled children at the local hospital. Many of the children immediately took to Marcia's warmth and personality.

2. Paul is a skilled musician, but is very shy. He loves to play guitar, but refuses to take lessons. Some of his friends have asked him to join their band and help them notate songs from the radio. He can play a song simply by hearing it once. Paul agrees to help, but he still feels uncomfortable about taking lessons and about playing in front of others.

3. Marj loves to write stories about people she has met, but hates to hear any criticism of her work. The teachers actually think she writes well, but feel she should make minor improvements. Afraid to face rejection, she disregards their suggestions, saying, "They're just jealous of my ability."

SECTION 2
God's Love: A Mystery

Moral living is a difficult process for everyone, but it is more difficult, more painful, and more uncertain for people who do not or cannot believe in God's unconditional acceptance of them.

The New Testament assures us of God's acceptance: "In this way the love of God was revealed to us: God sent his only Son into the world so that we might have life through him. In this is love: not that we have loved God, but that he has loved us and sent his Son as expiation for our sins" (1 John 4:9-10). The normal way we are prepared to accept God's love is by experiencing love and acceptance from our parents during infancy and childhood. The family's unlimited and loving care in holding, feeding, and comforting an infant builds an assurance of personal worth and a trust in the goodness of the world.

God Works in Strange Ways

Many years ago, two men were traveling to a distant city. One man believed firmly in God's love; the other was skeptical. They had a dog, a rooster, a torch, and their life earnings.

Coming into a town towards evening, they sought a place to spend the night, but no one welcomed them. "You say God loves us?" commented the skeptic. "Yes. Wait and see," responded the believer. They went a little way into the forest and prepared to sleep on the ground. Suddenly, they heard a growl and a yelp and turned to see that a wolf had attacked and killed their dog and was dragging it away. "So God really loves us!" exclaimed the one. "The wolf might have killed one of us," responded the other.

Mystery: something that can never fully be explained.

Chapter 1   Gifted for Mission

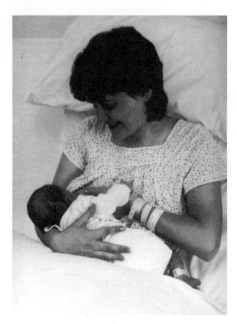

Isaiah 49:15 tells us that even if a mother forgets about her infant, God will never abandon us.

PRAYER FOCUS

Saint Teresa of Avila looked at the two wheels of her coach stuck deep in the mud. She complained to God, "If this is how you treat your friends, it's no wonder you have so few of them."

The saints often spoke frankly to God. They did not treat God as a fearsome, frightening, or unreachable being. In the same way, you can talk to God directly when life seems unfair, cruel, or puzzling. Be ready for an answer from any source—a friend, teacher, or even a current song.

As they were beginning to doze off, the rooster screeched in terror. The two men jumped up and climbed the nearest tree, just in time to see the wolf's mate kill their bird. In the next instant, a gust of wind blew out their torch. "God is working overtime tonight," said the skeptic sarcastically. "God is taking care of us. Our rooster warned us in time to save our lives, didn't it?" Just then they heard horses, but the riders sped by too quickly for the men in the tree to get their attention.

The next morning the travelers went back into the village to find that robbers had attacked every house and stolen all the money they could find. "You see," observed the believer, "if we had found a room in the village, we too would have been robbed. And because the wind blew out our torch, and neither the dog barked nor the cock crowed, the thieves didn't find us in the forest. God's love protected us four times last night. Praise God."

6. *Relate a true incident about an apparent tragedy that turned into a blessing.*

7. *What are some questions you have about how God treats people?*

God's Gifts Are Truly Free

God shows love in ways we may not understand. Good people ask why they suffer, why innocent children die painful deaths, or why criminals never get caught.

There is a tale of a clever talk show host who managed to schedule heaven's recording angel as a guest. The host thought she would settle the question once and for all. When she asked the angel what he recorded, he answered, "Only each one's efforts at unselfish love and their tears. You record your own wrong doing by the loss of inner peace." Very puzzled, the host asked how God knows who to reward and who to punish. The answer was a shock. "God doesn't reward anyone during his or her life. Neither does God punish anyone. All material benefits, including money, good health, and even a loving family are all gifts.

Living a Moral Life: Gifted and Growing

No one deserves them. They are given freely to the good and the evil. Unconditional love flows to everyone. Pain and tragedy are not punishments but results of material or human causes. They come to everyone, too.''

It is true. Good things are not rewards, but rather, are gifts. Suffering and misfortune are not punishments (see John 9:1-3). Natural disasters, for instance, show that the earth is changing according to physical laws. Jesus, by living and suffering with us, shows us that God is near.

God is often blamed for the sufferings inflicted by other people. Yet human beings also have the minds and abilities to alleviate much suffering in the world. "Mothers Against Drunk Driving" and "Students Against Drunk Driving" are examples of organizations where people work together to decrease the suffering caused by others who refuse to act responsibly. Many abuses that cause personal and social harm are the result of human choices. Even cancer seems to be caused in large part by chemicals put in our food, air, and water. The proper exercise of our free will can change the situations that cause suffering in the world. This is the challenge and responsibility of having a free will: to act as co-creators of God's kingdom on earth by working to build a better world.

Helping others is a great way to use God's gifts to us.

Practice This Skill

Psychologists use the word **affirmation** when they speak of unconditional acceptance. We need someone else to accept us, and when we accept their affirmation of us, we affirm ourselves. But love from another has to come first. If we only realized the power we carry to give other people life! No one can grow without being loved. Here are some ideas for those who need to be affirmed:

- *Don't seek affirmation by giving gifts, overworking, becoming a perfectionist, engaging in sexual activity, overdressing, or flashing money around. Affirmation must be freely given by **another.** By accepting this affirmation, we affirm ourselves.*

- *Don't be the "nice" person who lets himself or herself be used by others like a slave.*

- *Don't be afraid of hurting others' feelings by saying "no" when you want to say "no."*

- *Accept personal emotions, even at the cost of restraining action.*

- *Be willing to take chances. Live with a little more risk.*

- *Be gentle with yourself. Remember that God loves you.*

Here are some tips in helping to affirm others:

- *Compliment people on their gifts.*

- *Be generous with praise.*

- *Look others in the eye when they speak.*

- *Notice little things about others—a new hair style, the color of their eyes, their handwriting style.*

- *Tell people that you love them.*

- *Don't tease people about their physical traits.*

- *Don't force shy people to speak.*

- *Don't overprotect children. Let them experience life.*

- *Don't assume that others cannot be hurt deeply.*

◆

We might still question God's wisdom. Wouldn't it be better to send rewards and punishments throughout life to urge people to shape up faster? Wouldn't it be easier to avoid evil if we knew we'd be punished immediately? Most really evil deeds carry their own penalty, but it may be known only to the offender, such as inner loneliness and self-hatred. People are free to follow God at their own pace and in their own style. If God were to send rewards and punishments, people would respond out of fear and obligation. Therefore, free will was created so that we would choose God for the right reason—because we love God—and not because of any specific rewards or punishments we receive.

---

8. *What is your image of God now? Do any of these come close: strict parent, friend, party-giver, employer, police officer, mother, coach?*

9. *How do you feel about God not sending rewards or punishments but only gifts?*

10. *When have you felt the divine presence? Describe this experience in a short essay.*

11. *Recount a story of someone who trusted God without fully understanding why things happened.*

Summary

- God does not send specific rewards or punishments.

- All material and spiritual benefits are gifts, freely given to everyone.

- Abuses that cause personal and social harm are often the result of human choices, not God's.

- The proper exercise of our free will can change the situations which cause suffering in the world.

- God created free will so that we might choose to love God freely, not because of any rewards received in return.

Free will: the freedom to choose a course of action or make a decision based on one's own desires.

■ Review

1. Why is it said that "God works in strange ways"?

2. Does God send rewards and punishments to us? Why or why not?

3. What are some of the causes for suffering in the world? How should suffering and misfortune in people's lives be interpreted?

4. What does it mean to say that humans have free will?

5. What is the challenge and responsibility of having free will?

6. Words to Know: free will, affirmation, mystery, suffering.

■ In Your World

List and observe in the newspaper or on television examples of the sufferings humankind has fostered intentionally or through negligence. After making the list, identify the concrete ways you can address these problems as a co-creator of God's kingdom on earth. Be prepared to discuss possible remedies for these sufferings and misfortunes.

■ Cases

Discuss some ways you can act as co-creators of God's kingdom and use your free will to remedy these problems.

1. The rain forests of South America are being deliberately burned in order to make grazing land for cattle. Most of the beef is sold in fast food restaurants throughout the world, especially in the United States. Wild and exotic plant and animal life is in jeopardy of extinction because of this activity. In addition, the oxygen given off by the rain forests is essential to the ecosystem of the world. Plants convert the carbon dioxide given off by animals into oxygen, which is breathed in by animals. This process is essential for the preservation of life.

2. Homelessness is a serious social problem, especially in the United States. Thousands of families spend nights in shelters. Others are not so fortunate, and must find shelter on the streets. Along with the scarcity of decent, affordable housing, people are left to struggle with few job opportunities, either because of a lack of education or poor health.

SECTION 3
Free to Give Unconditional Love

Many people, even adults, find it impossible to accept themselves and use their gifts and talents fully because they lack self-confidence and self-esteem. They have always felt conditionally loved.

A Lack of Assurance

The world is full of gifted people, yet so many gifts are never expressed. Ignorance, fear, cowardice, and sinfulness are certainly obstacles to expressing these gifts. But often the biggest block to expression can be psychological, a lack of assurance that we are really good and that our gifts will make a difference in the world.

Conditional love says that one must fulfill this or that requirement before he or she can be loved. Think of all the television commercials that try to sell products or programs based on this idea. Weight loss programs and cosmetic products are often sold with the promise of love. Even cars are sold with the idea that once you drive the new car you will become the object of desire for others.

In contrast, unconditional love means that we are loved simply for who we are. Unconditional love recognizes that we may need to work at improving ourselves, but that we are not accepted on the condition that we improve. When we are loved unconditionally, we have no need to prove our worth. With such love, we can start to live creatively.

Standing up to ridicule and peer pressure is a sign of moral maturity and is a good way to use your gifts.

12. *Discuss specific ads that present a message of conditional love and acceptance. What "tricks" do advertisers use to make us feel conditionally loved?*

Jesus Lived Creatively

Before we can begin to fulfill our special mission, we need to be freed from our sense of worthlessness. This is what salvation is all about: God sent his son Jesus as our brother to free us by his love and to show us how to use our gifts creatively. A brief look at how Jesus used his own creative freedom will help us see the possibilities for ourselves.

Jesus' creativity showed itself in his knack for arriving at new solutions to problems and through unexpected behavior in almost all situations. His meeting with Zacchaeus is a typical example. As a popular preacher passing through the prosperous city of Jericho, Jesus was expected to lodge with one of the local dignitaries. Several of these self-important men were, no doubt, leading the crowd, ready to show Jesus to their home (Luke 19:1-10).

Included in the crowd was Zacchaeus, a man with a reputation for corruption, who had probably grown wealthy by overtaxing his own countrymen. Faithful Jews considered those who cooperated with Rome as traitors to their own people. Since a tax-collector's salary was based on how much he could collect from taxpayers, overcharging was a normal practice.

The "good" townspeople could not accept Jesus' unusual treatment of the corrupt official. But Jesus' complete acceptance of Zacchaeus, and his belief in Zacchaeus' sincerity, freed Zacchaeus from his sins. Zacchaeus promised to give half of his property to the poor and to repay four times over anyone he had cheated. Jesus' creative use of his gifts enabled Zacchaeus to love others unconditionally. In the same way, the creative use of our gifts can help us to love others unconditionally.

Channels of God's Love

Creative love doesn't belong only to Jesus. We can be channels of this love for one another. In fact, the usual way God gives love is through other people. The following people experienced unconditional life-giving love in very human ways.

- *"The gift of complete acceptance was given to me recently, and now I know its healing power. If I had only received it during my high school years, if there had been one individual to whom I could say absolutely anything, with whom I could be absolutely myself, I feel that I would have been free to grow beyond my power to imagine. But now that I have received this gift, I hope to give it to someone else"* (A homemaker, 27 years old).

Values for Life

Zaccheus' joy in the presence of God freed him from his past and allowed him to start a new life. The one thing that might have discouraged him from accepting this life was the fear of ridicule. Zacchaeus was a short man who knew he was despised by others. Because of his height, he had to climb a tree just to catch a glimpse of Jesus. The crowd roared with laughter when they saw this. Yet, Zaccheaus endured their ridicule. Jesus recognized this courage and singled him out by asking him to share dinner that evening.

It takes courage to be an individual and endure the ridicule of others. Yet Jesus assures us, "Blessed are you when they insult you and persecute you and utter every kind of evil against you [falsely] because of me. Rejoice and be glad, for your reward will be great in heaven" (Matthew 5:11-12).

"Now that I have received this gift, I hope to give it to someone else."

- *"It seems to me that people in high school are more interested in being accepted and in coping with the problems of grades and parents than in their moral growth. Interest in being good, I guess, begins from an experience of feeling worthy of love. My friend Vicky accepts me for who I am"* (A high school senior).

- *"My dad left home before I was born, so I could have felt rejected. But I've always known that I was born to win. I guess my mom built it into me. She was really a mother and father to me"* (A college freshman, state champion in cross-country).

"I've always known that I was born to win."

Living a Moral Life: Gifted and Growing

13. *What are some of the words or phrases the people quoted above used to describe themselves after they accepted someone's unconditional love?*

14. *Think of one person in your life who may be trying to accept you or assure you of acceptance. How would accepting that person's affirmation change your life?*

15. *How can you communicate that affirmation to another (parent, classmate, or neighbor) who might be hoping that you will love him or her unconditionally?*

Jesus Enables Us to Live Creatively

Being a Christian means being like Christ. But that doesn't mean being his twin. Rather, we are to accept him as a brother. This requires that we understand what it means to become his brother or sister.

Brothers and sisters share a common heritage, share a common name, and often share common values. Once we allow Jesus to free us from our selfish attitudes and self-centered ways of living, as he freed Zaccheaus, then we begin to participate in his family—sharing in the same inheritance God the Father offers Jesus. All we need to do is accept the offer.

Jesus thought of others as his brothers and sisters and treated them like family (Matthew 12:46-50). We are called to think and act in a similar way. How do we begin? We begin by realizing that we cannot do it alone. Jesus says, "I am the vine, you are the branches...because without me you can do nothing" (John 15:5). To become a brother or sister of Christ requires *metanoia*—turning away from sin. Jesus and his Father help us to experience *metanoia* through the gift of the Holy Spirit.

The Holy Spirit, the Third Person of the Blessed Trinity, is the personal living power of the love between the Father and the Son, and the moving force behind all of Christ's

> **Metanoia:** Greek for to turn around; to change the way one thinks.

activities. After his death and resurrection, Jesus revealed to us this divine person. The signs of the presence of the Spirit in the early Christian Church were seen first at Pentecost (Acts 2-3). The Holy Spirit first comes to you in baptism and prompts you to grow in your awareness of God's goodness, love, and power.

We begin to follow the guidance of the Holy Spirit when we accept God's unconditional love, letting it free us from our fears and sense of worthlessness. Once freed, we have the courage to use creatively our gifts to love others as Jesus did.

---

16. *What simple, good things have come into your life? Do you think the Holy Spirit had anything to do with this goodness? Why or why not?*

17. *What, for you, is the most wonderful thing Jesus did on earth? In what way might you accomplish what you admire in Jesus?*

The Jesus Difference

Christian morality is unique. While it has laws and principles of moral living, it is not centered only on law. Christian morality is centered on Jesus himself.

These are the essentials of Christian morality:
1. To direct one's life toward Jesus by using one's gifts.
2. To accept Jesus as our brother.
3. To look for Jesus in oneself and in others, and to listen to his Spirit in all decisions.

What Jesus as Savior brings to Christian moral living is twofold: (1) the power to overcome evil, and (2) the promise that a person's efforts will certainly lead to full freedom in the end. Christians are not given ready-made answers to life's problems, but with the help of the Holy Spirit and the guidance of the Church they find the answers themselves and are given enough strength to live with the problems.

Living a Moral Life: Gifted and Growing

■ Review

1. What is the difference between conditional and unconditional love? Give an example.

2. How does Jesus enable you to live creatively?

3. What does it mean to be a brother or sister of Jesus?

4. What is the meaning of *meta-noia*?

5. What are the three essentials of Christian morality?

6. Can people who do not know Jesus be saved? Why or why not?

7. What is the difference between morality and moral theology?

8. Words to Know: *metanoia*, morality, moral theology, salvation.

■ In Your World

Describe three people you know whose behavior make them a brother or sister of Jesus. Write down specific qualities that you have observed in them.

■ Cases

Consider these three students: Student 1 gets A's in school, but at the same time "cuts down" others and cheats on homework and tests; student 2 works honestly, tries to be sensitive to others, but gets poor grades in school; student 3 works hard to achieve a B, but cops out on chores at home and other responsibilities. Which student is making the most progress in Christian morality? Why? If Jesus were to talk to each of these students, what do you think he would say to each one?

1 Review

■ Study

1. Why is every person unique and irreplaceable?

2. What are the clues to following God's plan?

3. What is the purpose behind your talents and gifts?

4. Describe some of the ways you can discover your talents and gifts.

5. How is God's love shown to us?

6. How did Jesus live creatively?

7. How would you relate creatively to the gift of being unconditionally loved by God?

8. What makes Christian morality unique from all other moral systems?

9. How should one interpret suffering in people's lives? How should one interpret material rewards?

10. Why did God give us free-will?

11. What does it mean to be a co-creator of God's kingdom on earth?

12. How should a Christian view someone who claims to be an atheist but believes in helping others?

■ Action

1. Interview two adults and two peers using the following questions. Report your findings to the class.

    - ■ What are your deepest desires for yourself and for humanity?
    - ■ Do you think you can fully accomplish these desires?
    - ■ What could be your greatest obstacles toward achieving them?
    - ■ Why do you think God made each person unique?

2. Discuss ways in which people try to affirm themselves similar to the ways listed in the feature on "Affirmation." What ways seem to harm a person?

3. What relationship, if any, do you see between the content of this chapter and the fact that so many wealthy and otherwise "successful" people commit suicide?

4. Write a letter to someone you know or would like to know better. Affirm that person for the talents and gifts you recognize in him or her. Then, mail the letter.

5. Find five printed ads, TV, or radio commercials that appeal to your need to feel accepted and lovable. In what ways are the ads misleading?

■ Prayer

1. Write a short and personal prayer of thanksgiving for the gifts and talents you recognize in yourself. Name them and ask God that you may use them to discover and fulfill your unique mission in life.

2. Reflect on the words of Mary, the mother of Jesus, in the Magnificat and how it applies to the message that you are gifted for a unique mission, too. The Magnificat is found in Luke 1:46-56.

CHAPTER

2

Character and Conscience

OBJECTIVES

In this Chapter you will

- Define the nature of character.

- Recognize how you choose values.

- Consider how the Biblical command to "choose life" exemplifies Christian principles.

- Recognize how an adult's conscience is different from a child's conscience

God has created me to do Him some definite service...I have my mission...I have my part in a great work.
—John Henry Cardinal Newman

SECTION 1
Character: Your Deepest Self

The kind of person you are affects what you do day by day. Who you are is always more important than what you do. Yet what you do affects who you become. When you decide what kind of person you want to become, you make one of the biggest decisions of your life, a **character decision.** Actually, you make more than one character decision, but each builds upon the others to answer the question, "Who do I want to be?"

How Will Others Remember You?

One morning a man opened the newspaper and found his own death notice. As he read the obituary someone had mistakenly written, he was most shocked to find out what people really thought of him. Having amassed a fortune as the inventor of dynamite, he felt successful and thought everyone admired and respected him. Contrary to his assumptions, the article characterized him as a "merchant of death."

The man was so stunned he couldn't go to work that day. Was that how he wanted to be remembered—as a merchant of war and death? Then in a burst of inspiration he decided that he would become, instead, an agent of life and peace. He put his fortune in a trust fund to be given as prizes each year to women and men who would make outstanding contributions to humanity. That is how we come to have the Nobel Prizes, and it is for these humanitarian awards that we all remember Alfred Nobel.

Lech Walesa won a Nobel Peace Prize for his work in bringing change in Poland. Alfred Nobel is remembered today through these prizes.

1. *How important would a cause have to be for you to dedicate your life to it? Name a cause for which you would be willing to fight. Share the reasons for your choice.*

Building Character: A Lifetime Challenge

Character is one's whole self—actions, thoughts, gifts, beliefs—that answer the question "What kind of person am I?" Decisions which affect who you are are called character decisions. These decisions are strongly influenced by your idea of God, your acceptance of unconditional love, and your using your unique gifts. They are also shaped by the heroes and heroines you choose as role models.

Many people choose adults they admire and then gradually realize that Christ is the hero behind all their human role models. One example is Steve Van Zandt. Also known as Little Steven, he had a very successful and high-salaried position playing guitar with Bruce Springsteen. But Steve had the habit of asking himself when he woke up every morning, "What am I here for?" Answers like "money" and "success" didn't satisfy him deep down. So he left Springsteen's band to write and perform songs about world issues such as violence in Central America and hunger in Africa. He felt called to use his gifts to awaken his listeners to the sufferings of other people. His was a character decision that changed his life in very visible ways. Know that you can make character decisions that will have a positive impact on the lives of others as well.

Jesus is the most important moral example that Christians have, and you can choose him as a hero even before you understand fully what he's asking of you.

Living a Moral Life: Gifted and Growing

2. *Give three examples of decisions, made by yourself or someone else, that reflect your or the other person's character. After citing an example, describe the type of character that would make that decision.*

3. *Choose two heroes or heroines in your life. What kinds of character decisions do you suppose these people had to make in their lives?*

Sting gives his time and talent to benefit causes that matter.

Values Reveal Character

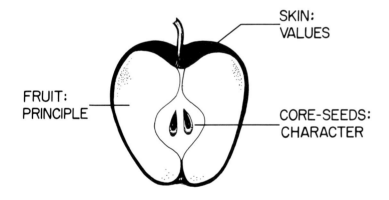

SKIN: VALUES

FRUIT: PRINCIPLE

CORE-SEEDS: CHARACTER

When you cut an apple vertically, you see several levels. At the deepest center lie the seeds which give promise of ongoing life. Built around the seeds is the thick layer of fruit designed as protection. Surrounding the fleshy pulp is the tough skin which acts as a shield against the sun, wind, insects and bumps which may endanger the seeds at the core.

Value: something having worth, or being desirable in and of itself.

Making A Moral World

You will probably never be in a position where you have to stand alone in conscience against the entire United States, including its Catholic leadership. Yet that was the position of Saint Thomas More when all of England accepted King Henry VIII, instead of the pope, as the head of the Catholic Church of England. Saint Thomas believed that no king could claim the power of the pope. His conscience was clear, but he suffered for his decision. He lost his office, his reputation, his home, his savings, his freedom, and ultimately his life. Today, more than four hundred and fifty years after his death in 1535, More is viewed as a model of integrity and moral strength. Despite the personal costs, Saint Thomas More followed his conscience.

You might imagine your character as your secret, life-giving core. It is the power to keep your whole self growing in a wholesome and healthy way. It can also lead to your destruction. As the news media remind us everyday in recounting the lives of great characters who have fallen, if the center grows corrupt, whether through cheating, lying, sexual excesses or substance abuse, the whole person is destroyed.

What are the safeguards built around your character to protect it? The values and principles by which you choose to live are like the thick layer of fruit around the core to protect it. These can be seen as somewhat soft, allowing you to adapt to the changing circumstances of your life. But like the apple, you have a yet firmer protection. It acts as an external skin—tough and objective. It consists of the laws, regulations and guidelines by which society measures which actions give life and which destroy it. The Bible states it clearly: "I set before you life and death. Choose life, then" (Deuteronomy 30:19).

Your character, of course, is the habits of choice you develop. It is made up of the hundreds of decisions you make every day. No one of those actions alone determine your destiny—not a single lie, not one act of service to another—but the whole. But there is a mystery about where good really takes hold and where corruption becomes fatal.

On the program, "60 Minutes," a police chief, dedicated to eradicating evil in his community, told how he became part of that evil. Just by wetting his finger to pick up a very small amount of cocaine lying in a bag he had recovered in a drug bust and, out of curiosity, putting that finger to his nose, he became addicted. He began to steal coke from the evidence room and then started buying it. Finally, he was discovered and went to jail. His career, his reputation, his family honor, and his freedom were all lost through a moment's indiscretion.

Evil doesn't always overtake us that easily. Not everyone will react as the police chief did. But it is important to give heed to the protections available to us. The most important protection is the values and principles you yourself choose to live by. Values are standards which, through trial and error, human beings learn are essential to life, but they don't become values until you recognize their worth and deliberately adopt them as your own. If the police chief had really made the value of life his own standard, he would never have taken the slightest chance of endangering it and could have averted his personal tragedy.

Good values are ideals which human beings strive to attain because they lead to personal happiness and society's well being. They guide your decisions and shape your character. True personal values are often few in number, usually expressed in simple words, and always supportive of life. Some familiar values are closeness to God, life, love, human dignity, growth, truth, compassion, wisdom, community, justice, freedom, respect, friendship, and health.

Just as the basic flavor, color, and texture of an apple depends on the tree, soil, sunshine, water, and climate, values are strongly influenced by parents, relatives, friends, religion, and the role models a person chooses. Your values both protect and reveal your character.

---

4. *List several of your values. Explain, if you can, where you got these values.*

5. *If the soft brown spot on an apple isn't removed, the whole apple rots, along with any other apple it touches. What in your life can be compared to this soft brown spot? Why?*

> **Ideal:** a standard of perfection, beauty or excellence; an aim or goal of one's efforts.

Principles Promote Values

Principles are statements that reflect values. You begin to learn principles from the adults around you who say things like "Always share with your sisters," "You shouldn't hurt your friend," "Respect Life," and "Always tell the truth." These principles reflect the underlying values of generosity, kindness, life, and honesty towards others. "Always tell the truth" is a statement that reflects the values of honesty and integrity. As you grow older, you keep adding new principles, and sometimes you have to let go of less important ones that don't improve life or promote greater values. For example, a child may blurt out embarrassing things said by her parents because she wants to "tell the truth." That child will eventually learn the principle, "Silence can protect a reputation." Silence is often a more prudent response than anything you could say.

Two important principles that guide moral decisions are these: (1) Whatever supports life and community is good. (2) Whatever destroys life and community is evil. When we deliberately choose to promote life in the long run, we are doing something morally good. Likewise, whenever we deliberately choose to endanger or harm life, we are doing something morally evil. Moral evil can be sinful. Just as there are degrees of damage that may be done to life, there are degrees of sin. Even as we can be healed of a wound, so we can be healed of the damage of sin by God's grace, especially through the sacraments of Baptism, Eucharist, and Penance.

A balanced set of moral principles for Christians should include these principles:

- *Accept God's love.*
- *Love God and depend on divine guidance.*
- *Love yourself as a good person gifted by God.*
- *Act justly.*
- *Respect each person's dignity.*

Living a Moral Life: Gifted and Growing

A Law That Fails to Support Life

Laws don't always change for the better. In 1973, Supreme Court Justice Potter Stewart wrote a majority opinion for the Court in the case of *Roe v. Wade.* Prior to this case, many states had laws forbidding abortion, except in the cases of rape, incest or the protection of a woman's life. Some states had laws that have made it a criminal act to attempt to have an abortion, or to assist someone to have an abortion, for any reason. The state abortion laws were designed to protect the life of the unborn child, placing a higher value on this life than on many of the woman's other rights.

In *Roe v. Wade,* Justice Stewart found that the Constitution supported the right to privacy. In this case, the right of privacy allowed a woman to make a decision about her body, without state interference. The court ruled that this right of privacy was a greater value than the unborn child's right to life, at least until he or she reached viability, that is, the ability to live outside the woman's body, around the seventh month of pregnancy.

Catholics, and other religious denominations, believe strongly that the right to life of the unborn child supercedes all other rights. Many Catholics, along with the Catholic bishops of America, have labored to have the law changed. Others have worked to change the minds and hearts of people so that they, too, can recognize and appreciate the value of the right to life.

Principles: statements of basic rules of conduct that reflect values.

Moral evil: an action or thought that has destructive effects or consequences.

Sin: an action or thought that harms your relationship with God and others.

Attempting new things is part of the challenge of growing to maturity. It is okay to take risks, with proper precautions.

Laws and Rules

Laws and rules are more specific external guides to behavior than are principles. They are formulated by society—civil or church—for the common good. Rules are very closely related to our daily actions and practical needs. Just as our daily actions and practical needs change with circumstances, so must our rules. But a rule should be changed only when it no longer supports the value it was intended to support. For example, carrying a gun was once seen as a legal right for self-defense. Now, to make society safer, guns are illegal without permits.

Success Includes Failure

Success in character growth has a quite different meaning than success in competitive sports, in school, or in business. In the area of character, you are successful if you keep moving in your chosen direction. You will never reach your ideal by your own efforts, and you will fail many times. You must not expect to be a perfect human being. When Jesus said, "You must be made perfect" (Matthew 5:48), he did not mean for you to be flawless. Instead, he meant that you must love universally—respecting and caring for the welfare of each person. He asks you to strive to be faithful to your mission from God and to allow God to assist you. Occasional failure, no doubt, will be part of that mission.

Here's a simple story which illustrates this point. Art was learning from his best friend, Mario, how to climb mountains. At one point, Art was in a dangerous position and had to take a risk in order to get ahead. He reached for a handhold higher up, but missed and fell. Suddenly, Art was dangling from the safety rope. He was feeling terrible about his failure when Mario called to him, "Hey, Artie boy, great fall!"

Living a Moral Life: Gifted and Growing

Sometimes you have to learn the art of falling if you want to continue climbing. It's crucial to learn from your failures, and not to judge yourself too harshly. Failure is often more important than success. Why? Perhaps failure holds a valuable lesson to help you complete your mission. So, it is important to realize that success, and especially failure, are opportunities for growth in wisdom and faith. A close friendship with Christ can help you handle the depressing feeling of failure. No one can please everyone! Christ also encourages you when you don't please other people. He helps you to remember that the important thing in life is to be faithful to him and to your own ideals.

6. *Name some rules that are broken in order to protect life.*

7. *Give three school rules. After each one, name the value it supports.*

8. *How can success make a person a failure?*

9. *Can you call a person a failure if you do not know his or her life goal? Give a reason for your answer.*

Summary

- Character is the sum total of distinctive qualities of an individual. It answers the question, "What kind of person am I?"

- A value is something having worth, or is desirable in and of itself.

- A principle is a statement that promotes or reflects a value.

- Laws and rules are specific, external guides to daily actions established by society.

■ Review

1. What are character decisions?

2. How are character decisions made?

3. Define the word "value." Give two examples of values.

4. What is a principle?

5. How does a principle differ from a value?

6. How do laws and rules help us to live our values?

7. What is necessary for success in character growth?

8. Words to Know: value, ideal, moral evil, sin, principle, character.

■ In Your World

Think of a city, state, or country that has laws and rules which do not support Christian values. What are these laws and rules? Be specific. What Christian values do they not support? What can you do to change such laws?

■ Cases

After reflecting on the following story, consider the questions below. Be prepared to discuss them in class.

Lee is an award-winning skater and a skilled athlete. However, the students at school think that skaters are "weird." In fact, Lee is often mocked for not being in a "normal" sport. Lee feels that he is doing what he likes and using his talents well. Often he wonders if there is something wrong with that. He knows he is not "weird," but gets depressed thinking about how no one his age cares for his sport.

■ Name one thing that Lee sacrificed when he made his choice to be a skater.

■ Name one value he chose to live by when he made his choice.

■ Was Lee's choice to take up skating rather than a more popular sport a character choice? Support your answer.

■ Have you experienced a similar dilemma? If so, describe the reasons for the choices you made.

Living a Moral Life: Gifted and Growing

Conscience Is Character in Action

Conscience is the name often given to that "little voice inside" when we make moral decisions. Actually, conscience is much more than a voice that tells us what is right. Conscience is our capacity to think and act morally. It involves a range of powers.

The Nature of Conscience

Conscience is, first, a general awareness that there are right and wrong actions and thoughts. We can abbreviate this as C-A (Conscience: Awareness). Second, conscience is a memory storage of values and principles that guide our judgments. This aspect of conscience is C-M (Conscience: Memory). Third, conscience is the power to think before making a moral decision. This can be abbreviated as C-T (Conscience: Thought). Finally, conscience is the urge to follow the best moral judgment we can make in a particular situation. Conscience: Urge can be abbreviated as C-U.

When a person can feel that wrong has been done, or that he or she has done wrong, then he or she is beginning to be aware of right and wrong, good and evil. This general sense (C-A) usually develops in children by the age of seven.

C-M is the storehouse of experiences that shapes our values. As we observe other people, study morality, and experience good and evil ourselves, it continually expands. Sometimes our memory storehouse may be lacking principles to guide a particular decision. That is why we can't always depend on our conscience alone to know what is right.

C-T is the power to think about a situation and evaluate it in terms of our chosen principles and according to the advice received from others. Further, C-T is the power **to decide** on what is the best course of action to take.

No matter how much we are supported by our C-U, when all is said and done we can still decide to ignore its judgment and do something else. When we follow our conscience, we will feel whole, at peace, and more like ourselves. When we don't follow our conscience, we will feel broken, uneasy, and restless.

Who's In Charge?

Although moral decisions can only be made by the people themselves, many people persist in believing that some authority—such as God, the Church, or parents—determines the moral choices they are obliged to obey. A conscience decision is an act which comes from within a person and expresses a person's own truth. Just as no one can eat for you, no one can make a conscience decision for you.

Following your conscience should simply mean following the advice of your best self in a particular situation. A true decision of conscience flows from chosen principles and all the information at our disposal. But sometimes we confuse following our own conscience with following our moods, feelings or immediate desires.

The Case of Rosalie

Rosalie considers herself a mature freshman. Her parents consider her too young to date or even to spend time with boys. They refuse to let her go out with Gary, a senior basketball player. Rosalie judges that her parents are wrong and that she was ready for a boyfriend. All season long she meets Gary after the games. She enjoys being with him and feels herself growing as a person. She also has definite convictions about sex being limited to marriage. One night, Gary suggests that they have sex. Rosalie refuses. "My mother wouldn't like it," She says. "What has your mother got to do with it?" Gary demanded. "She'd say it isn't right," answered Rosalie.

PRAYER FOCUS

The early Christian theologian Origen wrote that "God became human so that human beings might become God." This is what happens when you accept Christ into your life in faith. You're united with Christ in the center of your personality. Yet, this bonding is practically useless until you become aware of it. When praying each night, recall the choices you made and see if you did, indeed, choose according to your stated values. Then, ask God, who is within you, to guide you. By listening to this divine presence within, you will become more like God.

Living a Moral Life: Gifted and Growing

10. *Which parental principles does Rosalie accept? Which does she reject? What do you think of Rosalie's answers? How would you have answered?*

11. *Why do you think Rosalie used her mother's authority to support her decision? Would you expect the same kind of dependence on parents when Rosalie is twenty-five? Why or why not?*

12. *Why do teenagers often get into trouble by exercising their freedom to "follow their conscience"?*

Adding New Principles

Try to recall the first time you said, "That's not fair." A sense of fairness is basic to justice, a universal moral value. When you sensed that some action was unfair, your conscience was awakening to an awareness of right and wrong. This moral sense became more skilled at recognizing life-giving or destructive behavior as you learned more and more principles to guide you.

Twenty years ago, society did not need principles concerning test-tube conception or cloning. Now it does. At this time in your life, you may not need to know the moral principles behind labor strikes, but as an adult you may. Because you will continually face new moral situations as you grow older, you will have to add new principles and revise old ones for yourself. Taking part in the life of the Church helps you develop and then expand your set of moral principles.

A Child's Conscience

A child does not make his or her own choices. The child repeats or imitates approved behavior. A child's "conscience" operates on imitation, fear, and guilt feelings. A mature person, on the other hand, one who does not operate out of a need for approval, adapts to situations with creative solutions. A mature conscience relies on one's inner principles.

Fairness: an attitude or action which is equitable, just and unbiased.

Cloning: reproducing an exact replica of a person or organism from a cell of the original.

For a person with a child's conscience, getting caught is what makes something wrong.

A person with a child-level conscience:

- *performs actions for the approval and acceptance of others.*

- *repeats actions without truly understanding why those actions are important.*

- *responds to the order of an authority figure without question.*

- *determines degree of guilt by the degree of negative reaction from an authority.*

An Adult's Conscience

The development of an adult conscience does not automatically accompany physical growth. An adult can retain a child's conscience all through life. Many adults behave like children with some people and more maturely with others. An executive who makes mature decisions at the office, at home may be afraid of disobeying her mother. Many people carry remnants of a child's conscience around with them all their lives. A mature conscience operates on freedom, responsibility, and creative obedience.

A person with an adult-level conscience:

- *understands and promotes chosen values.*

- *functions creatively in each situation.*

- *adopts values because of their importance, not because of public opinion.*

- *supports chosen values whether or not an authority figure approves.*

- *is concerned with growing in one's decision making ability.*

- *determines the amount of guilt by the harm done to the corresponding value.*

Living a Moral Life: Gifted and Growing

Test Your Skill

Using the distinctions between a child-level conscience and an adult-level conscience, place each person on this continuum by considering his or her motive for the choice.

0   1   2   3   4   5   6   7   8   9   10
Child-level   **Adult-level**

1. Kim drives within the speed limit because speeding endangers lives, wastes fuel, and pollutes the environment with added exhaust fumes.

2. Sam drives within the speed limit because he's afraid of getting a ticket.

3. Consuela turns in a lost wallet because once she lost a wallet and it was returned to her. She would have been angry if someone had taken her money.

4. Al finds a purse and returns it to the owner. He tried to imagine how the owner must have felt losing her possessions.

5. Connor joins a walk to support the rights of people with disabilities because he believes everyone's rights should be protected.

6. Ray doesn't join the walk for people with disabilities because he doesn't know anyone with a disability and would rather watch TV.

7. Even though she is tempted to keep it, Danesha hands back extra money a clerk gave her by mistake because her little brother is with her, and he sees the mistake. She knows he looks up to her and will imitate her.

In some situations, we may know that we are making the best moral choice. Our conscience is certain, and we follow it. In other situations, we are not reasonably sure which choice is right. Our conscience is doubtful, and we need to pray and ask advice before acting. Before acting, most people want to be as certain as possible. If we act hastily when in doubt and find out later that we were wrong, we are responsible for the harm done.

When a principle determines if an action is right, it is **objectively** right. If it only seems right within one's mind, it is **subjectively** right. It is possible that one's certainty of what is right may actually be based on wrong information or principles. In Mark Twain's, *The Adventures of Huckleberry Finn,* Huck learns a wrong moral principle from his father: It is all right to steal a chicken if you give one away when you have it. Huck accepts this principle and poaches chickens without feeling guilty. Huck's conscience is certain, but misinformed. He may follow the principle until he begins to doubt its correctness or until someone shows him why he is misguided. Until then, he is doing something wrong, but he's not morally guilty.

A person who has done something objectively wrong, but who knows no better, is required to repair the evil that has been done, once he or she becomes aware of the evil. That is, morally Huck should have attempted to replace the chickens he stole, and not have stolen anymore, once he knew that his principle was wrong. He should not feel guilty, however, unless he was aware at the time of the choice that it was evil, and did it anyway. Would Huck be punished? Possibly by others, but not by God. Would the evil harm him? Perhaps. Every evil deed, whether intended or not, brings harm to the world. Yet if we, like Huck, learn from our errors, good can also come of the situation. Growth in wisdom and moral knowledge can take place.

Huck's subjectively moral principle concerning chicken stealing was morally wrong.

13. *If Huck is subjectively innocent of poaching chickens, does that make poaching right for him? Give your reasons.*

14. *If you were Huck's friend and knew the correct moral principle about respect for property, how would you inform Huck that he is mistaken?*

Summary

- Conscience is the capacity or ability to think and act morally.

- The four aspects of conscience include: **awareness** of right and wrong; **memory** or "storehouse" of moral principles and values; the motivation or **urge** to do the right thing; and the power to **think** before making a decision.

- A child-level conscience operates on imitation, fear, and guilt feelings.

- An adult-level conscience operates on freedom, responsibility, and creative obedience.

- **Objective** morality involves standards of behavior which are based on factual circumstances in the world. **Subjective** morality involves the individual's personal perspective on how to react to these moral issues with one's conscience.

Objective: anything that can be demonstrated as a fact.

Subjective: one's own personal perspective or opinion.

Poach: to steal.

Guilt: the fact of having violated a just law or moral principle.

■ Review

1. Define in your own words the meaning of "conscience."

2. Define what is meant by conscience-awareness

3. How does conscience-memory help you make a decision?

4. What is meant by "conscience-urge?"

5. Name the final level of conscience and explain how it works.

6. What are the differences between a child-level conscience and an adult-level conscience? List as many as you can.

7. Explain how you can be objectively wrong in an action, but not be guilty of sin.

8. Words to Know: conscience, subjective, objective, doubtful, certain, fairness, guilt.

■ In Your World

Recall a time when you did something morally wrong, but were unaware it was wrong. How did you learn it was wrong? Think of an issue in society about which people personally (subjectively) believe something to be right, but that you know to be objectively wrong. Discuss this in class. How are you to treat them? How would Christ treat them?

■ Cases

For each situation, write down what you would do and why. Your answers and reasons should give you an idea of the maturity of your conscience now. See how many characteristics of an adult-level conscience you have already developed. Be prepared to discuss your answers.

1. During a test you have a chance to copy answers you don't know from someone else's paper. The teacher's back is turned so you won't get caught.

2. You are supposed to be home by midnight. You will make it if you leave your friend's house now, but you are in the middle of watching a really good television show.

There are other situations in which our consciences may not be functioning properly. Some people know what is right, but choose not to act on that knowledge. Others are too strict and believe everything is potentially sinful. Both are dangerous extremes. Finding a balance between these two attitudes is the proper course. At other times, people feel guilty but don't know why. These problems need to be addressed to understand the nature of a healthy conscience.

Guilt and Guilt Feelings

Feeling guilty is not the same as being guilty. Humans feel guilty when they have violated one of their principles. But they may also feel guilty when they feel the disapproval of a person in authority. If one has grown up with very strict parents or teachers, he or she might feel guilty for doing very innocent and even good things. For example, a boy might feel guilty simply because he is attracted to a girl. He has been erroneously taught that sexual attraction is sinful. On the other hand, he would indeed be guilty if he intentionally harmed his relationship with a friend or acted indifferently to someone in need.

A Scrupulous Conscience

One distortion of conscience is scrupulosity. Scrupulosity is a psychological disorder, an unrealistic fear of having committed a serious sin when no sin was present. People can become scrupulous if, as small children, they are expected to be perfect in everything. An exaggerated fear of God's wrath and punishment are often strong indications of a scrupulous conscience.

Ordinarily a person with a scrupulous conscience needs the help of a priest or counselor to overcome this disorder. He or she needs to reflect on God's mercy and trust in God's love. Feelings of false or neurotic guilt may never disappear completely, but knowledge and acceptance of God's unconditional love can relieve the person of his or her excessive worries about sin.

> **Scrupulosity:** a psychological disorder that makes one find sin in mistakes or innocent actions.

Having a lax conscience does not excuse a person's behavior. "Being your own person" is no excuse for being a slob.

For Example

We often mask our faults in fine phrases. "I'm easy going" may really mean "I'm lazy and careless." "I'm agreeable" may mean "I prefer to accept things rather than to stand up for the right." "I'm quiet and good" may mean "I'm too proud to risk making a mistake or being corrected." "I'm the independent type" may mean "I'm really selfish and stubborn." "I'm strong in my beliefs" may mean "I'm really opinionated and have no respect for others' ideas."

A Lax Conscience

Another conscience distortion is being lax or lazy in moral matters. People are lax when they easily excuse immoral behavior or refuse to recognize it. Usually they are just too lazy to do the good that needs to be done. A number of things contribute to the formation of a lax conscience.

First, society does not teach clear, strong moral principles. It accepts as standard practice such things as paying off an officer to avoid arrest or jail; overeating; drinking to excess; sexual abuse and many other actions contrary to Gospel morality. Constant immersion in an environment of low moral standards makes it difficult for a person to recognize wrongdoing.

Second, people accept laxness as part of their personalities. They excuse themselves on the grounds that they are only human. They say they are "laid back" and "tolerant of different viewpoints." Such an attitude often masks an unwillingness to accept adult responsibility for their actions and to challenge the immoral actions of others.

Living a Moral Life: Gifted and Growing

Third, people prefer to be passive. Some think that it is easier to avoid evil by doing nothing, rather than by doing something. For a Christian, this thinking is unacceptable. Christ challenged his followers to be active, caring people, energetic in addressing the needs of others, not merely careful to avoid direct evil.

Responsibility for Others

Depending on your own moral maturity, you may sometimes be responsible for helping others form good consciences according to Christian principles. If you belong to a group, you have some responsibility for its behavior.

Groups of any sort—friends, clubs, or corporations—act on a set of principles which direct their activities. If one member sees that some principles are immoral, he or she has several options: A) stay in the group, face opposition, and try to make others aware of the immorality; B) stay in the group and accept the immoral principle; C) leave the group; D) try to find another group with a higher level of maturity and join it.

As a member of a group, you share some of the responsibility for the group's behavior. You may need to leave the group if it refuses to listen to your counsel.

15. In these Scripture passages, decide what kind of conscience is being illustrated (in some cases, there may be two kinds): Matthew 6: 1-4, Matthew 12:9-12, Matthew 18:21-35, Matthew 25:41-46, Matthew 26:6-13, Luke 3:10-14, Acts 5:27-32.

16. Of options A, B, C, and D above, which would violate the dissenting member's conscience? Does that member have an obligation to try to inform the others of the immorality of their actions?

17. How would you go about awakening the consciences of members of a group?

18. Cite an example of when you would leave a group, even at the risk of being a loner.

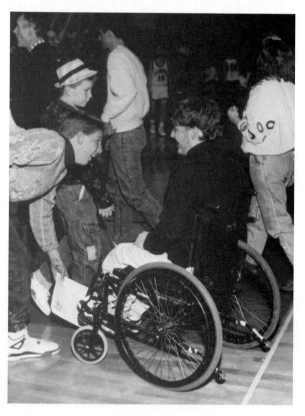

Friendship is a special gift. Share it with people in need of a friend.

■ Review

1. What are the seven suggestions for growth mentioned in this section?

2. Explain the difference between feeling guilty and being guilty.

3. What is a scrupulous conscience? Explain.

4. What is a lax conscience? What are three reasons why people have lax consciences?

5. To what extent are you responsible for the formation of others' consciences? Explain your answer.

6. What are your options when confronted with immoral principles of a group?

7. What is an informed conscience?

8. Words to Know: scrupulosity, lax conscience, guilt, guilt feelings, indifference.

■ In Your World

When have you been confronted with immoral actions or principles either at school, work, or social event? How did you feel? What, if anything, did you say or do? Were you afraid to challenge the group? Why or why not? Who agreed with your actions? Who disagreed and why?

■ Cases

Some people feel guilty about the following actions. Discuss whether or not they are actually guilty.

1. Crossing a street against the light when no cars are in sight for several blocks. Doing the same at the next intersection, but with young children standing next to you at the corner.

2. Opening another's personal mail without his or her permission.

3. Missing Sunday Mass to care for a sick member of the family.

4. Repeatedly promising to take your younger sister to the zoo and then always being too busy to do it.

Karen also mourned at the death of her substitute mother, but since she had kept in touch with Sadie over the years, Karen was not riddled with guilt. She recovered from her sorrow much sooner than Ed.

1. *What principles did Aunt Sadie forget when she was jealous of her sister? How might she have seen her role in her sister's life? In the life of the children? How would a different attitude have changed her? How would that change have affected her actions?*

2. *How did Ed fail to integrate the different time periods of his life? What were the effects? What are the causes of Ed's feelings of guilt? How might he lesson his feelings of guilt?*

3. *Why could Ed not forgive Sadie? What did Ed gain from his treatment of Sadie? What did he lose?*

Our Need for Freedom

Because we are called to love God and develop to our potential as images of God, we need freedom. But freedom has several dimensions. First, there is our **freedom of choice**—that is, the use of our freedom in daily actions. Second, there is our basic **freedom of self-determination.**

Freedom of Choice

The easiest kind of freedom to understand is the freedom of choice. This freedom governs your daily decisions. It is like the freedom you exercise in a cafeteria line or at a smorgasbord. You freely choose certain things and reject others. This type of freedom has limits from itself and from you. You can't choose mushrooms if the salad bar doesn't offer them. And if you are diabetic, you won't choose rich chocolate cake, even if it is offered.

Different objects have different dimensions—a piece of paper is two dimensional. A book has three dimensions. Theologian Karl Rahner said that freedom is multi-dimensional. It is like a coiled-spring with several constantly changing dimensions. Another example is that of an onion. Peel off one level and you find a new layer below.

Through your choices, you take responsibility for your life. But there are limits. The temperament you inherit will limit you in some degree. You might not be able to think of witty comebacks or make instant decisions. If you are hypersensitive to smoke, you cannot hang out with friends where people do smoke. These things are genetically determined. In addition, there are environmental limits affected by where you live—climate, culture, society.

However, neither your genetic nor your environmental limitations fully determine your freedom. You can cop-out and refuse to accept responsibility for your actions by blaming your limitations ("I can't help myself. I'm just like my father."), but as a person of moral capability, you are challenged to achieve the freedom available to you. This is one of the purposes of education. It helps people to step beyond their heredity and environment. With Christian education, good will, and God's help, people like Aunt Sadie and Ed can lessen their misery and live in greater happiness and peace.

Freedom of Self-Determination

Not all your choices are equally weighty. Choosing cookies instead of jello for dessert cannot compare with decisions like choosing the priesthood over the Peace Corps. There is a deeper use to which you can put your freedom. It is the basic freedom of self-determination. It is the choice you make to be in a loving relationship with the ultimate end of life—God.

The fact is that you operate out of a number of levels all the time. Within one hour you may decide on a certain jacket to wear to a sports event (level of possessions) and courageously say something positive about a person whose reputation is being put down by a group of friends (level of conviction).

But the most influential shaper of your life is your "heart." No, it's not the physical organ that pumps your blood, but your deepest, innermost, and most secret feelings, emotions, and judgments; it is the place where your identity is most concentrated whether you are good or bad. While the love of God springs from the heart, Jesus adds that evil springs "out of the heart" as well (Matthew

Living a Moral Life: Gifted and Growing

Choosing where you will attend college is a major decision in your life.

15:19). As lovers express their feelings through phrases like, "I give you my heart," hardened criminals are said to be "rotten to the core."

This wonderful power you have to shape yourself and your life makes it of utmost importance to look very closely at your core or heart—the dominant direction in which you are going. Are you moving closer to or further away from God in your actions and lifestyles? Because your basic or core choice is in the center of all that you are and do, it constitutes your personal identity, your self. The fundamental choice, or fundamental option, that lives in your heart expresses the kind of person you choose to be—either loving or self-centered. It lends meaning to all the other choices you make.

Although your fundamental stance or position toward God is always subtly at work shaping your actions and life, it will appear clearer on certain key occasions. This can be illustrated by the case of Betty and her little sister whom Betty generally regards as a pest. But when in a car

Core: from the Latin for heart; the center.

accident, Betty spontaneously threw herself over her little sister in protection. Betty showed that, although she was often annoyed with her sister, on a deeper level she really loved her. The more you can pull all your levels together and act out of your true and deepest intentions, the more satisfying and more wholesome your life becomes.

Times of great decisions might be adult baptism, confirmation, a test of friendship, the choice of a profession, or a commitment to just action. All these moments are rooted in our fundamental relation to our identity, God, our commitment to others and our responsibility for the world.

---

4. *Which of these limitations of freedom did Aunt Sadie or any of the characters in her story experience?*

5. *Describe an experience, perhaps from your early childhood, where your freedom seems to have been limited by ignorance or some other factor.*

6. *Why can we never judge the conscience of others, even though we may know that objectively their actions are evil? What does Jesus say about this in Matthew 7:1?*

7. *Why would it be difficult to switch your fundamental options often? Why do you think habits of substance abuse or chronic lying or cheating, which others can so easily see, often go unrecognized by those who are addicted?*

Our Relationship with Christ

Developing a sound Christian morality, then, is akin to developing a very special relationship. We choose Jesus as our friend and brother, and then make day-by-day decisions according to the values he taught and lived by. What makes this relationship unique is that Christ is also the Son of God. As a source of guidance in moral decisions and a faithful keeper of promises, God and the Son that God sent us will always help those who ask.

Living a Moral Life: Gifted and Growing

Every person old enough to have a human friendship also has some kind of relationship with God, although he or she may not be aware of it. Every time someone responds to goodness in any form, he or she is responding to and coming closer to God. All people, even non-believers, can be sensitive to the values of love, truthfulness, fidelity, and protection of the helpless. When they support these values, they are living moral lives according to God's plan for the human race. When they deliberately attack or ignore these values, they are sinning.

Faith Is the Difference

Faith in Christ is the difference between Christian morality and humanistic morality. When your devotion to goodness becomes devotion to the Divine Person of Jesus, who is the source of goodness, you have the gift of Christian faith. Christ is that person with whom you can talk and share difficulties, and from whom you can receive help. Once you have a deep relationship with Christ, you will find it harder to sin, just as it is undesirable to ignore or hurt a person you love.

8. *Describe your relationship with Christ. How did you first meet Jesus? How has your relationship grown?*

9. *Given the various levels of relationship with God, at what level are you? Which level do you find most unusual? Why?*

Mystic: a person who directly experiences the knowledge and love of God through prayer.

Humanism: a doctrine which asserts the dignity and worth of human beings without the need for religion or God.

Threat: an expression of intention to inflict evil, injury or damage.

Threats to Relationships

A relationship doesn't show its real strength until it is tested. Some of the tests come from the ups and downs of the friendship itself or from other forces. Others come from collective irresponsibility or personal weakness. All relationships are subject to internal and external threats.

The earth is threatened by our careless use of resources.

Making A Moral World

Kung Fu Tzu, or Confucius, as he is known in the West, was a teacher who lived in China over 500 years before the birth of Christ. As a teacher, he believed that family relationships are the best indication of whether or not a society is peaceful. If the children do not respect and care for their parents, then whom will they respect? Likewise, if the parents don't respect and care for their children, then it is unlikely that they will care much for anyone. Confucius believed that if society is to be strong and peaceful, then children and parents must have respect for each other. Respect is essential for a moral world.

A threat to a relationship may weaken or kill a friendship. A man who becomes involved in heavy gambling abandons his friend who refuses to gamble. Eventually, one of the men will have to change, or the once close relationship will die. The nongambler may remain loyal and even try to help his friend overcome his addiction, but unless the gambler responds, the friendship will come to an end.

Other relationships are subject to threats as well. Our relationship to society is threatened when we find it convenient not to follow a law or rule. People may be hurt and, ultimately, we ourselves are hurt. Our refusal to participate in the electoral process may result in unacceptable legislation, which may, in turn, infringe on our own rights. Threats to a relationships are not always the product of active choice or intention. They may simply result from an indifference or a refusal to accept responsibility.

Our healthy relationship with the earth is also threatened. Pollution in our air, water, and soil is prevalent, and because people often have difficulty admitting their contributions to environmental problems, they may never take any steps to restore the earth. Acid rain is one example of environmental irresponsibility. The product of coal burning and the use of gasoline-powered engines, especially in automobiles, acid rain now endangers the precious forests and lakes of North America.

Living a Moral Life: Gifted and Growing

Relationships between nations can be threatened by national interests and corporate selfishness. Differences in political viewpoints often produce conflict. Wars are often the result of a nation pursuing its own, selfish interests. As a citizen of a democratic country, either through your action or inaction, you affect the course your government will take with respect to other nations. The responsibility to enact Christian values, then, belongs to every individual.

10. *List the many types of relationships that make you what you are. Next to each type, discuss the threats or pressures that threaten these relationships. What is the most common threat to these relationships?*

11. *How can these threats or pressures strengthen the above relationships?*

12. *In the case of the gambler, do you believe he is hurting his friend? If so, how? Relate this example to your moral life.*

Summary

■ A Christian lifestyle involves a network of relationships: between you and family, you and friends, you and society, you and the environment, and you and God. The challenge is to bring Christian values to all of these relationships.

■ Christian morality is centered not just on Christ's teachings, but also on having a relationship with Christ.

■ Every relationship may be threatened by human weakness or selfishness.

■ Review

1. How is Christian living built on relationships? What are some of these relationships? What does the Christian bring to these various relationships?

2. What demands are placed upon us by the fact that we are created living in a certain period of history, in a particular culture and on this earth? What powers have we been gifted with to meet these demands?

3. What kinds of freedom do we have? Which is most important? Why? What limits to our freedom do we experience?

4. How is your relationship to Christ similar to a human friendship? Explain.

5. What is the difference between a Christian morality and a humanistic one? Explain.

6. Why does having a personal relationship with Christ make it less likely that a person will sin?

7. List four types of relationships and how they are sometimes threatened. Use examples to illustrate each type.

8. Words to Know: humanism, mystic, Christian lifestyle, threat, relationship.

■ In Your World

Describe what you feel threatens your family and school relationships. How do you contribute to the threat? How can you resolve the threat?

■ Cases

Identify the relationships and the potential or actual threats to each of the relationships in the following case.

John enjoys working long hours at the office to impress his boss. He feels that he is a family man and good Christian. Currently, he is working on a project for raising cattle at lower prices. Unfortunately, this will involve the destruction of some of the rain forests in South America. He thinks that this is an acceptable loss, especially because of the good that this food will do for hungry nations. He rarely sees his family, although he supports them financially. To relieve his hectic pace, he smokes cigarettes, averaging two packs a day.

Sin and Relationships

At times you may be under strong pressures like lack of time for worship, or a need for money to buy clothes, pay for a car, practice a hobby or support an expensive habit. These may threaten your relationship with Christ, but they can also work to bring you closer to him. Catholics believe that people are given the help they need to face all their difficulties. This help, called grace, is God's gift of divine life and power. The only thing that can really weaken our friendship with God is the separation created by sin.

Missing the Mark

Sin does not refer primarily to evil actions. In the Hebrew Scriptures there are several words for sin. One means "missing the mark." Like throwing a dart off target, to sin is to miss full life and happiness with Christ. Sin is the process of turning away from Christ's love. Any person or thing—even yourself—loved in preference to Christ can be the cause of sin.

A second meaning of sin is that of an inappropriate response to God. This is the deeper meaning of the two words. It implies that, through interior revolt or rebellion, we do not value God's covenant with us. Most of us act more by our hearts than our heads. It's what we love—or hate—that leads us to action. That's why it's so important to learn God's love, not just through study, but through personal experience. Personal experience of the love of God comes through prayer, the sacraments, and loving service to others.

When you experience for yourself that you are loved, you respond with love. In other words, if your heart is directed toward the Lord you won't deliberately and willfully break this relationship, although you may occasionally act as if you don't care.

Your target in life is Christ. When you sin, you have missed that mark.

The New Testament proposes another view of sin. In this view, it's not the noble "love for love" notion that rules. Rather, sin is rejecting your relationship with God. You might think of how you would act toward an employer who provides you with a job, a weekly paycheck and generous benefits. The two of you are definitely in a relationship, although you may not feel bound to her or him by personal friendship. You don't maintain the bond out of fear, but through good common sense.

As a baptized Christian who receives all you are and have from God, you would ideally want to develop the close ties of the relationship Jesus hinted at when he said, "I have not called you servants, but friends" (John 15:15). Sometimes your emotions are strongly pulled in other directions. At such times you need to remember the losses you will suffer and act deliberately with fidelity, gratitude and obedience, even if you don't feel like it. Jesus understood this well when he spoke of the need to consider the hell we make for ourselves in preferring anything to God's love (Matthew 5:22, 29, 30; 10:28).

Because people act from a variety of motives ranging from the purest love of God to sheer fear of hell, we cannot judge anyone. Nor can we judge whether someone's action reflects a serious break in his or her relationship with Christ or an uncharacteristic lapse. There is certain behavior which is always morally unacceptable. For instance, murder, stealing, cheating and quarreling are evil. Yet in the case of apparent sin, we cannot judge a person's degree of guilt. Jesus said we shouldn't even try: "Judge not and you shall not be judged" (Matthew 7:1). Yet there is one case you can know something about—your own. Only you know whether your life is firmly anchored in Christ.

Kinds of Sin: Venial and Mortal

Every family experiences tensions. Sometimes the tension is caused by a simple argument which is quickly resolved. At other times, the tension is caused by a serious problem, with one member eventually choosing to leave the family over the difficulty. Sin is like the tension in our families. It can either cause a rift in our relationship with God (venial sin), or it can lead to a total break (mortal sin).

Living a Moral Life: Gifted and Growing

Mortal sin is not so much what we do, but the degree of self involvement and personal investment that a deed expresses. If a person's fundamental option or core direction is toward God, the relationship will be so strong that a single action, regardless of how serious, will not destroy it. On the other hand, a person full of love for God will not intentionally choose evil in an action that will separate her or himself from God.

Is it possible for teens to sin mortally, and in so doing, kill their relationship with God? Most people would say, "Yes." Is it possible for teens to easily "fall" into mortal sin? Not only is it not easily done, but a teen would have to really work at being in such a serious state.

---

13. *What actions would be serious enough to destroy your relationship with God? What would it mean for you to freely choose to do this?*

14. *How would it be possible to do something wrong and yet not fundamentally reject God?*

15. *How can we tell the difference between venial sin and mortal sin? In your opinion, why do people completely reject God's love?*

The Effects of Sin

Since 1980, thirty-three states have legalized gambling, either through a state lottery or through casinos. Many of these states had to first change their constitutions in order to make gambling legal. One of the arguments offered to justify legalized gambling is that it allows people to engage in a small sin without hurting anyone. Whether or not gambling is a moral evil is a question for debate. However, the use of the word "sin" here is misleading, because if gambling is a "small sin," then it would hurt everyone touched by the evil. Even the smallest sin affects you, affects others, and yes, even affects God.

Is legalized gambling sinful? How about illegal gambling? How would you decide?

LOTTO
ILLINOIS STATE LOTTERY

TICKETS ON SALE HERE

How Sin Affects God and You

Sinning affects God by disrupting the divine plan for the human race. You have a unique mission that is an essential part of God's plan. The more open you are, the happier and healthier you become. The less honest you are, the less peaceful you become. By pulling away from God, you become less and less an instrument of divine intent. As a result, the human race loses the benefits of your contributions.

When you sin, you lose your inner peace. You cut yourself off from your primary source of love and goodness. Your freedom is actually decreased. God's laws aim at freeing you to be yourself and accomplish your mission. When you turn away from God, you lose your freedom and become a slave to sin.

Sinning can have visible effects. For example, lying may cost you the trust of your best friend. The deepest effects of sin are always personal and interior, damaging the sinner's relationship with God.

How Sin Affects Others

Every sin hurts somebody. You live and grow in a whole network of relationships. Every relationship changes you. What you are changes others. Your choice of evil, even in secret, decreases your ability to love. Sin has a subtle weakening effect on you and on all who touch your life. Your sinfulness makes it easier for you to influence others to cooperate in sin.

Living a Moral Life: Gifted and Growing

Saint John of the Cross on Sin

Saint John of the Cross, a mystic who lived during the sixteenth century in Spain, wrote about sin and how it harms our relationship with God. Saint John believed that a very deep relationship with God could be achieved through love. He called this the "union of kindness." A person who truly loves God begins to resemble God in all activity. Saint John likens this to the sun shining on a window.

God is like the sun, the soul is like a window. God's presence is seen through the soul as the sun shines through a window. When the window is smeared and covered with dirt, the sun cannot illumine it. In the same way, the soul, when concerned with things other than God, is unable to reflect God.

As the soul grows in love for God, it rejects any obstacle that might get in the way of the love God communicates through grace. When the window is entirely clean, the sunlight so illumines it that it appears to be the light. Yet, regardless of its total resemblance to the light, the window remains separate from the nature of the sunlight. Similarly, when the soul is completely purified of everything unlike God, when it is entirely conformed through love, the soul then resembles God.

Saint John compared God's grace in us to sunlight through a window.

People's evil choices eventually become part of the social structures of family life, school systems, business, and government policies. Every person's sin has a social effect, but there is also social sin. Social sins are actions which affect society, for which no one individual may be directly responsibility, but for which all people are indirectly responsible. Racism has been called a social sin by the American bishops. Even though you may personally treat everyone equally, if you support a system which is racist, you share in the responsibility for racism. Anyone who supports an evil system or chooses not to fight against it participates in its sin.

Making fun of another person's problems can be sinful.

Punishment for Sin

Every moral choice registers within you, increasing or diminishing your ability to love. God does not punish sinners by sending sickness or disasters, or by taking away family or friends. But God does not prevent the pains brought on by sin either. Although the sinner feels unhappy, God still continues to love the sinner and to be a friend. What we call "eternal punishment" is eternal separation from God. That is the state of mortal sin. It is always freely chosen by an absolute rejection of God's love.

16. *Describe a situation in which you discovered that an action was sinful. How did you discover that it was sinful? What convinced you?*

17. *Describe a situation where negligence or refusing to act could be sinful.*

18. *How do you know when you have sinned against another person?*

19. *Why does God allow the sinner to feel unhappy?*

Sin can be easy because it often grows out of good things that we let become too important. We continue to enjoy the pleasure of the thing even when it has become sinful. Sin can also be easy because we have evil impulses. The more often we follow even slightly evil ones, the easier it is to follow the more serious ones without feeling guilty.

Sin seems easy when a person sees only the immediate gain and blocks out the long-range harm to oneself and to others. It is easy for passions to become very strong, very quickly. If not kept in control, passions can blind reason. The person says, "I don't care about the consequences, I want it anyway." When it's over she or he says, "I couldn't help myself, I just got carried away." Finally, when others seem to be getting ahead by doing evil, sin can look very attractive.

20. *What are some factors that make sinning seem easy?*

21. *Is a sin less serious if it is easy for you to commit? Give reasons. What if the sin has become a habit?*

Social sin affects many people, like those forced to live in abandoned buildings or on the street for lack of adequate housing.

Summary

■ Sin is anything which separates you from the love of Christ. Sin literally means "missing the mark." The mark is Christ.

■ Mortal sin is a state of completely rejecting God's love. Though not a complete break from God, venial sin is the process of choosing things over God, or choosing self-satisfaction over concern for others.

■ An evil action is not a sin unless it is done with personal freedom, knowledge and deliberation.

■ God does not punish sinners by sending sickness or disasters.

■ Review

1. What are three ways in which sin can be defined.

2. How does it harm your relationship with God? Others? Yourself?

3. How does mortal sin differ from venial sin?

4. Why is mortal sin called a state of being, not an action?

5. What three factors must be present in the individual in order for an evil action to be sinful?

6. Are feelings good indicators of morality? Why or why not?

7. Does God punish sinners on earth? Explain.

8. Words to Know: grace, sin, social sin, mortal sin, venial sin, deliberate, fundamental option, forgiveness.

■ In Your World

Describe a real-life tragedy or misfortune which many people feel is God's way of punishing sinners. Why do you think people believe that God punishes people on earth? What can we learn, then, from sinful actions or personal tragedies?

■ Cases

In the following situations, identify whether the occurrence is sinful. Be able to support your answer with reasons. Recall the three conditions that must be fulfilled in order for an action to be sinful.

1. Randy's younger brother Joey watched as he shoplifted a tie at a local mall. Later that week, Joey's parents received a call from mall security. Joey had been caught shoplifting at the same store. When asked why he took the item, he replied, "Randy did it, so I thought it was okay."

2. Lyford is a well-known reporter on assignment in the Middle East. At gun point, he was forced to stop a motorist, drag the man out of his automobile, then depart in the same vehicle with his captors in the backseat.

SECTION 3
Forgiveness and Healing

If sin is something we allow to get between us and Christ, then forgiveness is the open arms of Jesus accepting us back into a close relationship with him. Just as in a human friendship, it is important to get to the bottom of the offense. Just as sin is an interior, personal rejection, sorrow must be an interior, personal desire to return to Christ.

Turning Away from Sin

Christians aspire to be Christ-like. Again, this is experienced in *metanoia*—a turning around in how we think and act. A person who has reversed his or her course—has turned around—will not only behave differently, but will feel the need for contrition. Contrition is genuine sorrow; we have turned away from our sin and have promised not to sin again. It may involve emotional feelings of sorrow, but not necessarily. Some persons feel very little guilt over their sins. Some have no feeling of sorrow, though they may be genuinely moved to change their lives for God's sake. A very emotional sorrow may be a sign of shame or embarrassment at what other people think rather than the realization that we have been resisting a loving God.

The sign of true contrition is conversion *(metanoia)*, a genuine change in the whole person. You begin to rearrange your life according to God's love and goodness. It is as simple and complete as that. Contrition is not a brief attempt to feel bad. It is not a quick "Act of Contrition" said before or during the sacrament of Penance. Rather, it means to turn towards God and rearrange your life so that it reflects Christ's love.

Celebrating the reunion of friends after a serious disagreement is a very natural thing. An exchange of gifts or a meal together helps to heal the sting of the quarrel and seals the renewed closeness.

Catholics have many ways to celebrate God's forgiveness, but one way is through the Eucharistic liturgy. The opening penitential rite invites us to admit our sinfulness and accept God's mercy. The sacred words of consecration show how central forgiveness is to Christ's sacrifice: "This is the cup of my blood. It will be shed for you and for all so that sins may be forgiven" *(Order of Mass: Eucharistic Prayers).*

Sacrament of Forgiveness

The proper name of the sacrament that celebrates forgiveness is Reconciliation, or Penance, not confession. Reconciliation means the healing of a conflict. Penance means making amends, acting out of sorrow for previous behavior. Confession is just one part of the reconciliation process, and not even the most important part. What happens with the priest is not merely a spiritual housecleaning chore or an embarrassing, though secret, revealing of one's sins. The sacrament is a celebration of a renewed relationship with Christ.

Because all sin and conversion is social, the celebration of forgiveness is social. We confess our sinfulness to a priest by naming the sin that has been harming our relationship with

The sacrament of Penance offers people an opportunity to seek forgiveness for their sins.

Living a Moral Life: Gifted and Growing

God. We have already admitted it to God and "been converted." Now, with the priest, we celebrate God's mercy. The priest's role is to speak the words of God's forgiveness, witness our sincerity and rejoice in our reconciliation with God. God pardons us and welcomes our renewed friendship.

Continuing Conversion

Before the priest gives absolution, he assigns or asks for an "act of penance." The act is symbolic of conversion, the rearrangement of our lives. Besides healing our hurt relationship with God, we need to heal any damage that our sins have done. Our act of penance may be to begin communicating again with our parents, or to ask forgiveness of someone we have injured. If we have stolen something, it will include the return of the item or money as far as we are able. Sin always includes a responsibility for its damaging effects. Therefore, contrition must include a repairing of this damage.

Why Confess to a Priest?

God surely can and does forgive us outside the sacrament of Penance. But Jesus told his disciples to forgive in his name. Jesus knows that we need the personal assurance of forgiveness, since guilt feelings can burden us long after the guilt itself has been removed. The act of coming to celebrate the sacrament brings us into actual contact with the humanity of Jesus through the priest. It is the healing touch of Jesus that strengthens us to renew our life. The Gospels show Jesus laying his hands on those he healed and forgave. Today, we experience that same power as the priest lays his hands on us while giving absolution. This healing touch is not received by simply confessing to God in our heart.

There is a second reason for confessing sins to a priest. The social effects of sin make it right that there is a social side to forgiveness. The priest represents the whole Church that we have wounded and made less holy by our sin.

Third, we need encouragement and guidance to rearrange our life. The priest is able to advise us in our continuing conversion and recommend acts of penance that will help us continue the journey to Christ.

Fourth, the Church, to which Jesus gave the authority to grant forgiveness in his name, obliges us to confess all serious sins before being assured of forgiveness. Serious evils, which may be mortal sins, include theft of large amounts of money or property, murder, abortion, serious damage to a reputation, adultery, repeated heavy drunkenness, drug abuse, large-scale vandalism, or deep hatred. These evils, when deliberately and freely chosen, hurt the individual and the Church so much that God wants the person to be healed through the sacrament of Penance.

Depending on the degree of our sinfulness and the seriousness of our separation from God, we may go to the sacrament of Penance either out of necessity or out of devotion. It is necessary to receive the sacrament when we are guilty of serious sin or are in a state of mortal sin. A person should not receive the Eucharist if he or she has not confessed mortal sins. In a confession of devotion, we express any obstacle to our love; Christ strengthens us in a particular area of our life. In an emergency, if no priest is available, we can receive forgiveness directly from God because sin and sorrow are primarily between the individual and God.

PRAYER FOCUS

"Lord Jesus, you turned and looked on Peter when he denied you for the third time. He wept for his sin and turned again to you in sincere repentance. Look now on us and touch our hearts, so that we also may turn back to you and be always faithful in serving you, for you live and reign for ever and ever. Amen" (*Rite of Penance*, Appendix II #25).

What are some of the reasons for confessing sins to a priest?

Living a Moral Life: Gifted and Growing

22. What does it mean to turn away from sin? Describe ways in which you can turn away from sin?

23. Why is it important to confess your sins to a priest? Why can't you simply tell God directly?

24. Why would "acts of penance" help you complete your conversion process? Give an example which explains your answer.

Feelings of Guilt and Shame

Feelings are never accurate indicators of morality. Guilt feelings are closely linked with feelings of shame. These arise out of fear of being disapproved of by persons in authority or by the people we admire.

True guilt is the realization that we have chosen evil instead of good. The sacrament of Penance can help alleviate guilt feelings associated with sin. Once the sin is forgiven, there is no longer a need to feel guilty.

Just as feelings do not indicate the presence of sin, they also do not indicate its absence. If an action that feels good promotes life, love, and community, it is good. Sex between loving, married people is a source of pleasure. It not only feels good, it is good. It is love in the right order, balanced with all the other needs and duties of life. On the other hand, a married man may have intercourse with a very attractive woman who is not his wife. He may feel no guilt about the experience, but he still sins through his adultery.

Within us are impulses for both good and evil. If a man or woman consistently chooses to follow his or her good impulses, this behavior will become natural. If he or she habitually follows evil impulses, evil behavior will seem natural.

For Example

You may feel guilty if you are angry with someone who hurt you. The feeling of anger is not a sin, despite the fact that your parents may have taught you never to get angry. On the other hand, you may be guilty of sin by getting subtle revenge on a person who hurt you. Revenge may make you feel satisfied and justified, even though you have sinned by refusing to forgive.

Eucharist: holy communion, the body and blood of Jesus offered at Mass.

Often we confuse true guilt with feelings of guilt. Guilt feelings can be the product of shame. Shame can either be healthy or toxic (unhealthy).

Toxic shame gives a person a sense of worthlessness, a sense of failure and a sense of falling short as a human being. It is experienced as "I am flawed and defective as a human being." It is important to realize that these feelings are not good indicators of guilt, either. Feelings of shame, instead, reflect on one's childhood experiences.

Healthy shame, by contrast, may come as a moment of embarrassment over one's human failures or as timidity and shyness in the presence of strangers. Healthy shame functions as a signal that we need to love and have caring relationships with others. It also lets one know that he or she is not all powerful. The important difference between healthy and unhealthy shame, then, is indicated by one's basic sense of self-worth: "Do I truly believe that I am a lovable and capable person?"

---

25. *Vote "Yes" or "No" on the following statements. Be ready to give reasons for your choices. a) Guilt feelings indicate true guilt; b) If it feels good, then it must be right; c) The good thing will usually be the most difficult; d) If something gives pleasure, it must be sinful; e) Feelings are not controlled by your conscience.*

Living a Moral Life: Gifted and Growing

The Source of Unhealthy Shame

In *Healing the Shame that Binds You,* John Bradshaw explains how feelings of guilt might really be feelings of unhealthy shame.

We need to know from the beginning of our life that we can trust the world. As young children, we need to know that we can count on someone outside of us. If our parents and loved ones demonstrated unwavering affection, then we developed a basic sense of trust in others. This sense of trust is crucial for self-worth. Many psychologists believe that toxic or unhealthy shame is the result of some childhood memory of feeling abandoned by one's parents or guardians. At some point, the feeling of trust was shattered between the parents and child. If a child did not receive positive attention and affirmation, then many parts of that child were alienated. For example, Joseph was never allowed to express anger in his family. His anger became an alienated part of his self. He later experienced feelings of shame when he felt angry. Although anger is a necessary emotion, and should not normally be a source of shame, Joseph was always feeling like he was bad.

Such memories of childhood can easily make a person feel unloved later in life. Many adults and teens find help through counseling or discussions with understanding companions.

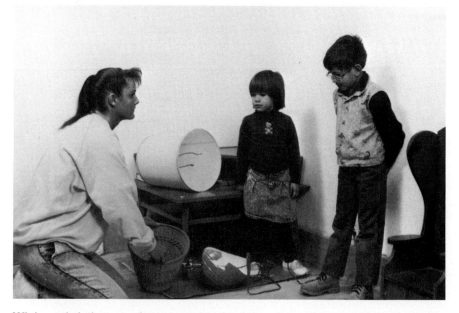

While guilt helps people recognize when they have done wrong, shame can wound a person, causing life-long problems.

Summary

■ Contrition is genuine sorrow for one's sins and the intention not to sin again. The true sign of contrition is conversion *(metanoia)*.

■ Conversion is a change in one's whole self—to rearrange one's life according to God's love—and to heal any damage the sins have done.

■ Though we may seek forgiveness directly, there are spiritual advantages to receiving the sacrament of Penance. Through this sacrament, Catholics celebrate their renewed relationship with Christ, receive spiritual direction from the priest, and reconcile with the Church community.

■ Review

1. How does contrition relate to conversion?

2. What are two ways Catholics celebrate forgiveness? Explain each.

3. What is penance? In addition to healing your relationship with God, what else must be healed?

4. When is it necessary to receive the sacrament of Penance?

5. What is a confession of devotion?

6. Why confess to a priest? Give four reasons.

7. Words to Know: contrition, conversion, *metanoia*, reconciliation, penance, shame.

■ In Your World

1. Name some common fears that prevent people from seeking reconciliation with others. Why are people discouraged from actively seeking reconciliation and forgiveness from others?

2. Are teen less likely to receive the sacrament of Penance than their parents? Conduct a brief survey at your parish after a Sunday Eucharist. Speak to five adults and ask "How often do you celebrate the sacrament of Penance?"; "When was the last time you experienced the sacrament?"; and "What are your reasons for celebrating the sacrament as often (as seldom) as you do?" Conduct the same survey in your school and compare the results.

■ Cases

Ben is a freshman who came to college on a full scholarship for having the highest grades in science class. Narrowly, Ben beat out Tracy, who was the favored candidate for the prize. Now, as a freshman, Ben began to feel guilty. He knew that his family could afford the tuition if he took a part-time job. He knew that Tracy's family was not so fortunate. They couldn't afford any of the tuition. But what really began to gnaw away at him was the fact that he had cheated often in high school, thus gaining an unfair edge for the college scholarship. Are Ben's feelings of guilt a true indication of being guilty? Explain your answer. How can Ben seek reconciliation? What must he do before receiving forgiveness?

3 Review

■ Study

1. How does the Christian lifestyle influence relationships?

2. Describe each of the four stages of relationship with God.

3. How does Christianity differ from humanistic morality?

4. List the various types of human relationships and how each can be threatened. Use examples for each type.

5. Give one effect that sin has on each of these: God; the sinner; other people.

6. Explain this statement: "Every evil action is not necessarily a sin."

7. What are the various types of freedom which you exercise? Which of these freedoms is most important.

8. What does it mean to say that a person has made a "fundamental" decision? How does this relate to mortal sin?

9. How did Saint John of the Cross view sin? Explain the analogy he used.

10. Why are most sins considered to be social? Explain.

11. Give two examples illustrating the difference between mortal and venial sin.

12. Explain this statement: "Feelings are not accurate indicators of morality."

13. How does contrition lead to conversion?

14. Why is penance a necessary part of reconciliation?

15. What are the advantages of confessing to a priest? Explain each.

16. How does shame relate to guilt feelings?

You Are a Decision Maker

You won't get through a day without making many decisions. So much of what you do is a matter of choice—sifting through options, choosing a course of action. Some decisions—what record to listen to, what clothes to wear, what route to take to school—are not really important. Some decisions, on the other hand affect your whole life. Decisions affect your relationships with people and with God. Learning the steps for making good decisions, then, is crucial to achieving happiness.

Choosing a Career

One case study incorporates the steps of decision making.

"Around my sixteenth birthday, I became aware that I had to decide what to do with my life. I went through childhood believing that when the time came I'd know what I was going to be. But at sixteen, I noticed that the seniors were having anxiety attacks over whether they would enter military service, college, trade school, or the workforce. Most were pretty uncertain about the future.

"I wanted to avoid the hassle, so I made up my mind that I would prepare ahead of time for my career. First I looked at the things I **liked** to do. I liked school, and did well in my grades. I enjoyed sports and I really liked people, particularly younger kids.

"Eventually, I found myself leaning towards a teaching career. That tentative decision shaped my choice of college, courses, job, and recreational activities.

"I talked to teachers I admired, asking how they had chosen their careers. I listened to their negative experiences as well as the pleasures and challenges they met. Despite the difficulties, the idea of becoming a teacher stuck with me. I found myself spending time with the teachers who really cared about their mission. "Before long, I had a goal. I would focus on history with a minor in physical education, two subjects I thoroughly enjoyed.

"Now, after eighteenth year of teaching, I have a master's degree. I have also been a head coach in three sports. I still look forward to going to work in the morning. I realize that the sense of fulfillment I now enjoy goes back to the process that began when I was a sixteen-year-old facing life choices. What was then my goal has become my life."

1. *What steps can you identify in this career choice? How would you evaluate the process of this case study?*

2. *Read Mark 10:17-22. What goal did the young man aim at? What did he choose? How do you know he didn't really want what he chose? Do you think he will find happiness? Why or why not?*

Successful Decisions

Four ingredients go into successful decision making: (1) goals, (2) motives, (3) obligations, and (4) consequences. We will look at each ingredient in more detail.

Long-Term and Short-Term Goals

When you make a choice toward a goal, you must in turn sacrifice something else. If you find that what you have chosen leaves you unsatisfied, look more closely at what you gave up. You may find that you let go of a long-term goal for a short-term gain or pleasure. Short-term gains and

Living a Moral Life: Gifted and Growing

Obligations

A third aspect of decision making is obligation. Besides considering your own desires, you have to keep your obligations to others in mind. Every relationship you have includes obligations for both you and for the other party. You have a moral duty to fulfill these obligations as far as you can, even if it means cutting back on fulfilling your own desires.

Some obligations are built into your life because you belong to a family, a church, or a nation. You agree to some formal obligations when you sign a contract, buy a product, or take a job. You agree to some informal obligations when you make friends or make a promise.

You aren't the sole determiner of your obligations. God's law, the needs of society, common courtesy, and other factors dictate what your obligations are.

Obligations seem to limit freedom. You may find that you can't go to the dance because you promised to babysit. In reality, obligations actually ensure freedom. Without obligations, no one would care for the young, protect the weak, or educate the alien. Faithfulness to obligations contributes to the welfare of all.

Consequences

The final aspect of decision making is its consequences. Every choice has consequences that affect you personally. You can't have the freedom to choose unless you are willing to take responsibility for the consequences of your actions. You lie to a person to get a date. When your lie is discovered, your date may never trust you again. That's one consequence of your lying, not to mention the hurt feelings your action has caused. In addition, when you make one choice, you must let go of alternatives. You can't go shopping, work out, and study for a test at the same time. You choose the consequences along with your decision.

Consequences are so closely linked with decisions that you can't prevent them once the decision is made. But a truly free person stops to consider the possible conse-

Good Motives? Bad Motives?

How many motives can you identify in the following examples? Determine if they are good motives or bad.

- *Kathleen wants to be homecoming queen. Her mother is always talking about what it was like when she was queen. Kathleen also thinks that if she's elected queen, she could get a date with the star soccer player.*

- *Peter has just convinced his parents to let him get a used car. He argued that, with a car of his own, he could get to work without bothering his parents. He also promised to drop his younger sister off at school each morning, and to run errands for his folks when asked. Peter also dreams of the girls he will attract with a car of his own.*

- *Sarah wants to be a teacher when she finishes high school. She loves to learn, and has had some really exciting teachers over the years. When asked why she wants to be a teacher, Sarah talks about shaping people's minds. When Sarah acts as a Student Moniter in homeroom, she always manages to find a student to report for breaking a rule.*

- *Danny plays guitar in a band. He sees music as a way of getting out of the house for good, away from his fighting parents and his severely retarded younger brother. Danny has had to steal from his folks in order to buy his guitar and costume. Now he has to lie about his age to play in a nightclub that sells liquor. If he gets caught he goes to juvenile hall, the club loses its license, and the band loses a job. Danny will risk anything to be successful.*

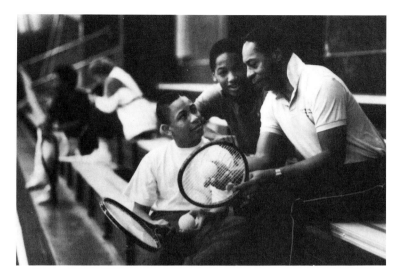

"I owe the joys of my life to decisions I made when I was sixteen years old."

pleasures aren't wrong, and are often important steps to a long-term goal. But if you always choose short-term pleasures instead of your real life goals, you may find your life not moving in your chosen direction.

The ability to choose for the long-term over the short-term is a sign of maturity. A baby wants a bottle **now**—without concern for the parents' sleep. A child wants to play **now**—without concern for the wishes of brothers and sisters. An adolescent wants to drive **now**—without weighing the consequences for the future. Signs of maturity include the ability to delay immediate pleasure for long-term goals and to accept responsibility for personal actions and choices.

The Holy Spirit leads you to choose for the long haul instead of for the short ride. Faith is the ability to trust that God directs your life. Hope inspires you to build for the future. Love helps you to sacrifice something that seems good now for the benefit of a better good to come. Inner peace results from wise decisions. It is the experience of inner peace that encourages you to continue reaching for long-term goals.

Goal: the end toward which effort is directed, what one hopes to accomplish.

It will be years before this tree provides shade from the sun, but it is a benefit worth the wait.

Motives

Another important aspect of decision making is motivation. Industries spend millions of dollars every year on motivational research. Teams of psychologists study people's reasons for buying certain kinds of cars or shampoo. If the car industry can discover what in a car attracts this or that kind of person, it can capitalize on those features to increase sales.

Motivations are your reasons for which you choose an action. "Why am I doing this?" is the question that helps you get at your motivation. People usually accept their conscious motives as their real—and only—ones and may be surprised when a choice brings to light some unconscious motives which have guided their actions. It isn't easy to discover unconscious motives.

Some motives are better than others. You might buy a friend a gift because you want to make him or her happy. Or you may want to impress the person with **your** generosity. Which motive is the better one?

Even though you may struggle with your motives for deciding, developing the habit of facing your motives openly and honestly goes a long way to make you a more mature decision maker.

For Example

Domenico says he drank a lot because he enjoyed the feeling the alcohol gave him. He also says he drank to be one of the gang. The real motive for Domenico's drinking, however, was his desire to escape from a very difficult family situation, but that motive was a little too scary for Domenico to face. Drinking, he admits, would not be such a problem if things were better at home.

Living a Moral Life: Gifted and Growing

Consider the consequences of your actions before making a choice.

quences before making a decision. If the consequences are unacceptable, then the option being considered is unacceptable.

---

3. *What is one of your long-term or life goals? What sacrifices must you make to attain this goal?*

4. *Why is it always difficult to determine other people's motives? What information would you need to understand other's motives?*

5. *Think about obligations that you have toward others and that other people have toward you. How did they come about? How do you feel about them?*

6. *Share an incident when you acted without considering the consequences. How did you feel about the outcome?*

Summary

- The four ingredients for successful decision making are goals, motives, obligations, and consequences.

- Recognize that the decisions you make concerning yourself will also affect the people around you and the society in which you live.

Obligation: something that one is committed to do.

Consequence: the effects of a certain decision or action.

SECTION 1
Checkpoint!

■ Review

1. Explain the difference between short-term and long-term goals.

2. How do conscious motives differ from unconscious motives? Give some examples.

3. Describe how goals influence your decision-making process.

4. How do obligations ensure freedom? Use an example to illustrate your answer.

5. Why is considering possible consequences part of any decision?

6. Words to Know: goals, motives, obligations, consequences.

■ In Your World

Make a list of the many things in your life which influence you when you make a decision. Include as many influences as possible. Be sure to consider friends, family, advertisements, as well as your own personal desires. Compare your lists with others in the class. Be prepared to challenge them about things that should be on their list but are not— like popularity—and be prepared to be challenged in return.

■ Cases

Read each of the cases below. Then, describe how goals, motives, obligations, and consequences affect each case.

1. Roger's father loves him very much and has always protected him. When Roger stayed out all night, his Dad told the school that his son was sick. When Roger couldn't decide between a motor bike or a car, Dad bought him both. When Roger was driving under the influence of alcohol, Dad got him the best lawyer in town.

2. Danesha was kept out of school for a week by the flu. When she returned, she had hard choices to make. Should she spend her time after school catching up in her classes required for college, or should she attend her voice lesson? She explained to the voice teacher why she could not attend her lesson. The next day the head of the music department blamed Danesha for wasting the voice teacher's time. Danesha felt angry and hurt.

Living a Moral Life: Gifted and Growing

SECTION 2
Decision-Making Processes

Very few decisions are isolated, clear-cut choices made with full freedom. Instead, (because of your previous decisions) most decisions are half formed before you make them. That is why it is so important for you to have a conscious process for making decisions. The more you practice, the easier it will be for you to make good moral decisions.

The OPTION Arrow

Here is a simple process for you to use when you are faced with a decision—especially a moral decision.

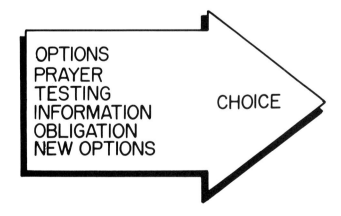

OPTIONS
PRAYER
TESTING
INFORMATION
OBLIGATION
NEW OPTIONS

CHOICE

The steps in the OPTION Arrow will help you organize your thoughts, look carefully at the options you have, and move from those options to the choice you make.

Here are the steps in the OPTION Arrow process:

1. **O**ptions—When making a decision, list your options on separate sheets of paper. Next, consider all your motives (especially ones you are not proud of), the consequences you see, how each option helps you reach your long-term goals, and what you consider to be the mature response.

2. **P**rayer—Present all of your options to God, and pray for guidance, as well as the moral courage to choose the one that best fits your life's goals—not necessarily the easiest or most pleasing one!

3. **T**esting—Weigh each option against your personal and religious values. Which option supports what is really important to you? Which one is most in line with the ideas you want to live by? Which are in keeping with your moral principles?

4. **I**nformation—Consider the facts for each option. Consult with other people, especially those whose maturity and judgment you trust, and who may have faced similar decisions. To be free to choose, you must know what you are choosing.

5. **O**bligations—Do any of these options conflict with current obligations, like the need to study or an after-school job? Remember that your relationship with the Lord has its obligations as well.

6. **N**ew options—In working through this process, have any new options or combinations of options surfaced? If so, go back to step one and consider them as well.

Eventually, even if you are not absolutely sure of the rightness of your choice, you must come to a decision. If you follow the OPTION Arrow, and if you trust in God's guidance, you will be better prepared to live with the consequences of your choice.

PRAYER FOCUS

Try this form of prayer when making a moral decision. Sit quietly and think about being with Christ. Tell him the choices you are facing and the struggle you are going through. Then ask Christ for the power to choose well.

7. *Compare the way you currently make moral decisions to the OPTION Arrow process? Which way is more effective? Why?*

Perhaps the best way to learn the process is to go through it with someone else's moral decision. Read the case below, then, see how the OPTION Arrow process helps Ricardo face a very difficult moral decision.

Ricardo has been offered two job opportunities. The first job is full-time, working at an automobile repair shop. He has always been good with his hands, and loves to work on cars. The problem is that if he takes this job, he will have to drop out of school before earning his degree. The second job is working in a bank as a mail clerk and delivery person. This job is part-time, four hours a day, five days a week, immediately after school. Ricardo is excellent with numbers and thinks he would enjoy a career in banking. The full-time job pays three times as much as the part-time job, and he could use the money. He has one week to make a decision.

Let's look at how Ricardo reaches his decision using the OPTION Arrow process.

Options

Ricardo considers his present options.
1. He can accept the job in the auto shop, quitting school immediately, but with the intention of finishing up at night school over the next year or so.
2. He can take the part-time job, finish school, then go to college.
3. He can choose to take neither job and wait for a better opportunity to arise.

As you consider each of these options, try to put yourself in Ricardo's position. Remember that nobody uses this decision-making process with cold, intellectual precision. Fear, anxiety, hope, and longing are only a few of the emotions you'll face.

Option 1—AUTOMOTIVE REPAIR
■ *Positive features*—Full-time employment. Immediate cash. New car. Own apartment. High school diploma delayed, not forgotten.

Ricardo is facing a difficult decision. How can the OPTION Arrow help him choose wisely?

Option: choice; the power or right to choose from two alternatives.

Ricardo loves to work on cars, but taking this job would mean quitting school.

- **Negative features**—Leave school. Give up his dream of going to college. Away from friends. Parents' anger.

Option 2—BANK

- **Positive features**—Part-time job. High school diploma. Money for dates. Saving for college. Weekends with friends.

- **Negative features**—Not enough money to buy a car or get an apartment.

Option 3—DO NOTHING

- **Positive features**—Not having to make a difficult choice.

- **Negative features**—Passing up two good job possibilities. No money for tuition or dates. May have to take a job flipping burgers.

Prayer

Ricardo considers his options and prays for direction. He asks his patron saint for help, prays for Mary's support, and asks Jesus for the wisdom and maturity necessary to make such a big decision. Through prayer he recognizes that the Do Nothing option is really not an option at all. He also recognizes that he needs to test these options as well as seek more information and guidance.

Testing

Ricardo weighs the options against his own values—the things that are really important to him. He values school and his friends and family. But he also loves the lifestyle that a car and a place of his own would bring him. He tries to understand the moral consequences of this decision.

Information

Ricardo learns that the owner of the shop started out as he would, at the bottom. He also learns that the turnover rate for employees is high, that salaries are low, except for the foremen, that weekend work is expected, as well as many evening hours.

Living a Moral Life: Gifted and Growing

From the people at the bank he learns that several of the Vice-presidents started out as mail clerks. Ricardo also learns that this bank has a program that encourages employees to go to school, even during work hours. And if he stayed with the bank for a minimum of two years, they would pay a portion of his college expenses. Finally, he learns that while he starts out at a smaller salary, if he becomes full-time at the bank in a year, he will be making a better salary—with better benefits—than at the auto shop.

By the time he speaks to the counselor, Ricardo has pretty much made up his mind. But, feeling the need for advice, Ricardo explains the choices to the counselor, who listens intently to Ricardo, asking many questions. Ricardo is especially concerned for moral guidance in his choice. What help can the traditional teachings offer to his decision? When Ricardo finishes, the priest repeats what he understands about the options, asks if Ricardo really understands his options clearly, and suggests that they pray together for moral guidance.

Ricardo is then able to present his options to his parents. He apologizes for not speaking to them earlier, then presents his options. His parents listen quietly, then offer their hopes and expectations for Ricardo. They assure him that, while they will be very disappointed if he leaves school to take the job, they will continue to love him dearly, but that ultimately, the decision is his to make and his to live with.

Ricardo decided not to speak with his parents until after he explored the options for himself. When do you think he should have spoken to them?

A Shorter Process

All too often, you must make decisions almost immediately. The following process, a shortened form of the OPTION Arrow, can be used in these situations.

1. Mentally review your **Options,** exploring the consequences of each.

2. **Pray** for God's help and guidance.

3. **Test** each option against your values, principles, and obligations.

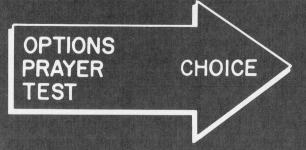

Choose the option that seems to best support your principles, and which will have the best consequences. Then follow your conscience.

Obligations

Ricardo recognizes that his obligations to his family include being faithful, to live up to his potential, to make his parents proud and to be a good example to his brothers and sisters. To his friends, Ricardo is obliged to be available, to share experiences, to grow together. To himself, Ricardo owes respect for his abilities, for his faith and his values.

New Options

Through his search, Ricardo recognizes that he can find additional ways of getting a car and moving out of home than he first thought possible. These new options help him finally make a decision.

By taking his time, and using the steps of the OPTION Arrow, Ricardo realizes that he knows the right thing for him to do. He will go to the bank and work, choosing the hope of a long-term career over the immediate car and apartment.

---

8. *Can you think of additional advantages and disadvantages for each of Ricardo's job opportunities? List them and reconsider this case.*

9. *What additional information would you need to know before making such a decision?*

10. *What additional obligations would you have?*

11. *If you found yourself in this situation, how would you make a decision?*

Summary

- The steps in the OPTION Arrow are: consider your **O**ptions, **P**ray for guidance, **T**est the options against values, seek **I**nformation, know your **O**bligations, look at any **N**ew options. Then make your decision.

- The steps in the OPT process are: list your **O**ptions, **P**ray for guidance, **T**est options against your values. Then make your decision. Use the OPT process when a quick decision is needed.

■ Review

1. What are the steps in the OPTION Arrow process? Explain each of the steps.

2. Explain the steps in the OPT process.

3. What are some of the factors which might have a negative effect on your ability to make good decisions?

4. Where can you go to receive appropriate information before making a final decision?

5. Words to Know: OPTION Arrow, option, testing, information, obligations.

■ In Your World

1. Evaluate a decision you must make using the OPTION arrow. After illustrating each step, go back and evaluate the same decision again, but this time use the OPT process.

2. Discover at least two different ways that people your age make decisions. How are they like the OPTION Arrow process? How are they different?

■ Cases

Read each of the cases below. Then, work through the decisions involved in each case.

1. Todd considers himself a fairly good Catholic. He has made two youth retreats, even giving a witness talk at one. His French class is planning a trip to France. This trip would really boost Todd's scholarship chances. But there is no way he or his parents can afford the trip. He knows that students are being recruited to sell "crack" on campus. Todd feels sure that he wouldn't get caught, and he knows he would quit as soon as he got back from France. He really wants to go! (OPTION Arrow)

2. Contemporary music is often about relationships and the decisions those relationships require. Pick one of your favorite songs. List the decisions that are mentioned in the song. Using the OPT process, try to judge whether or not the song is leading you toward a good decision. Explain your conclusions.

Living a Moral Life: Gifted and Growing

Problems with the Process

Everybody is aware of external obstacles to making sound decisions. Society sometimes has values which proclaim quite different choices from those a Catholic Christian is taught are right. Nobody is ever in complete control of a situation. So, there are bound to be problems. Another sign of maturity is the ability to face those problems and to work toward overcoming obstacles. The biggest of those obstacles may be inside yourself, not outside.

Obstacles to Freedom

In many situations, there is an obstacle which gets in the way of the decision-making process, limiting the person's freedom to act, and making a good decision harder to reach. Four which turn up on a regular basis are: **ignorance, fear, bad habits,** and **addictions.**

In moral matters, these obstacles cannot be used as excuses for making the wrong decision. While they may lessen moral responsibility to some degree, they do not remove moral obligations.

In the following situations, which obstacle (ignorance, fear, bad habits, or addiction) interrupts the decision-making process?

■ *Dino sees a student cruelly mocking a classmate. He wants to stop the student, but he is afraid of speaking out against the larger (and more violent) boy. Dino feels anger, but cannot act upon it.*

■ *Phil is beginning to realize what alcohol is doing to him, but he has to have a drink or two just to cope with a normal day.*

Bad habits can hinder your ability to make wise decisions.

- Vida wants to attend college. She needs financial aid. She finally decides to skip college and go to work. She has not researched the other options open to her.

- Jackie is so used to lying that even when she has a good reason for something, she tends to make up a story.

12. What internal realities affect your ability to make decisions? How can you overcome these obstacles?

Internal Conflicts

Sometimes you may try to make decisions following either OPTION or OPT, but you cannot seem to resolve the conflict between your knowledge and your emotions. This is a very normal conflict. You may recognize that your head tells you to call your friend and tell her calmly that she hurt you, but your feelings tell you to pay her back for her thoughtlessness.

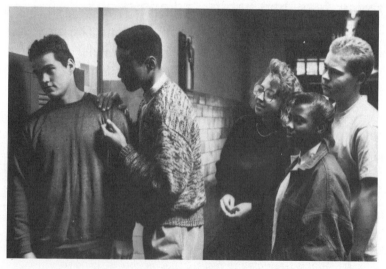

Emotions and peer pressure may influence you more than you think possible.

Games People Play

Here is a list of some of the games people use to fool themselves into believing that something bad is actually good.

- ***Wait-Watchers*** *say, "If I wait long enough, someone else will take care of the problem."*

- ***I'm the Star*** *people think that their moral irresponsibility can be excused because of their fame, fortune, or community standing—even the high school community.*

- ***Gamblers*** *take chances with moral decisions, attempting to avoid the consequences by luck.*

- ***Let's Make a Deal*** *players believe in fair exchange. "I'll go to Mass if you go to Mass."*

- ***Perfection Paralysis*** *people are so afraid that they'll make a mistake that they don't even try.*

- ***Big Spender*** *people choose to live beyond their means rather than be responsible for their debts.*

- ***Guilt Grip*** *people are afraid to trust anyone, even those they love. They are frozen in their usually unnecessary guilt.*

- ***Follow the Leader*** *players watch what others do before acting.*

- ***Grab Bag*** *people take all they can get now, and to heck with tomorrow.*

- ***Lone Rangers*** *make decisions without outside advice. They can do it alone.*

Emotions and the Mind

Your emotions need the direction and guidance of your mind. So, it might seem that you should disregard emotional messages and do what your mind advises. But your emotions are a very important part of you and should not be put aside. Your feelings are giving you important information.

Emotions are the voices of your past experiences and of your unconscious fears and needs. These emotions also respond to the feelings of others. However your mind is often too busy to consciously notice what another is feeling.

Before acting, it is important to think through questions such as the following.

1. Why are my feelings really so opposed to what my mind is telling me?
2. Am I afraid of something I can't or won't admit to?
3. Do I have a need that my mind cannot see—a need that must be satisfied?
4. Am I certain that I am correct? Or am I only seeing surface facts?
5. Am I being guided by a prejudice that has an emotional rather than a factual source?

Emotions can also keep you from doing what you should at times. Several professional athletes have had their careers cut short because they were afraid of flying. A deep-seated fear of death or of growing old can prevent a person from speaking with or caring for an aging grandparent. By tracing your emotions, you can free yourself to do the good you want.

Game Playing

If you have followed a reliable decision-making process, obtained the facts, and governed your emotions, nothing should stop you from making a good moral decision. Right? Wrong! It is entirely possible for you to use these processes to fool yourself. When people want something very intensely, everything inside works toward getting it. If the desire is not good, you can try to fool yourself into thinking that it is good—or at least, not as bad as it really is.

Values for Life

Christianity has recognized many virtues which, when developed, help us to be honest with our decision making. The opposite of ignorance is the gift of the Holy Spirit, knowledge. The virtue that overcomes fear is fortitude. Prudence and temperance are virtues that replace bad-habits and addiction. These virtues are known traditionally as the "cardinal" or primary virtues.

Living a Moral Life: Gifted and Growing

Dressing to impress others is a "game" many people play.

It isn't hard to recognize the games we all play. However, even if you are an expert in game playing, you need to face these difficult questions:
1) What is it inside of me that tries to pull me away from what is good?
2) What urges me to choose the wrong thing, even after I have tried to choose correctly?

Saint Paul felt the downward pull as well and wrote: "What I do, I do not understand. For I do not do what I want, but I do what I hate" (Romans 7:15). He identifies the pull as the mystery of evil. Sometimes it comes from your own choices to do what is wrong. Sometimes it comes from the evil example of others.

13. *How can feelings make it difficult to make good moral decisions?*

14. *How can you understand these feelings and deal with them?*

15. *What are some of the ways you fool yourself?*

16. *Which of your relationships help you make good decisions? Which get in the way of good decisions?*

Instead of leaving a book of rules to fit every situation, Jesus spoke of relationships. "You shall love the Lord, your God, with all your heart, with all your soul, and with all your mind...You shall love your neighbor as yourself" (Matthew 22:37,39). "Whoever wishes to come after me, must deny himself, take up his cross, and follow me" (Matthew 16:24).

As your personal friend, Lord, and guide to the Father, Jesus gives you his Spirit. He places you within a worshipping community who believe in him—and in you. Together, under the leadership of the bishops, the community interprets the Bible and the experiences of the community for the guidance of its members. Every time you make a moral decision, you can draw on the strength you have in these relationships.

Neither Church members, teachers, nor even the Bible, is meant to replace your own attempt to follow Jesus in the particular situations of your life. Christ is present in this community, in the sacraments, and in the companionship of its members. Through them you can develop confidence in yourself, in your common sense, and in your conscience. The support and guidance received here will be invaluable when you are faced with moral decisions.

---

17. *Whom do you go to when you need advice on an important issue? Why do you choose that person?*

Summary

- Be on the lookout for the power of your emotions and the ways you might be fooling yourself.

- Learn to recognize the games people play to keep from making an honest, moral decision.

- Remember that relationships with God, your family, the Church, and your friends can be very helpful in overcoming these internal obstacles.

■ Review

1. What are some of the internal obstacles that get in the way of the decision-making process?

2. How can you deal with these internal obstacles?

3. Why don't these internal obstacles "take you off the hook" if you make a bad decision?

4. How does "game playing" affect your decision-making ability? Give an example.

5. What role can emotions play in the decision-making process?

6. Words to Know: internal obstacles, ignorance, excuse, game playing.

■ In Your World

Describe a situation in your life in which you feel an internal conflict over a decision. This need not be a big decision or even a moral decision. Try to get in touch with the sources of the conflict. How might you fool yourself?

■ Cases

Read the following cases. Describe what internal obstacles you find in the case. What are the emotional needs here? How will these needs affect the person's ability to make decisions?

1. Dana fears she is the cause of her parents' recent divorce. She has moved to another city to live with her grandmother, and she wants to be accepted by her new classmates. She is invited to a party at the home of a boy who is believed to use alcohol and drugs.

2. Bob has been depressed since the death of his mother. He needs Karen's personal support and love. He has urged her to have sexual intercourse with him, but each time she has refused. Karen's feelings tell her to go ahead because Bob needs her, but her mind tells her she will do him no good in consenting to jeopardize their relationship with the Lord.

CHAPTER

4   Review

■ Study

1. How is it possible to choose what you want to do and still not feel satisfied about it? Give an example.

2. How do your long-term goals affect your decision making?

3. Give an example of how a short-term pleasure can derail the decision making process.

4. Explain the role of maturity in decision making.

5. Give an example of how motives are important in making moral decisions.

6. Why are obligations an important element to consider when making a decision?

7. Give an example of how you can have good and bad motives for the same action.

8. How can you know that you are accepting the consequences of your actions?

9. Why is it important to develop skill in making good moral decisions?

10. Describe in some detail the OPTION Arrow process for making moral decisions.

11. Which of the steps in the process seem most difficult for you? Why is this the case?

12. Describe the OPT process. When would you use it?

13. In your own words, how can you be obedient and still be free?

14. What are four obstacles to freedom in decision making? How do these obstacles affect your moral responsibility?

15. How do society's laws guide you in your moral decision making? How can these laws conflict with decision making?

16. What is the role of feelings in making a moral decision?

17. How can relationships help you through internal conflicts in making moral decisions?

"I started looking at each customer as if he or she was Jesus."

was lifted from my shoulders. After that night, I decided to continue visiting the prayer group. Gradually, over the next three years, my life took a new course. I became less concerned about things I couldn't control and focused, instead, on what I could do.

"I met another guy who seemed to really care for me. But this time, I wasn't looking for a husband, just a close friend. I kept my job at the restaurant and started looking at each customer as Jesus. I began praying for them, too. I realized that the Bible spoke about me when Jesus said, "For I was hungry and you gave me food, I was thirsty and you gave me drink...whatever you did for one of these least brothers of mine, you did it for me" (Matthew 25:35-40). Before, I wondered where God was. Now I saw that God was at my tables every day.

"My friend and I have been married for fifteen years now and we have three children. I still read the Bible everyday. I don't always get direct answers to my prayers, but I do receive insights that help me in my decisions. I feel drawn to welcome others to meet Jesus as I did years ago at that prayer group. When I help just one person find a relationship with Jesus, I feel that my life has a purpose—a purpose I only began to realize after I gave my worries to Jesus."

Living a Moral Life: Gifted and Growing

I, the Lord, Am Your God

Faith can be described as a personal "Yes!" to the love God offers. Yet, faith in God always has been and always will be difficult for human beings. It means accepting the words and actions of a mystery we cannot see or understand as good. It also means letting this mystery direct our lives.

It Changed Everything

"I went to Catholic schools but I guess my values were the same as those you see on TV: look beautiful, stay young, get rich, have fun, and life will be happy. In my job as a waitress, I tried to live by these values, but I wasn't happy. What caused me the most worry was that I wasn't married yet. Everything seemed hopeless. I soon lost interest in going to church because I didn't get anything out of it.

"Then I met a guy who invited me to a prayer group at a local Catholic Church. I pretended to be interested because I thought he was cute. When I showed up, there was this room full of people I had never seen before, but the guy who invited me was nowhere to be found. He stood me up! Too embarrassed to say anything, I decided to stay. The group really wasn't strange. They spoke about God in a way which seemed real to me. They praised God and asked to be released from their worries and burdens. Then, it hit me! I had never really given my life to God. I had never asked for God's will. Instead, I was always too wrapped up in myself, or trying to copy some TV personality.

"I told Jesus that I would surrender all my worries to him. I put my concerns about marriage, career, and future into Jesus' hands. Suddenly, I felt as though a heavy burden

1. *What people in this story were channels of God's love to someone else, even without knowing it?*

2. *Relate an incident in which an everyday happening or an ordinary person brought God's message to you.*

3. *What is the key to this woman understanding what her life is all about?*

God Is a Compassionate Lover

God is not like a shrewd boss who promises fair wages (salvation) for a good day's work (obedience and worship). God is not like an overly-strict parent who demands that people straighten out their lives by laws and commands. Rather, God is more like a passionate and compassionate lover who offers personal tenderness and wants love and fidelity in return. The Lord makes a personal choice to love each one of us and asks for an individual response in return.

This is how the prophets experienced God's love for Israel.

- *"I remember the devotion of your youth, how you loved me as a bride, Following me in the desert, in a land unsown" (Jeremiah 2:2).*

- *"I had thought: How I should like to treat you as sons, And give you a pleasant land, a heritage most beautiful among the nations! You would call me, "My Father," I thought, and never cease following me. But like a woman faithless to her lover, even so you have been faithless to me, O house of Israel" (Jeremiah 3:19-20).*

- *"For he who has become your husband is your Maker; his name is the Lord of hosts; Your redeemer is the Holy One of Israel, called God of all the Earth. The Lord calls you back, like a wife forsaken and grieved in spirit, A wife married in youth and then cast off, says your God. For a brief moment I abandoned you, but with great tenderness I will take you back" (Isaiah 54:5-7).*

The Jews have a special covenant relationship with God.

In the book of Exodus, God freed the Israelites from slavery for no other reason than compassion. God liberated and cared for the chosen people through the covenant. The Israelites accepted the offer, promising to love no other god and to shape their lives around these laws. In return, God assured the Israelites that they would be given a homeland where their descendants would prosper.

The Heart of the Law

For a believer, morality has its deepest meaning in loving and respecting the true God. Through the Hebrew people we have the Ten Commandments, the heart of Hebrew Law. The first three commandments deal with humanity's relationship with God. These commandments forbid believers to manipulate God's power by making idols, by using magic, or by controlling the powers of the earth through labor. Through the first three commandments, one learns that God freely chooses to love us, not because we honor a graven image, but solely as a gift. People are to remain free from fear, never again becoming slaves who worship the sun or the seasons.

The fourth through tenth commandments deal with relationships between people. These commandments forbid the neglect of and disrespect toward parents and elderly members of the community (4), murder (5), adultery (6), robbery (7), perjury (8), and greed (9,10).

In addition to the commandments, Christians have access to an additional well-spring of God's love. It is through Jesus that the commandments are understood and interpreted by the Christian believer.

The New Covenant

Christ did not come to set aside the Ten Commandments; he came to fulfill them. Jesus' New Covenant is sealed in his blood. God sent Jesus so that he could be even closer to us and share in our sufferings and joys. We can begin to realize God's passionate love for us only through the passion and death of Jesus. A tremendous new energy comes to us, too, through the death and resurrection of Jesus. We possess his Holy Spirit. Following Christ is more

Living a Moral Life: Gifted and Growing

The Covenant and Themes of Exodus

God's commitment to the Israelites was shown in their deliverance from slavery. The Israelites had been taken captive by the Egyptians. During this period of enslavement, the people hoped and prayed that God might free them. This hope was realized in the efforts of Moses who became Yahweh's prophet. Moses informed Pharaoh that he should free the Israelites. Pharaoh laughed and ignored Moses. But soon, plagues and numerous pestilences overtook the Egyptians, harsh warnings that the Egyptians should heed Moses' request. The struggle continued until the Spirit of God claimed the lives of every first born male, except those in homes where the door post was painted with the blood of a lamb. Pharaoh lost his son and allowed the Israelites to go free.

Eventually Yahweh led the Israelites into the desert and assured them of a promised land. God's faithfulness and saving action were shown in the form of the Covenant. God would remain faithful to the people as long as they kept the commandments.

The story of Exodus and its themes are still alive today in the struggles of the poor and oppressed. God continues to deliver people spiritually, physically, and mentally. You may want to read the book of Exodus for the whole exciting story.

than obeying a long list of written laws. Following Christ means to live his life.

Being a Christian means growing deeper in relationship with Christ and working with others to build a compassionate world. To work at friendship and community with others demands our entire heart, and is much more difficult than simply memorizing rules and keeping them.

Covenant: a two-way promise in which both sides benefit from the agreement.

Being a Christian means putting one's faith into action.

Keeping Faith Alive

Christ teaches his disciples to leave all human security behind and follow him. This is the lesson he taught when he invited Peter to walk across the water (Matthew 14:22-33).

This lesson can speak to us in several ways. First, we can learn that Jesus will always lead the way into the unknown future and that he will support our choices as long as they are made with the desire to reach him. Even if we lose heart in the middle of the journey, he will be there. Second, we can see that Jesus wants us to surrender to him. He wants us to give over to him our trust. Finally, we can begin to understand that Jesus wants us to meet him on his terms.

Keeping Love Real

Loving God is different from loving a human person. God's love for us works so mysteriously that we often do not understand it, and we do not always realize how it is transforming us. We only gradually learn how to respond totally in love. Loving God takes work, just as loving another person takes work.

When you say you "love" a person, that means that you have made a choice to care for that person, that you respect the other as he or she is, and that you will live for the well-being of the loved-one, no matter what the cost. The opposite of love is not hate, but indifference. Hate is an emotion. Indifference means that you don't care. It can be easy to be indifferent toward God because we cannot see God and because God is not pushy.

If you hate someone intensely, you may still want to be close to him or her. There is still a relationship. Indifference, however, is the absence of a relationship. You don't care if the person loves you, hates you, or ignores you.

4. *How has Yahweh delivered you from the enslaving forces in life? What enslaved you? How were you liberated?*

5. *Give an example from the Gospels to show that Jesus calls us to love, not just obey God.*

Living a Moral Life: Gifted and Growing

Love requires you to respect the other person as he or she is.

6. *What forms of self-sacrifice are necessary if you want to accept the New Covenant of Jesus Christ?*

7. *Read Matthew 14:22-33. Would you have gotten out of the boat to walk to Christ? Do you think you would have made it to him without sinking? Explain your answer.*

Summary

- Know that you are a channel of God's love to others.

- God offers love and compassion in the form of the Covenant, which is a mutual agreement between humanity and God.

- The first three commandments focus on humanity's relationship to God, whereas the last seven commandments talk about relationships among people.

- The New Covenant is Jesus himself. Through his death and resurrection, and with the gift of his Holy Spirit, it is possible to follow God without needing a long list of rules and laws.

■ Review

1. Give one reason why faith in God is difficult.

2. Explain the covenant God offers.

3. Explain this statement: "The Ten Commandments alone are not the heart of Christian worship."

4. What is the lesson of Peter's walking on water?

5. How is loving God different from loving a human person?

6. Words to Know: covenant, faith, love, hate, indifference.

■ In Your World

1. Think of "water" as a figurative expression for struggle, uncertainty, and self-doubt. Relate an incident in your life when Jesus helped you "walk across turbulent waters." In what ways did you feel like Saint Peter? Where did you get the courage to cross the "turbulent waters"?

2. What kind of forces can enslave you if you do not: a) honor the true God; b) obey just authorities; c) respect and protect life; d) respect marriage vows; e) respect property; f) tell the truth; and g) remain content with your vocation and possessions?

■ Cases

Some people feel justified in hating or not caring about God, or in loving themselves more than God. These are some reasons they give for breaking off their relationship with God:

1. God has sent me nothing but pain and struggle. I am punished when I don't do anything wrong.

2. You have to be selfish to be happy. If you don't take care of yourself, who will? The modern world is run by people who say "me first."

3. Life is too exciting right now to bother about God. What I love is the here and now. It satisfies me. What more do I need?

4. God is too narrow and rigid. Being good is dull. I need adventure and excitement. Why should I love a life-restricting God?

■ Which person above expresses what you see as the most common cause of people's hatred of God? Of their indifference toward God?

You Shall Not Have Other Gods before Me

When God made the original covenant with the Israelites, they had to be taught that their lives were not controlled by spirits within the sun, the wind, or the earth. They were forbidden to make statues of these gods, for as soon as the Hebrews made such an image, they believed they had "captured" a god's power. By honoring the image, they could force the god to help them. For this reason, the Hebrews were forbidden to make images of God. In doing this, the people were taught that they could not control God. They had to have faith that their God would remain close to them for God's own reasons (see Exodus 20:2-6). The challenge for us today is to recognize the images in our lives which we prefer to God.

The Message of the First Commandment

The message of the first commandment is that God wants to keep in close communion with us, free from forces that can isolate and enslave us. We are called to belong to a community that depends on the God who really loves us. Then we can support others in believing, hoping in, loving, and worshipping God. Mutual support is especially needed when the pressures from other people, materialism, or society threatens to cut us off from God. Through faith we can say a big, personal "yes!" to the love God offers us. But faith in God is difficult for human beings because it means accepting as good the words and actions of a mystery we cannot see or understand completely. It also means letting this mystery become the driving idea in your life.

Humility doesn't mean you can't be proud of your special skills.

PRAYER FOCUS

Doubts are an essential part of faith development. Doubt is the urge to seek deeper answers to the mysteries of faith. One way of working through doubt is to hand over to God your immediate desire for reasons and answers. Advice can be found in *The Cloud of Unknowing,* a book written anonymously in the fourteenth Century. The author explains, "A person may know completely and ponder thoroughly every created thing and its works, yes, and God's works, too, but not God himself. Thought cannot comprehend God. And so, I prefer to abandon all I can know, choosing rather to love him whom I cannot know. By love he may be embraced, never by thought." In prayer, thoughts about God's work can be helpful, but love is the surest way to develop an understanding of God, especially during periods of doubt. As you pray, love, then listen.

Humility: Being Yourself

Humility is an attitude required by the first commandment. Humility is admitting that God is your creator and that you are God's creature: You do not own yourself nor determine your own mission and purpose in life. Humility is an act of love, an accepting of God as God and yourself as a human being. Being humble before God does not mean degrading yourself as if you were worthless. Humility is feeling proud that you are good, gifted, and called for a specific mission. It is recognizing the truth about yourself and about God. If truly humble, you can accept a compliment with a simple "thank you" and not feel embarrassed or pretend that you don't possess the good that was complimented.

Pride Takes Many Forms

The opposite of humility is pride. Pride takes many forms. **Conceit** is holding too high an opinion of one's self in comparison with others. **Intellectual** pride is refusing to admit that one's ideas may be incomplete or wrong, even to

Living a Moral Life: Gifted and Growing

the extent of refusing to believe God's word. **Perfection-ism** is refusing to accept human faults and limitations. Perfectionists think they must produce flawless work; they cannot believe that God loves them even in their weakness.

Pride can drive people to prove that they are always better—better than they were last year, better than their friends, better than those in authority, better than any other human being. No compliment, prize, or success can fully satisfy the proud person.

Only the Spirit of Jesus can free us from the chains of pride. Little by little, he shows us that we are unique and valuable human beings, and that comparisons with others are unnecessary. Of course, this is not to say that we can't learn from others.

---

8. *Write a conversation between two conceited people. With a friend, dramatize this conversation in class.*

9. *How can you help a friend overcome perfectionism?*

10. *How would a humble person react to winning a scholarship? To losing an election? To seeing a beautiful sunset?*

Obedience: Letting God Be God

Obedience to God requires following the Ten Commandments, but it also involves much more than that. Obedience includes accepting God's design for your life. Walking along the way of God does not eliminate your freedom because God leaves plenty of room for individual creativity and decision making. God does not ask your obedience in order to limit personal freedom, but to do just the opposite. God wants to direct you to the happiest, most fulfilling life you can live, a life of great personal expression. Obedience helps you discover that life.

God's way is beneficial not only to the individual, but to the whole world. Your life fits into a larger plan that involves the good of others, especially since your mission is

For Example

One man ran for political office eleven times and lost seven of the elections. If he had given up his efforts, believing his losses were "God's will," Abraham Lincoln would never have been president of the United States.

Lincoln did not see his early losses as a reason to give up his political career.

connected with theirs. God never wastes a gift or talent, so every ability you have makes some contribution to your mission. When you develop your talents and follow God's direction, you adore God with humility, obedience, faith, hope, and love.

It may sound strange, but it is not God's will that you should know with absolute certainty what is in store for you. If it were, God would be sending direct messages every moment. Instead, you are given the powers of intelligence, imagination, and choice. God directs you step by step whenever you: use your talents, take good advice, pray, and act with confidence. You will be shown what is necessary for each decision and will be blessed for taking the consequences of a free choice, even though the choice turns out to be a mistake. A poor choice may be irreversible and it may hurt others. Still, God can help you learn to grow from this mistake and become a better and wiser person.

Living a Moral Life: Gifted and Growing

Twisting God's Messages

There are many ways to twist God's messages so that they fit our will. Some people lie about their abilities in order to get scholarships or jobs. Others use dishonest means to win competitions, or they manipulate people to get ahead. Some may even give their lives to Jesus for the express purpose of getting rich and then proclaim their wealth as God's seal of approval.

Of course, the opposite can also be true. People will attempt something, fail, and then give up saying, "It's God's will that I'm a failure." Such attitudes miss the mark badly. "God's will" should not be used as an excuse to avoid the hard work needed to fulfill your real mission in life. The general principle here is that if you are fairly sure you are doing a good thing and you have the ability to do it, go ahead and keep trying. Your mission may be depending on it.

Send Us a Sign

God occasionally sends clear messages to people about what is wanted of them, but usually we are guided indirectly through our talents, our relationships with other people, and through the circumstances of our lives. Yet some people keep trying to know God's will completely. They will not make a decision without assurance from their astrologer or their psychiatrist. Or, they will tell God to send a "sign" so that they will know they are doing the right thing.

You do not have to have complete knowledge before you can obey God. You honor God more when you trust the subtle guidance. The closer you come to God, the clearer you will be able to recognize God's direction. Saint Paul assured us of this when he said: "At present we see indistinctly, as in a mirror; but then face to face. At present I know partially; then I shall know fully as I am fully known" (1 Corinthians 13:12).

Subtle: difficult to notice or understand.

What If I Don't Believe?

Doubting and questioning are parts of developing a more mature faith. Sometimes you may be shaken when you find out that your friends don't practice their religion or pray. Then you may experience a period of doubt. This does not mean that you are bad or unlovable, or that you have been forgotten by God. Doubts about God may last only a few hours or for several years. In fact, darkness and doubt are often signs that you are being drawn closer to God, away from the pat answers of childhood faith.

11. *In what other ways can people try to twist God's will to fit their own desires?*

12. *How do you know that you are doing God's will?*

13. *Failure is often associated with weakness. Do you think men suffer more from fear of failure than women do? Explain your answer.*

14. *What are two inward signs that the Spirit of Jesus is guiding your decisions?*

Head and Face. ♈ ARIES, The Ram.

Arms.
♊ GEMINI,
The Twins.

Heart.
♌ LEO,
The Lion.

Reins.
♎ LIBRA,
The Balance.

Thighs.
♐ SAGITTARIUS,
The Bowman.

Legs.
♒ AQUARIUS,
The Waterman.

Neck.
♉ TAURUS,
The Bull.

Breast.
♋ CANCER,
The Crab.

Bowels.
♍ VIRGO,
The Virgin.

Secrets.
♏ SCORPIO,
The Scorpion.

Knees.
♑ CAPRICORNUS,
The Goat.

Feet. ♓ PISCES, Fishes.

Some people will try anything to know God's will clearly, even believing that their futures can be predicted by the stars.

Living a Moral Life: Gifted and Growing

The Jesus Prayer

The first commandment guides us to make God the center of our lives. The Jesus Prayer is a form of meditation that adores the Son of God. It was developed by the Desert Fathers in the fourth and fifth centuries. It is a way of entering the region of the heart where one can recognize and feel the presence of God.

"Pray constantly," said Saint Paul to the Thessalonians. The Jesus prayer is one way to achieve this goal. In *The Way of the Pilgrim*, a Russian peasant who lived sometime in the 1800s tells how he found God through the Jesus Prayer. He writes, "One day an old man, who looked like a member of some religious community, caught up with me. I asked him, 'Please, be gracious, Reverend Father, and explain to me the meaning of ceaseless mental prayer, and how to practice it.' The priest replied, 'The ceaseless Jesus Prayer is a continuous, uninterrupted call on the holy name of Jesus Christ with the lips, mind and heart; and in the awareness of His abiding presence it is a plea for His blessing in all undertakings, in all places, in all times, even in sleep.' "

At the center of the prayer is a mantra. Repeat the phrase, "Lord Jesus Christ, have mercy on me." Or simply say, "Lord Jesus" over and over, while focusing your attention on your breathing.

First, relax by breathing deeply. Place yourself in a comfortable posture, but one that won't let you fall asleep. Silently say "Lord" or "Lord Jesus Christ" as you breathe in easily and naturally through the nose and "Jesus" or "have mercy on me" as you breathe out. When distracting thoughts come, let them go and focus your attention back on the mantra and breathing. Practice this for about fifteen minutes. Afterward, open your eyes and sit quietly for a minute or so. Do this as often as possible. The presence of God will be felt more strongly in your life, and greater happiness will follow.

Mantra: a word or phrase repeated as a focus in meditation.

Adoration is the unique honor we owe God. As we grow to know God better, we can learn to adore God more spontaneously, sometimes without words. Adoration can be part of our amazement at a beautiful scene. Or we may adore God when we hold a child or embrace someone we love. Adoration is closely linked to thanksgiving. There is a difference, however. We thank God for the good we have received, but we adore God simply because of who God is.

Spiritual growth, like human love, never stops. Our relationship with God will become more personal and meaningful as we work to develop it. God is always reaching out to draw us closer. Later in life, toward the middle years of forty or fifty, many people pass through a period of doubt. Depression, marital problems, and career crises often occur at about this time. At the end of this period of spiritual growth comes a great peace, with a sense that one finally "has it all together." Life is still mysterious, but it has meaning and beauty. One simply way in which you can come to this peace is through adoration.

We owe God adoration that is private and personal, taking any form of prayer we choose. Our prayer can be just a thought, either of love or praise. It can be a special silence during which you simply rest in the divine presence without doing, saying, or thinking anything. The Christian community also owes God adoration that is public and communal—liturgy. Catholic liturgy includes the Mass, the sacraments, and the Prayer of Christians (the Divine Office).

15. *Recall the way you prayed when you were a child. How did you picture God then? How has your image of God changed?*

16. *How do you honestly feel about the way God is present or not present to you? Explain.*

17. *Name some of the concrete ways that you can show adoration to God. Be specific.*

18. *What does it mean to simply rest in the divine presence without doing, saying, or thinking anything?*

Spiritual growth, like love, never stops.

Summary

- God wants you to belong to a community that accepts God's gift of love. This desire is expressed in the first commandment.

- Humility means accepting the truth about yourself and recognizing God as your creator.

- When you doubt God, keep talking to God about the doubts.

- Thank God for the good you have received, but adore God because of who God is.

The Prayer of Christians: an arrangement of Psalms, Scriptures, and vocal prayers to be said at various times in the day.

■ Review

1. Why were the Israelites forbidden to make images of God?

2. Explain this statement: "Humility means not degrading yourself."

3. Why is perfectionism a form of pride?

4. When can religious doubt be a good experience?

5. How should you honor God? What makes this honor different from other forms? Give two examples of private adoration.

6. Words to Know: humility, obedience, conceit, liturgy, adoration, Prayer of Christians.

■ In Your World

1. What has caused you to doubt your faith in the past? In the present? Name the ways you can work through periods of doubt.

2. What does it mean for you to feel pride? To feel humility? Find examples in your life of false pride and false humility and write about these examples in your journal.

■ Cases

Read the following story about Lauren. Then discuss what enabled her to resolve her doubt.

On the way home from school one day when she was in the eleventh grade, Lauren was pondering whether or not she believed there was a God. Finally she decided that God was just a crutch for weak-minded people—something they could lean on instead of facing the cold, hard facts of life. It hit her that, without God, there was no reason or need for her to live. Any mission she might have been born for was now void. She felt alone, very scared, and very small. After an hour of these feelings, she decided that she needed God and that somehow her thinking was mixed up. She decided to accept God again.

Living a Moral Life: Gifted and Growing

SECTION 3
You Shall Not Worship Them

Some people rattle off prayers without thinking. Others keep a Saint Christopher medal in the car and then drive while drunk, putting their faith in an image rather than in Christ. Some seem to value Lenten ashes more than Sunday Mass and Holy Communion. In these cases, worship is turned into superstition.

Counterfeit Worship

Superstition is only one type of counterfeit or false worship. There are others, including practices that involve worship for wrong or misguided reasons. Some people worship idols or are members of cults. Beyond this, many people seek answers to their questions by calling on the supernatural realm. Practices of this nature are broadly termed "the occult." All of these practices destroy a true relationship with the living God.

Your friendship with God can be weakened or destroyed by various types of counterfeit worship. Counterfeit worship is any misguided or abusive religious practice. Superstitions and religion for profit are two common examples.

Superstitions

Superstition is the abuse of an authentic form of worship. God is not a vending machine that dispenses spiritual candy bars provided the right prayer coins are inserted. Our prayer does not control God. Rather, it puts us in personal touch with God so that we can listen and be more open to God's will.

Chain prayers or letters are also forms of superstition. Usually the reader is promised a miraculous answer to prayer if he or she sends copies of the prayer to a certain number of people. Sometimes there is a warning of danger if the letter is not passed on. The best thing to do if you receive a chain letter is to destroy it immediately. The first commandment teaches that no one can control God.

Religion for Profit

A second form of counterfeit worship is the turning of religion into a big business. Some preachers and evangelists pepper their "healings" and sermons with promises of specific blessings to those who contribute money. These people "sell" religion for their own personal profit. The selling of sacred objects or religious services for personal profit has existed since the time of the Apostles. In Acts 8:9-24, Simon Magus tried to buy the power to work miracles. Today, such a practice is known as simony.

God's blessings, healings, or answers to prayer can never be bought, even through contributions to a church or a preacher. However, making sincere contributions to a church is a duty. Today, churches of all denominations care for large numbers of believers. They need buildings, qualified personnel, and many other material things to spread the Good News. Since people are influenced by television, radio, film, and magazines, believers need to

Some television evangelists have preyed on people's superstitions and fears to make money. Some have been convicted for their deceit.

Living a Moral Life: Gifted and Growing

invest money to use these means of communication to make Christ known. Contributions to your church keep it alive. Still, the giver needs to guard against superstition, and the receiver needs to guard against greed.

---

19. *Name some of the effects that collecting huge contributions and using religion for profit might have on a person's faith in the Gospel.*

20. *Describe a superstition that people you know follow. Where did the belief originate, and why do they continue to practice it?*

The Occult

The occult is a broad term that covers any activity or practice which involves seeking power, help or knowledge from the supernatural or spirit world. Divination, witchcraft, and satanism are the most common forms of the occult practiced.

Divination

Divination is any activity that calls on the supernatural or superhuman to obtain knowledge, especially of the future. Here are some of the more well-known or popular forms of such activities:

- *Astrology: The study of the positions of the stars and planets, with the belief that their position at the time of one's birth influences a person's entire life.*

- *Spiritualism: The belief in and practice of seances (SAY-ahnce) that attempt to communicate with the spirits of the dead through a medium, a person who claims to have the ability to converse with the spirit world.*

- *Ouija board: The method of contacting the spirit world by using a board painted with symbols and a free-moving pointer. Ouija (WEE-je) is from the French "oui" and the German "ja," both of which mean "yes."*

- *Palmistry: The foretelling of one's future by an analysis of the lines on the palm and the shape of the hand.*

- *Cartomancy: The foretelling of the future by interpreting symbols on cards drawn in chance order. Tarot cards are an example.*

Divination appeals to people who have difficulty accepting responsibility for their choices. Because of this, they seek answers from the spirit world or the stars. Other people want a message from a deceased loved one. This fascination with the unknown attracts many people.

Divination has some harmless forms, such as the fortune-telling or palm reading used at parties and fairs, or reading newspaper horoscopes. However, people who become seriously involved in any form of divination open themselves to psychological and moral harm.

When seriously pursued, all divination activities create dependence on forces other than God and oneself. They prevent moral maturity and gradually weaken one's freedom of choice. Eventually, they can end up taking the place of faith and prayer. In general, divination exploits people's need for security. Fraudulent fortune-tellers and astrologers grow rich on the misplaced faith of weak people. Tampering with spiritualism and the ouija board can open the way to satanic control of one's life.

Games of divination can be fun to play as long as they are not taken seriously.

Values for Life

Fortitude, or moral courage, is one of the gifts of the Holy Spirit. Fortitude is the strength "to take a stand" against the popular idols of your society. This does not mean that you must speak out, but it does entail having the courage to implement such convictions into your life. Some of the most powerful statements against idolatry come from those who simply and quietly live out the Christian faith.

If you are afraid and need greater moral courage, ask the Holy Spirit to guide you and give you that strength.

Living a Moral Life: Gifted and Growing

There are no harmless forms of witch-craft.

Magic and Witchcraft

Witchcraft is another occult activity which attempts to obtain power from the spirit world through the practice of magic. Traditionally, there are two forms of magic: white and black. White magic is an attempt to master the forces of nature for so-called good purposes or self-development. Black magic, by contrast, is an attempt to do evil, inflict harm, or gain riches by controlling the forces of nature with the aid of evil spirits.

Magic is as old as the human race. It appeals to the human thirst for power to control natural forces and fate. Fear of evil has driven people to worship the source of evil and to make pacts with spirits. Witchcraft has a great appeal because it claims to release extraordinary forces of energy within a person.

There are no harmless forms of magic or witchcraft. Even white magic requires a rejection of the true God. All forms violate the respect owed to other human beings because they involve casting spells on people. Even when no harm is done, these activities manipulate people's freedom, promote an unrestrained desire for power, money, and revenge, and reject moral laws. Many participate in magic out of a sense of fear for their lives, not out of a sincere desire or wish to do so. Their free will, then, is being threatened by such practices. In short, magic and witchcraft insult the true God, destroy human freedom, and endanger life.

Exploit: to use another's weakness for one's own profit or gain.

Fraudulent: a person who deceives others, usually for money.

Satanism

More serious than the occult practice of divination and magic is the direct worship of the devil. Satanic ceremonies always include desecration of Christian objects—especially the Blessed Sacrament—and perverted sexual practices. Sometimes the ceremonies include animal or even human sacrifices, and they always encourage various forms of violence and corruption. Worship of the devil is a direct rejection of God.

Evil and Deception

Satan is clever, fooling us into thinking that the frightening aspects of the occult are the devil's primary work. In reality, the most successful tactics are hidden ones. People are encouraged to make excuses for their immoral conduct. In this way, people are lured away from God gradually and comfortably. Not even Jesus was safe from Satan's temptations. Satan wanted Jesus to do God's will, but not God's way. Jesus was tempted to use dramatic demonstrations of power to force people to believe (see Matthew 4:1-11, Luke 4:1-13).

Two reliable signs of Satan's presence are confusion and lies. Signs of the Spirit of God at work are peace and clear truthfulness. Saint James says, "Resist the devil and he will flee from you" (James 4:7). Don't be afraid to pray, and then act on the strength of God's help.

---

21. *How would you treat a neighbor who says she is a white witch? How do you think Jesus would act toward her?*

22. *Why do you think so many young people are attracted to the occult? What are the potential dangers involved?*

23. *Satanism seems to be on the rise. Find newspaper or magazine articles about it and discuss them in class.*

24. *What are some of the hidden ways Satan tries to influence you? Be specific.*

Living a Moral Life: Gifted and Growing

Cults

When faith in an idol develops into organized worship, it becomes a cult. A cult tends to grow into an entire way of life with its own set of beliefs and practices. A cult differs from a sect or religion in these ways:

- *unusual demands are made upon its members;*
- *the leader of the cult claims to be either superhuman or divine and exerts almost total control over the group's members;*
- *independent thinking is discouraged.*

This denial of the person's free-will jeopardizes his or her relationship to the true God. So, participation in cult activity can be idolatrous, too.

◆

Cults, like that of Rev. Moon, promise freedom but actually trap many young adults.

Idols Around You

You can probably see how the occult and counterfeit worship can easily weaken your relationship with God. However, it may not be so easy to see how a good thing can become an idol or substitute for the living God, thus doing the same damage as the occult. Some Americans, for example, seem to worship money. It gives them a false sense of independence, a feeling of being self-sufficient and free. Any deliberate transfer of loyalty from God is forbidden by the first commandment.

The art, styles, and music of adolescents and young adults form a subculture and carry mixed messages and values. So, is there a moral danger in listening to these rock groups? As in any other moral situation, you need to review your morals and values. Simply listening to the music will

Sect: a religious group which separated from a major religion of the world.

most likely not win anyone over to immoral conduct. Still, if you listen carefully, you can soon see that many songs don't promote a normal, healthy way of life.

Moreover, it is important to realize that the entertainment industry is trying to sell you an "image," seeking to manipulate your interests and desires. In order to make informed decisions, you need to recognize this fact. If the values expressed in the rock group image conflict with your relationship with God, and you adopt those values anyway, then there is a problem with idol worship.

25. *Name two good things besides money that people rely on instead of God.*

26. *What are some examples of how popular culture can become an idol?*

27. *Describe an organized cult that gives people a way of life that replaces their devotion to God. Why do you think people join cults?*

Money and power can become idols. What other things do teens idolize?

Summary

- Counterfeit or false worship can take the forms of superstition and using religion for profit.

- The desire to know the future or control the supernatural, though it may seem harmless, can hurt your relationship with the true God.

- Satan is clever and usually works through our weaknesses or sinful habits.

- An idol is anything that replaces your devotion to the true God.

SECTION 3
Checkpoint!

■ Review

1. How can counterfeit forms of worship weaken your relationship with God?

2. What are three forms of the occult? Why are people attracted to the occult?

3. What are the two forms of magic? Explain each.

4. Why is satanism the most serious form of the occult? Explain.

5. How does Satan deceive people? Explain.

6. List various types of idols. How is each an idol?

7. Why is participation in cult activity dangerous to your relationship with God? What makes a cult different from a religion?

8. Words to Know: counterfeit worship, simony, occult, divination, idolatry, witchcraft, cult.

■ In Your World

1. Describe the "images" the media and entertainment industry try to sell. How do they "sell" these images? What do they promise in return if you accept them? How can you prevent these images from becoming idols?

2. List the values transmitted in two popular songs. Do these values conflict with your Christian values? Why or why not? How can following these groups become idol worship?

■ Cases

Read this report on a strange new cult, then answer the questions that follow.

A new cult has been discovered. Each room of its house has a shrine in it. Inside the living room there is an altar with worshipper seats arranged around it. Most worshippers seem willing to work long hours each day to support the cult. The people rarely speak to each other, although they know exactly what to wear, what to eat, and how to behave with the opposite sex. Some even have a personal shrine and seem to prefer it to homework or family gatherings.

■ What is the god of this new cult?

■ What are some of the features of this cult that make it different from religions?

CHAPTER
5   Review

■ Study

1. How can images harm your relationship with God?

2. Why does God request your obedience?

3. How is humility similar to truth?

4. What are some of the types of pride? How does pride affect your relationship with God?

5. Is religious doubt a sign of weakness in faith? Why or why not?

6. What is the unique honor you owe God? Why?

7. What is the ordinary way that God's will is made known to you?

8. How does the Covenant of the Old Testament differ from the New Covenant? Explain.

9. What does it mean to twist God's will? List some examples.

10. Explain one example of a superstition. How is it an abuse of a genuine form of worship?

11. If you were to commit simony today, how would you probably do it?

12. What are the various forms of the occult? How are these practices similar? In what respect are they different from each other?

13. List four reasons for the condemnation of divination by both Jews and Christians.

14. Distinguish between white and black magic. Why are both morally wrong?

15. What is idol worship? Describe the behavior of a person who worships an idol instead of the true God.

16. How do cults harm the follower's relationship with the true God?

■ Action

1. Present a television report similar to "60 Minutes," with segments on idols and cults in America. Be sure to include a description of the "images" which the media and entertainment industries are trying to sell the public.

2. Debate this statement: "Active hatred of God is not as harmful as complete indifference."

3. Research the ways cults try to get people to join. List the reasons why people join cults. Present your findings to the class.

4. Dramatize a discussion involving a pastor and some lay people. The pastor has asked their advice on how to get enough money to pay all the bills, including salaries of the teachers, the organist, and the custodian.

5. Write out the words of your favorite song. Then, answer the following questions: a) What values are promoted? b) What behavior is praised? c) What are the consequences of this kind of behavior? d) What feelings do these songs express? e) How would you know if a friend were being harmed by this kind of music?

■ Prayer

1. In groups of four, write a worship service, with prayers, petitions, and readings from the Scriptures. Choose your theme from the following ideas: humility, obedience, faith, religious doubt, devotion to God. Take turns presenting one liturgy each day at the beginning of class.

2. Reflect on these words from John's Gospel. How do Jesus' words apply to you?

   "As the Father loves me, so I also love you. Remain in my love. If you keep my commandments, you will remain in my love, just as I have kept my Father's commandments, and remain in his love. I have told you this so that my joy might be in you and your joy might be complete. This is my commandment: love one another as I have loved you. No one has greater love than this, to lay down one's life for one's friends" (John 15:9-13).

God Is Near

OBJECTIVES

In this Chapter you will

- Study reasons why worshipping God "in your own way" is not a substitute for Sunday liturgy.

- Discuss why cursing can be a form of violence.

- Recognize the effects that cursing has on others.

- Learn the meaning of keeping holy the Lord's day.

"I didn't think I'd ever find God. Then someone told me that no matter what, God would certainly find me."

Words Have Power

"Exult, you just, in the Lord;
  praise from the upright is fitting.
Give thanks to the Lord on the harp;
  with the ten-stringed lyre chant his praises.
Sing to him a new song;
  pluck the strings skillfully,
  with shouts of gladness.
For upright is the word of the Lord,
  and all his works are trustworthy.
He loves justice and right;
  of the kindness of the lord the earth is full"
(Psalm 33:1-5).

Words have power. They can be used to encourage growth in God's spirit or they can destroy that spirit. Words affect how others perceive you and how you perceive them. Think of the times you have been inspired by the words of a great speaker, or hurt by the cruel words of a peer. Or, think of a letter you wrote to a friend and recall just how carefully you chose the words, examining each word so that your thoughts and feelings were conveyed precisely. Built into this gift of language is a responsibility to praise God and affirm others. Yet, all too often, people overlook this responsibility and use the power of words to harm others and promote their own selfish interests. The choice of how you use your power is entirely up to you.

Dr. Martin Luther King, Jr., in his "I Have a Dream" speech, showed the power of words to inspire and motivate people.

What's in a Name

The second commandment forbids taking God's name in vain. This is the same as saying that God's name should not be used irreverently. Knowing a person's name gives you a special power to call on that person. You can probably recall the slight feeling of frustration when you've met someone whose name you did not know. Likewise, think of how comfortable and relaxed you felt after learning a person's name. Learning a name, then, is the first step in developing a relationship with another.

The same is true with God. God's name is shared with people so that they might come to know God personally and call on God in a more intimate way. But this intimacy is not to be abused.

The original meaning of the second commandment was similar to that of the first. Both idols and magic formulas containing the names of gods were used by ancient peoples

Living a Moral Life: Gifted and Growing

to control the divinity's power. Many people believed that if they knew the name of a god they could force the god to act in their favor. The true God asked people to treat the divinity not as an impersonal power that could be manipulated by magic, but as someone who would always be close.

The Jews were sensitive to the power of God's name and gave it such reverence that they preferred to say *"adonai"* (lord) instead of God's proper name, *"Yahweh." "Yahweh"* was written but never spoken. To use God's name in any way was to blaspheme. Silence became the preferred expression of reverence because words cannot capture or adequately express the majesty and grandeur of God. We can still recognize the reverence of silence when we communicate with God through silent prayer.

"When you pray, mean what you say" is a saying some parents use when teaching their children to pray. Whenever we say prayers, we speak to God, and God listens. If we rattle off the words like a machine, God hears rattling rather than the thoughts of a friend. Still, prayers composed by other people need not be meaningless. People love to read poems and sing songs that others have composed, when they put their hearts into the words. That is the difference between simply repeating prayers and actually praying them.

Your name is important. It identifies who you are and is how you are known by others.

Yahweh: the Hebrew name for God meaning, "I am who am."

Blaspheme: to deny God or to insult God directly.

One way of making Mass, prayers, and other recited words more meaningful is to spend some quiet time in preparation for the service, simply reading a few lines of a prayer (or the Scriptures) at a time. Say the lines in different ways and rearrange the order of the words. This will encourage you to ponder the meaning of each word. Then, the next time you hear these prayers, the meaning found in quiet meditation will enrich their verbal expression.

1. *Choose a modern song that might hold a message from God to you. Write out the words and explain the message.*

2. *How can you make the words of prayer more meaningful to you? Explain.*

3. *How do you discover the name of a person you want to meet? After learning that person's name, how do you use it?*

4. *What are some ways that a person's name can be abused?*

Bless Words

Words can transform the world. Think of the words the priest says at the Liturgy: "This is my body. This is my Blood which has been given up for you." These words of the Eucharistic Prayer call upon Jesus to be present in a powerful way on the altar. Look at the words of Baptism, "Be baptized in the name of the Father, Son, and Holy Spirit," a change in our very being and acceptance into the Christian community are signified.

Words can also heal others. "I am sorry," "You are absolved of your sins," "Peace be with you," and "I forgive you" are examples of phrases that convey a healing power. Phrases or words that encourage reconciliation or growth in God's spirit are a part of courteous speech.

Living a Moral Life: Gifted and Growing

Words of praise make you feel special.

Courteous and gentle speech requires effort and self-control, as does every good habit. But developing a habit of "bless words" can help a person overcome the use of curse words. If people are embarrassed to say "God bless you" along with "good-bye," they can at least say it to themselves. They are then using God's name as a prayer. You can bless anything, and thus praise God for this particular sign of divine goodness. Blessing the thing that is irritating you can keep you from physically abusing it. Sometimes all a difficult situation needs is a calm, healing word.

5. *How can bless words resolve a conflict between you and another? Use examples.*

6. *Describe a time when a bless word helped you deal with a difficult situation. How did you feel?*

Misusing the Power of Words

Words can harm as well as heal. Words have the power to alienate and cripple our relationship with others. Consider how the world has been harmed by words misused.

War and violence are often the products of misused words. The critical and intolerant words of the Afrikaaners toward the black native peoples in South Africa is an example. Afrikaaners have sought to defend apartheid through words of intimidation and acts of aggression. Consider the cruel words of the Ku Klux Klan or "Skinheads" against other races, or the words of disrespect used by some children toward their parents. Words have the power to convey feelings as well as thoughts. What a tremendous gift and responsibility to use words peacefully.

Swearwords

In English, swearwords, curse words, and street language are similar. A few of these words include sacred names, a few are family related insults, and many of the rest refer to bodily functions. Usually, swearwords are vulgar. Other cultures have more imaginative curses than we find in the

The Ku Klux Klan has used the power of words to incite racial hatred and violence.

Living a Moral Life: Gifted and Growing

Jesus Is the Word

God's Word became flesh: Jesus Christ. As one baptized into the faith, Jesus dwells within you. Let that Word speak through you and transform the world.

We participate in the living Word of Jesus Christ when we enter into a relationship with him. Through the sacraments of Baptism, Confirmation, and Holy Eucharist, we grow in that relationship. By accepting Jesus as the Word Incarnate, we are called to be sons and daughters of God. In this way, we share in the heritage of Jesus and become part of the Word—called to share Jesus' message and life with all.

Present at all times and in everything, God is in each cell of our bodies, sees every secret effort, and knows all our hidden feelings. Because of God's presence, there is nothing in the world that is not sacred. Since everything is good, then everything can be enjoyed according to its purpose. Sacredness is not the same as seriousness or solemn boredom. It is close to life, wonder, and surprise. Deliberate damage or disrespect to anything sacred is called sacrilege. The most serious form of sacrilege is deliberate desecration of the Blessed Sacrament.

◆

English language that in no way refer to God, sex, or excretion. One Yiddish curse goes: "May you lose all your teeth but one, and in that may you have a toothache."

The question of offensive language should be kept in perspective, however. It is not always a serious destroyer of relationships. At worst, it is a symptom of a violent society. Many people appear shocked at hearing a swearword, even though they themselves break promises and harm others by gossip without a twinge of guilt. Practical charity, honesty, and forgiveness are just a few of the obligations that are more strictly binding than clean language.

Afrikaaners: Dutch settlers (and their descendants) who came to South Africa in 1652.

Apartheid: a policy of racial segregation in South Africa.

Ku Klux Klan: a post-Civil War secret society advocating white supremacy.

Vulgar: a word, phrase or action that is morally crude or offensive.

Yiddish: the language used by Jews in eastern Europe.

Making A Moral World

Think of speakers who have inspired you. How has their style moved you to consider what they were saying? Words can convey profound feelings as well as thoughts. Jesus spoke in parables which touched upon the everyday things of the world, things which have meaning to people. Parables enabled Jesus to spread his message to the people of his day in a way that they could understand. Jesus considered his audience before he spoke: he used words to challenge the leaders; he used words to heal the suffering of the people; he used words to reveal the truth about himself. Before you speak, always consider the audience you're speaking to and the most effective way to convey your message. If your message develops a moral theme, and is tempered with compassion, you will affect positive changes in the world.

Friends might claim that using a swearword is harmless, say, while playing a sport or watching a game on television. Some people think that using such words in jest is acceptable and understood as such by friends. It may very well be the case that using such language is understood between friends, but what sort of character does it reflect? Some people use swearwords in every part of speech because they can't think of other words to express themselves. Generally speaking, the frequent use of swearwords reflects a dull and unimaginative mind.

Curses

The real meaning of a curse, in contrast to a blessing, has to be understood. Ancient peoples believed that the human word had the power to produce actual physical effects, good or bad. A spoken curse was believed to bring harm, while a spoken blessing was believed to bring benefits.

To curse or bless in God's name meant that God was called upon to back up the words. For the most part, people today have lost that sensitivity and respect for holy names and objects. Nevertheless, to use any sacred name carelessly displays ignorance of the fact that God is deserving of honor. It demonstrates a lack of respect toward those who

Swearing and calling people names, even when done in jest with friends, can lead to hurt feelings.

Living a Moral Life: Gifted and Growing

truly care for God, for God's followers, and for God. The seriousness of each case depends on the speaker's intention to be irreverent, the emotion of the moment, and the amount of hurt or insult in the words.

7. *Is there a difference in harm between saying "damn it" when your car doesn't start and saying "damn you" to a person's face? How would you evaluate the saying of "God damn you" to someone?*

8. *Do you, as a rule, prefer to be with someone who does not use offensive language? Why or why not?*

9. *How would your parents perceive a friend who habitually used offensive language? How would a potential employer view this person? Do you think this friendship would influence how others view you? Explain.*

10. *Describe some real and visible damages that have resulted from misusing the power of words. Draw examples from other nations, your society or a personal situation.*

Summary

■ Words have the power to heal or harm. Choose words carefully, especially when you are angry or upset with another.

■ Learning someone's name is the first step in building a relationship. The Divine name was revealed to us so that we might enter into a more personal relationship with God.

■ A curse is calling on God to effect harm or injury on another.

■ Swearwords may be curses or they may simply be bad habits.

■ Jesus is the Word made flesh. You become that word when you enter into a relationship with Jesus.

SECTION 1
Checkpoint!

■ Review

1. How can words build up the spirit of God? Use examples to explain your answer.

2. What does it mean to take God's name in vain? What was the ancient belief about knowing God's name?

3. How and why did the Jews show reverence for God's name?

4. How do swearwords differ from curse words?

5. What does it mean to say, "We become the word of God"?

6. Words to Know: sacrilege, blaspheme, vain, vulgar, apartheid, Yahweh, adonai.

■ In Your World

1. Count how many times you hear or see swearwords at school in one day. Do the same for bless words. Which did you encounter more often? What might be the reasons for the proliferation of one over the other?

2. Watch a movie or TV program from the period prior to 1960 and a more recent one. Should there once again be a publically accepted language code? Be prepared to defend your statement.

■ Cases

Would you consider all of the following actions forms of sacrilege? Why or why not?

■ Hanging an obscene poster on a statue of the Blessed Virgin.

■ Reading a Bible passage for a mock religious ceremony held during a Halloween party.

■ Using the Lord's name in vain.

■ Swearing at a priest or minister.

■ Taking and saving the Holy Eucharist at Communion, then using it to bless pets, plants, or personal items.

Keep Holy the Lord's Day

The third commandment extends the meaning of the first two commandments. God is Lord over all creation. The third commandment calls for a spirit of reverence for the mystery of God in the world. Human beings are fully immersed in the world. They use land, trees, minerals, air, water, animals, and light for their comfort and progress. This in itself is good, but when people irresponsibly dominate the earth and exploit its resources merely for profit or some other selfish motive, they show that they have lost sight of God's life and mystery.

To Be Holy

Holiness means being made whole. A holy person is a well-rounded person, socially, academically, athletically, and spiritually. How is this possible? Once we recognize our union with God and witness the presence of God in all of creation, we become whole again. Christ can heal us and make us complete. Holiness is showing reverence for the Spirit of Christ within us and within creation.

Keeping holy also means learning when to let go, to say "Some things are beyond my control." Instead of leaving us completely on our own, God wants to work wonders for us. God can't do that unless we allow the divine presence to fill us. This happens when we actively trust God and let go of unhealthy pride and selfish interests.

Many people feel especially close to God while hiking or being outdoors.

PRAYER FOCUS

The Benedictine Monks have a motto, "Ora et labora", which translates "Work and pray." Life needs a balance between work and prayer. Work can be a form of prayer. Martha wanted to cook for Jesus. That was her way of showing reverence for the Lord's presence. Mary, on the other hand, simply wanted to sit and listen quietly to the Lord. In life, we must be both "Martha" and "Mary" (see Luke 10:38-42). You can offer your work as a prayer. In leisure, you can listen quietly to the words Christ speaks to your heart.

11. *Describe the qualities of a holy person you know or have read about. Which qualities reflect a well-rounded person?*

Let God Be God

God asks us to appreciate creation and to celebrate the renewal of life offered through Jesus Christ. Many Christians believe that "keeping holy" means merely fulfilling their obligation of Sunday Mass. Celebrating the Lord's Day means much more.

The God of the Sabbath is the protector of everything that is personal, fragile, and mysterious. To celebrate the Sabbath means to take time out regularly, to let go of our control, to trust God, and to look more closely at our personal relationships. Taking time out from work and simply relaxing is a very good way of showing reverence for the Sabbath. The heart of religion is respect for the holy in everything, even relaxation.

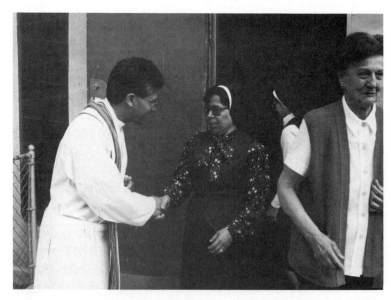

Sunday worship is a way of showing respect for God and giving thanks for all God's blessings.

Living a Moral Life: Gifted and Growing

Jesus taught this by his whole life. He was respectful to the poor and outcast, and he controlled his anger. Yet he loved spontaneity and personal honesty, reprimanding those who had rules for every little thing in life. Jesus praised the sister of Martha for sitting down and listening to him instead of fussing in the kitchen over the meal (see Luke 10:38-41).

To observe the Sabbath means to live the belief that the world is not our possession. Instead of working all the time, we are called to relax and enjoy life's beauty, deepen our relationship with God, and increase our appreciation of the goodness in others.

Jesus loved to go to parties and dinners, and told several parables about parties and celebrations. They were important to him as times to relax and get to know people. There are too many people who don't know how to relax, or to let go of concerns over work and money. They act as if they really could run the entire world and solve all its problems.

The laws and rules of the Pharisees were such that even helping others was considered work and was outlawed on the Sabbath. When Jesus healed the sick on the Sabbath and was criticized by the religious leaders for his actions, he replied, "The Sabbath was made for man, not man for the Sabbath" (Mark 2:27). Laws and rules serve their purpose when they help people to grow in God's Spirit. Regulations which don't allow for this growth must be discarded. The focus of the Sabbath, then, is on life, not on rules.

---

12. *What does Jesus say about people who think that they have their lives under control? Read Luke 12:16-21 for a clue.*

13. *If your job requires working on Sunday, how can you still observe the spirit of Sabbath rest?*

14. *What are some of the ways people try to take complete control of their lives? When does the need for control become unhealthy or even sinful? Explain.*

From Jewish Sabbath to Christian Sunday

Being good Jews, the early followers of Jesus continued to observe the Jewish Sabbath. But very soon they gathered in a believer's home on the following day—the first day of the week—to celebrate the ritual Jesus left them—the Lord's Supper. They believed that Christ was in their midst when they assembled. As so often at meals during his life, they experienced his presence "in the breaking of the bread." Because the first day of the week marked the anniversary of Jesus' resurrection it became known as the Lord's Day.

Near the end of the first century, Christians attended both the synagogue and the Lord's Supper. Because the Jews of the synagogue lacked faith in Jesus as the Messiah, understandably they would not allow the Christians to preach in their synagogues. This finally led to the expulsion of Christians from the Jewish services. Christians transferred the readings, psalms, hymns, and prayers from those services to their Eucharist. In a spirit of fellowship in Jesus, the early Christians would share a meal as part of the Lord's Supper. Today, you can seek out that same fellowship of the early Christians by coming together as a family or community on Sundays.

The Lord's Supper

Christians of the first centuries chose the first day of the week to celebrate the resurrection, as the Jews had celebrated creation on the sabbath. The Lord's Day, Sunday, signified the first day of the new creation—the renewal of creation in Christ. The weekly celebration became known as the Lord's Supper, or the Eucharist, a word meaning thanksgiving. At Eucharist, the community joins the priest in participating in the sacred mystery of Christ's death and resurrection.

The Holy Eucharist requires active participation of the community—in thought, prayer, and song. It begins with deep gratitude for all God's gifts, especially for the gift of Christ our Savior. Out of love we decisively accept Jesus' invitation to join him in worship of the Father.

15. *Cite some concrete ways you can participate in the celebration of the Eucharist.*

16. *Describe the parts of the Eucharistic liturgy that most appeal to you. Why? Describe the parts that are confusing or not especially interesting to you. Why?*

Your gifts are a welcome addition to the community's celebration.

Summary

- A holy person is a well-rounded person who recognizes his or her union with God, and continues to grow in that relationship.

- You are called to celebrate the Lord's Day by taking time to relax, enjoying life's beauty, and appreciating the good in others.

- Christians chose the first day of the week to celebrate the renewal of creation in Christ. Sunday is a time to renew our relationship with Christ and others.

Eucharist: literally means "showing gratitude."

■ Review

1. How does holiness relate to being whole? How does God make us whole?

2. How should you observe the Lord's Day? Explain.

3. Explain this statement: "Learning how to let go of a need to control everything is a step towards holiness."

4. Why is the Eucharist more than just a memorial celebration? Explain.

5. How did Jesus observe the Sabbath? Why was he criticized by some of the Jewish leaders?

6. Words to Know: Eucharist, Sabbath, holiness.

■ In Your World

1. Interview three or four adults to find out how they honor the Sabbath. How was the Sabbath observed when they were children? What do they think about this change? Report your findings in class.

2. How do teens feel about Sunday Mass? Interview several teens in your parish and find out. Ask them to identify one thing that could be done to make the Eucharistic celebration more valuable to them.

■ Cases

Given the situation, what are some ways that these people can keep holy the Lord's Day?

■ Julie is a student who is traveling in the Far East. She is a devout Catholic, but is unfamiliar with the local language and some of the local customs. She is having difficulty finding a Catholic Church.

■ Roy is a father of four children. He has many bills to pay, and must plan for the children's futures. His boss has insisted that he work on Sunday.

■ Becky's parents are atheists and believe religion to be a waste of time. In her late twenties, she converted to Catholicism. During the summer, the family invited her on a camping trip, but wanted to know first what she plans to do on Sunday if she joins them.

SECTION 3
Worshipping Today

Once you understand that the commandments are a response to God's covenant, it is much easier to put them into practice. Reverence for God and all God's creation is the value behind everything a Christian does or says.

Living the Liturgy

Praising God in word and deed is a way of living out the meaning of Sunday liturgy. Sunday—all day—should be a celebration of Jesus' resurrection, and our participation in his new life. Celebrating the Mass is just the beginning. The entire day is an opportunity to renew and appreciate our relationships with one another as well as with God. Keeping the day holy means showing appreciation in word and deed, for the gifts of life, family and creation. Enjoying a picnic in a park is just one form of thanksgiving. Sharing a meal with other members of the family is another. Sunday is the day above all others for celebrating God's creation through the use of our own creativity. Our creativity reflects the power of the Creator. We can use it to strengthen and renew all our relationships: social, environmental, and spiritual. We can use it to renew ourselves and enrich our world by exercising our gifts in hobbies and games.

Reverence the Earth

The American Indians are noted for the way they showed reverence toward nature. The Great Spirit of their religions was seen in all aspects of nature: water, plants, animals, sky, hills, and plains. One way the Indians lived out this understanding was in how they conserved natural resources. The Indians did not see themselves as separate from nature, but intimately a part of it. So, whenever they took something from nature, they tried to repay the gift with something given in return. Whatever they took, they replaced—either with a prayer of thanksgiving or with some deed. This is how they kept holy God's creation. For example, when the Indians killed a buffalo, they made sure to use every part of that animal. Nothing was to go to waste. The meat was food, the hide provided clothing and warmth, the bones were fashioned into tools and ornaments, the muscles were used as bow strings. Whatever they couldn't use, they would bury. This enriched the soil. This attitude of conservation is an attitude of reverence for God's gifts. Indians would sometimes set a place of honor at the feast celebrating the kill for the dead buffalo's spirit. Are we to show the same reverence toward creation?

In Genesis, God blessed human beings saying, "Be fertile and multiply; fill the earth and subdue it. Have dominion over the fish of the sea, the birds of the air, and all living things that move on the earth. See, I give you every seed-bearing fruit on it to be your food; and to all the animals of the land, all birds of the air and all living creatures that crawl on the ground" (Genesis 1:28-29). God has given us charge over his planet, to take and use the gifts of his creation. How should this gift be revered? How should holiness apply to our use of God's creation?

If we look at modern society, we can see the positive and negative effects our industries and technologies have had on the planet. There is a growing concern that the pollution we discharge into the air is causing a global warming effect, called the "Greenhouse Effect." As pollutants increase in the air, the earth's temperature is rising. Just a small increase in the earth's temperature will result in large-scale ecological changes. Tides will rise and certain animals and sea-life will perish, all as a result of human beings not showing reverence for the earth. Another example of the

Values for Life

"Blessed are the meek, for they will inherit the land" (Matthew 5:5). The meek are those who know the truth about themselves. They praise God and show reverence for God's gifts. The meek also endure suffering or injury with patience and without resentment towards others. Such people set a powerful example that no trial is too difficult to bear, no hardship is so strong that it can break their relationship with God. These are the people who will not only possess the earth, but transform it through their steadfast spirit and devotion to truth.

Living a Moral Life: Gifted and Growing

Native Americans show a reverence for all of creation.

effect of modern technology upon nature is how certain fishing practices have jeopardized the survival of dolphins. Other animals and forests and seas are threatened with extinction because many people do not recognize the responsibility of having "dominion over the earth."

Having dominion does not simply mean to govern over, but rather, to act as God's caretakers, too. Keeping holy the Lord's Day means exactly this. We have a responsibility to see to it that all of God's gifts are not taken for granted. If someone were to receive a birthday gift without thanking the giver, we would say that person is rude and ungrateful. Likewise, when we show disrespect for God's creation, it is the same as accepting a gift without saying "thank you." Only here, our thanks need to be demonstrated **in how** we treat the earth. That is showing reverence for creation, keeping holy the Lord's Day.

Reverence: to show profound respect or honor.

Worship in the World

Hinduism, the predominant religion of India, is a polytheistic religion. A Hindu can worship at a temple or at a shrine in his or her home. There is no regular weekly worship, but there is worship on frequent holy days. On holy days the people may gather at a temple dedicated to a particular god. Normally, worship is completely individualized. Each person worships the god or gods of his or her choice. Usually flowers, incense, or other gifts may be offered to the gods. Candles are lit, and prayers are said silently.

Islam, the main religion of the Middle East, requires all Muslim men to worship Allah (God) at the mosques every Friday at noon. This worship includes readings, meditation on the Koran *(Qur'an),* and prayers. Five times each day, Muslims must stop work and say a short prayer. Prayer must include the following observances: hands, feet and face must be washed; shoes must be removed; the place of worship must be clean; the follower must face the East toward the holy city of Mecca (Saudi Arabia); and he or she must stand, kneel, and bow while praying.

Some Chinese Buddhists worship the Buddha as a god, while others consider him to be only a holy man. Most followers meditate before the statue of the Buddha. Silent meditation directed toward reaching a state of pure detachment from all desires is the main element of Buddhist worship. Occasional services may include group chanting, offering incense, and a sermon.

In Judaism, the Sabbath, which is the holiest day of the week, begins in the home on Friday evening with the lighting of the Sabbath candle, the blessing of wine, and a special meal. The Sabbath continues until Saturday at sunset. Some Jews attend a service of readings, prayers, and a sermon in the synagogue on Friday evening; others worship together on Saturday morning. The Sabbath is a day of rest and family unity.

Living with the Word

Praising the good in others is another way of honoring the second and third commandments. Through our words, we can bring Christ to others, affirming the good in them. All goodness comes from God. So, our praise of others is a praise of creation—keeping holy the Lord's Day.

Likewise, we live out the second commandment when we affirm the good and holy in another person. God is present in all creation, especially in the baptized members of the Church, and therefore, is praised when we speak with compassion and love toward them. On the other hand, if we speak with unnecessary criticism towards others, in effect, we speak to the Lord in such manner. "Amen, I say to you, whatever you did for one of these least brothers of mine, you did for me" (Matthew 25:40).

---

17. *Describe some creative ways you can keep holy the Lord's Day. How can your creativity be used to show reverence to God through creation?*

18. *How can you be a caretaker of God's creation at home? school? work?*

Sacredness of Time and Space

How we keep holy the Lord's Day also requires a certain sensitivity to the sacredness of time. Certain times of the year are holier than others. At Christmas, we prepare for the birth of our Lord during the season of Advent. At Easter, we acknowledge our weaknesses and sinful ways during the season of Lent. Ash Wednesday marks the beginning of the Lenten Season, when we remind ourselves of our absolute need for God and the ultimate sacrifice Christ made for us.

Muslim: a follower of Islam.

Mosque: an Islamic church.

Koran: *(Qur'an)* the Holy Book of Islam.

Synagogue: a place of Jewish worship.

Often, when people face difficult decisions, they find comfort by praying in Church.

You may feel closest to God while praying in your own room.

Time is sacred. The choices we make now will affect the kind of life we will lead in the future. When God became man, God entered into time and affected history. Time, then, was made sacred. In each moment of each day, we have the opportunity to realize God's presence in the here and now, in our time. A real attentiveness to God's presence in time can provide a positive influence in our use of time.

Space is sacred. Places have functions. You might visit a bank and notice how the furniture and atmosphere is arranged to facilitate business tasks. But step inside a great cathedral of Europe and you might feel a purpose far greater. Structures are built to enclose space for a reason. A church is a place where the space is set aside so that a person might encounter God. That is sacred space.

A room in your home can function as sacred space. Virtually any place where you raise your heart to God becomes sacred space. Another way of reverencing the Lord's Day is through your use of God's space. No matter where you are, you can transform a profane place into a sacred spot through an exchange of kind words with another, or through the lifting of a quiet prayer to God.

Living a Moral Life: Gifted and Growing

Jesus said, "When you pray, do not be like the hypocrites, who love to stand and pray in the synagogues and on street corners so that others may see them. Amen, I say to you, they have received their reward. But when you pray, go to your inner room, close the door, and pray to your Father in secret" (Matthew 6:5-6). That "room" or place of solitude is the sacred space of your heart. You need not go into an actual room to pray in private. The privacy you seek is the privacy of your own heart. There you may enter the sacred space where God is present and hears you. Remember this when you are standing in a place of business where the space doesn't seem so sacred.

19. *Name some times of the day or year which are sacred to you. Why?*

20. *Name some sacred places other than a church. What makes those places sacred to you?*

Questions about Sunday Worship

■ *"Is it necessary to attend Mass every week or can you go occasionally?"*

In Kara's family, everybody went over to Grandma's house for Sunday dinner. It was the time to get the family news and, even more, to show Grandma that she was still important. When Kara got to high school, she didn't want to go anymore because there wasn't anything interesting to do. She couldn't go a few times because of sports practice, and then she used school activities as an excuse. Several months went by and Kara got interested in baking bread through some friends. She loved the smell of bread in her grandmother's kitchen and took her friends to meet her grandmother and learn some of the secrets of baking. They went over several times to try out some old family recipes. Then Grandma invited Kara and her friends to help cook one of the Sunday dinners. Now Kara feels sad when she has to miss a family gathering.

When Kara became interested in baking, she began to enjoy visits to her grandmother's.

In the same way, Mass is an opportunity to learn more about Christ and what gifts he offers us. If you want to get something out of attending Mass, then you must actively seek ways to make it new each time you go. Christ does not want spectators at Mass, but active participants in the celebration. Being an active participant means taking ownership of the liturgy—realizing it is as much your celebration as it is the priest's.

■ *"Which is worse: not going to Mass or going to Mass and not paying attention?"*

External behavior is hard to judge. Only you and God know what is in your heart. Only God knows if you are trying to show love by going to Mass, even though it may be hard to pay attention. And God knows if you stay away because you don't want to pray at all or because you will pray for an hour at home. A rabbi was asked the same question. He said, "The discipline of doing the action faithfully will lead you to understand why you do it. Believe it has meaning first." Maybe you don't feel you get anything out of Mass, but Jesus is giving you a message every Sunday, even if only through one word.

Living a Moral Life: Gifted and Growing

■ *"Every time I go to Mass I just sit there and don't listen to the readings. I always drift off into space. Why is it so boring?"*

Mass may seem boring to many people because it is slow and quiet, but worship is full of energy. If you find the Eucharistic celebration to be boring you may wish to find a parish where there is a lively liturgy and attend there. The readings can be more interesting if you read them to yourself ahead of Mass, and try to translate one of them into your own words. If the homily is truly boring (and some are), try to meditate quietly during this time.

■ *"Both my sisters have left the Catholic Church. One is a Baptist and the other goes to the Church of the Nazarene. Both really love their churches and enjoy their form of praise. Will they be punished for leaving the Catholic Church?"*

Each person has to search for God and respond to love as his or her own conscience guides them. God loves and blesses all people and wants deeper friendship with everyone.

■ *"Is missing Mass a mortal sin?"*

Mortal sin is a chosen attitude of completely rejecting any relationship with God. Usually one single choice to neglect Sunday Mass does not mean that a person wants to end his or her relationship with God. But repeated neglect of Sunday Mass is like repeatedly closing the door in God's face. When a person no longer wants to be bothered with God's love, he or she is in a state of mortal sin.

---

21. *List some of the difficulties you have with attending Mass. Then, next to each item, state one positive way to resolve that difficulty.*

A Call to Service

Christ calls us to a life of service. One very powerful way to show gratitude for God's gifts is through a life of service. You may be called to serve God as a priest or a man or woman religious. Your vocation may be the very important one of bringing people close to God through family life. Lay ministries are calling many people to serve as campus or youth ministers, as lectors, or in volunteering service to soup kitchens for the poor, in hospice programs, and in assisting terminally ill patients. Service isn't limited to something you can do; true service is an attitude of putting others first. Dorothy Day, founder of the Catholic Worker Movement, wrote "To serve others, to give what we have is not enough unless we always show the utmost respect for each other and all we meet." Showing respect for others, then, is at the base of all we do to reverence the Lord's Day.

---

22. *What are some career options that involve a life of service? What is appealing about these careers?*

23. *Describe a person you know or have read about that has dedicated his or her life to serving others. What appeals to you about his or her life? What frightens you about living that life?*

Summary

■ Keeping the Lord's Day holy means showing appreciation for God's gift of family, friends, and creation.

■ Praise the good you recognize in others, and thank God for the gift of creation.

■ Both time and space are sacred. Watch for the presence of God, here and now, and speak to God in the "private space" of your heart.

■ You may show reverence and gratitude to God in a life of service to others. Service is more than a deed; it is an attitude of respect for the welfare of others.

Checkpoint!

■ Review

1. What are some of the ways you can live out the liturgy of the Holy Eucharist?

2. How can you show reverence to God today?

3. What is the responsibility that comes from having "dominion over the earth"? How is this a form of reverencing God?

4. What does it mean to live out the message of the second commandment today?

5. How was time made sacred?

6. What is sacred space, and where is it located?

7. How can one make Mass a more fulfilling experience? Explain.

8. How does a life of service incorporate the message of the second and third commandments? Explain.

9. Words to Know: service, profane, sacred space, sacred time, Koran *(Qur'an)*, reverence, dominion.

■ In Your World

Examine your and your family's attitudes towards the earth. How do you treat the earth? What are some of the ways you don't show reverence for the earth? After listing examples, determine ways that you might be encouraged to develop a healthy reverence for God's creation. Present these problems and solutions to the class for discussion.

■ Cases

Jason has heard that it is important for Catholics to worship on Sunday. He has made a couple of retreats where he began to sense God's closeness. But Jason's parents don't go to church except on Christmas and Easter and rarely bring up religion at all. The parish church is too far to walk to and Jason is too young to drive.

■ What options are open to Jason to get to a weekend liturgy?

■ If he can't worship at a church, what other options are open to him?

■ Role play a scene between Jason and his parents. Jason has figured out a way to get to Mass on Saturday evening, and now his dad wants him to help repair the porch.

6   Review

■ Study

1. Give at least three ways in which swearwords can harm your relationships.

2. Is it logical to say that violent language is a harmless substitute for violent actions? Defend your answer.

3. Is there a difference between swearwords and curse words? Why or why not?

4. Explain this statement: "Jesus is the Word made flesh. We become that word when we enter into a relationship with Jesus."

5. How can you develop a habit of using bless words?

6. Why was God's name revealed to the Israelites? What power is there in knowing another person's name? How did the Israelites show reverence to God's name?

7. Why was the first day of the week chosen as the day for Christian worship?

8. Why does it offend God when you try to control every event in your life?

9. When should laws and rules be disobeyed?

10. Explain why the Pharisees were critical of Jesus' behavior on the Sabbath?

11. When does missing Sunday Mass become mortally sinful?

12. Debate this statement: "You are keeping holy the Lord's Day only when you attend Sunday Mass."

13. What is our responsibility in having dominion over creation? How does this responsibility relate to the message of the third commandment? How did the American Indians demonstrate this form of reverence?

14. Why is time sacred?

15. Explain this statement: "You can transform profane space into sacred space."

16. Why is service more than performing good deeds? How is service part of celebrating the third commandment?

1. *How did Frank Tugend's family "honor" him?*

2. *Discuss whether keeping an aging parent at home with the family shows greater respect for the person than placing the person in a nursing home would. Give reasons for your answer.*

3. *What do you think Dan and Mark mean when they say that they "chose to let him die at home, with his dignity intact"?*

Parent's Personal Uniqueness

Sometimes the fourth commandment is thought to refer exclusively to a child's unquestioning obedience to a parent. Christian obedience is broader. It encompasses compassion in the one who commands and understanding in the one who obeys.

Parent-child relationships are not meant to be based on force or fear. A family is not a "prison" situation where "inmates" obey "guards" to avoid being beaten. Relationships based on force or fear do not respect the uniqueness of family members, and are far from the level of the fourth commandment. When parents and children appreciate each other's uniqueness, accept each other as they are, and allow each other the freedom to grow as God intended, both obedience and authority become Christian.

Communicating with Parents

Although there is no direct commandment that says "Thou shalt communicate with thy parents," you cannot have a loving, compassionate, human relationship with your parents without communication. Isolation, loneliness, misunderstanding, deep hatred, and even greater evils can result from a lack of communication.

Parents can often feel isolated from their children. They don't know the popular music stars, or they may feel ignorant of the advanced subjects being taught in school.

Developing good communication habits with one's parents is crucial to a healthy family relationship.

They may simply be afraid of finding out about problems they're not trained to solve, or they themselves may be going through inner emotional crises that they may not fully understand.

One good conversation with a parent can encourage both the youth and the parents to realize that real support and harmony are possible and that love is alive in the family. If a first attempt at a reasonable talk seems to fail, wait a while and try again. Perhaps mom or dad wants to talk but does not know how. Hopefully, both parents and teen will be more able to communicate the second time around.

The following eight basic rules can help improve most attempts at communication:

1. **Show respect**—Be respectful in your choice of words and tone of voice. Nothing closes another person to communication as quickly as an insulting remark or a sarcastic, offensive tone of voice. Speak with control and respect to parents and anyone else in authority. Respect tends to make communication easier and calls for respect in return.

Living a Moral Life: Gifted and Growing

2. **Avoid accusations**—Report how you feel or how you see the situation. Don't accuse the other person. For example, instead of "You never listen to me," say " I don't know if you understand what I'm saying." "I-messages" are helpful even for short conversations. Instead of yelling, "Who took the newspaper again?" try saying, "I can't find the paper. Does anyone know where it is?"

3. **Listen**—Whenever possible, stop what you are doing and listen intently to whoever is speaking, looking directly at him or her. You will be surprised at the result. Preoccupied listeners are really saying, "I'm not interested. Don't bother me."

4. **Confront the issue**—Face problems instead of ignoring or postponing them. Little irritations or misunderstandings can worsen if they are not faced promptly. Studies of heavy television watching families show that they escape from conflicts by turning on the set. Conflicts don't go away when they are avoided. Instead, they continue to grow until they cause great harm. Prepare a person for a conversation about a problem by saying "Something's been bothering me," or "I'm kind of upset about something—do you have time to talk about it now?"

5. **Touch**—Many angry, frustrated, or fearful emotions can be released by warm, gentle hugs or other forms of touching. When you feel another person's tense muscles relax, you learn how important a loving hand can be. Did you ever notice how arguing people often move away from each other? It is very difficult to strike a person when you are hugging, kissing, or touching gently. On the other hand, simple physical displays of affection encourage patience and understanding.

Making A Moral World

The fourth commandment emphasizes respect for all legitimate authority, not just for members of the family. The society of the ancient Hebrews understood that social order would not be preserved unless people respected legitimate authority. Whenever you consider an act or comment that would be construed as showing disrespect, ask, "What are the consequences of my actions?" If the consequences do not give life to the other or to society, then you will want to reconsider your comments.

6. **Plan ahead**—Planning ahead for long conversations on a difficult subject will ensure some success. First, pray for the other person and yourself. Ask God for the wisdom to use the right words and to be with you during the conversation. Then, wait until both parties are in a positive emotional mood. Angry discussions only generate more heat. Choose a time when you can talk in a leisurely way, and choose a place that is private, comfortable, and unthreatening.

7. **Be open**—Begin by assuring the other person that you are really open to his or her ideas, that you want to listen, and that you are willing to change. "Dad, I'd really like to know what you think about..." It helps if you can sincerely compliment the other person in the beginning. For example, "Mom, you read a lot and I know you think about things. Have you ever read about...?" Be sure to use "I-messages" whenever you introduce an idea. If the other person gets angry, keep your cool. Let the anger come out. Listen to the feelings beneath the anger. Say something like, "I didn't know you had such strong feelings about..." Anger is often an expression of fear or hurt. Don't bring up old grievances or problems, but stick to the topic.

8. **Resolve anger**—Finally, never end a conversation in anger. If the other person should leave, don't end the day until you resolve the anger. Anger is not a sin, but withholding forgiveness can be. Try to keep the conversation open even when you stop talking. Leave the other person with the assurance that you are going to think about it, that you have learned something, and that you want to continue talking another time.

Living a Moral Life: Gifted and Growing

"I-messages"

Change these "you-messages" to "I-messages" and give another "I-message" as an answer. Here is an example:

- *You-message: "You're always comparing me to Bob."*
- *I-message: "I feel that I'm always being compared with Bob, Mom."*
  Answer: "I didn't know you felt that way. Maybe I do judge one of you against the other."

1. "You made me miss the bus."

2. "Why did you wear my sweater again?"

3. "You don't like any of my friends."

4. "You don't trust me."

5. "You're always comparing my life to yours twenty-five years ago."

6. "You don't understand the situation."

7. "You never like our music."

8. "You don't want me to have any fun."

9. "You just don't know what kind of teacher he is!"

10. "You treat me like a child."

4. *What are some practical ways to show your parents that you are aware of their unique qualities?*

5. *Describe the last time you had a real conversation with either of your parents about a matter of concern. What made it a "real" conversation?*

6. *Which of the eight basic skills in communicating do you find most effective? Which are the most difficult to practice? Why?*

7. *Within the next three days, experiment with using "I-messages" and "You-messages." Observe the different results in the conversations and share these with the class.*

Honor the Elderly

"Gray hair is a crown of glory; it is gained by virtuous living" (Proverbs 16:31). The story of Gramp points out the value of older adults. When you think of parents, it may be difficult to recognize that the fourth commandment's original interpretation was primarily aimed at gaining respect for the elderly. The elderly deserve the respect of the whole community. What happens when the older generation is not honored can be seen clearly in this folk tale.

Once there was a very old woman who had to live with her daughter's family. Because of her weakness, the old grandmother could not always manage the dishes and silverware and occasionally broke her daughter's china. Finally the daughter made her mother eat her meals alone in her room, using an old wooden bowl. After the old woman died, and the family was disposing of her belongings, the daughter noticed her little son hiding the grandmother's wooden bowl and spoon.

Living a Moral Life: Gifted and Growing

"What are you doing with those things?" she questioned.

"I want to save them for you, Mother, for when you get old," the little boy replied.

Even though your own parents' old age may be a long way off, the way you treat your grandparents and other elderly persons now will influence the way you treat your parents later. Likewise the example you set for small children, especially your own children, will influence how you might be treated by them someday.

An elderly person is a unique individual with the rare advantage of having already experienced many of life's gifts and challenges. He or she can evaluate what is important and pass on this wisdom, but it cannot be shared unless someone comes to receive it. Many older people are afraid to be a burden on younger people, and so they are unwilling to offer their wisdom unless they are asked to do so.

Showing respect for the elderly is the original meaning of the fourth commandment.

Your elders can share with you insights into the purpose of life and the value of love, money, work, and suffering. They can teach you loyalty, gentleness, gratitude, and patience. They can offer you the wisdom of their experience. If they are your relatives, they can pass on the family heritage, facts and stories about your roots, ethnic values, customs, and an appreciation of your family history.

In return, you can give hope to the elderly by offering them a listening ear. You can assure them that you want to carry on their ideals. You can encourage them, compliment them on their gifts, help them realize that they are still people of dignity and value. You can play cards with them, sing, write letters for them, or bring them homemade cookies or fresh fruit. When you have questions or problems, turn to them for support and guidance. When you treat people, old or otherwise, as if they are valuable human beings, they feel good about themselves, and not as if they were a burden to you and society. Whatever you do with an older adult, don't patronize, don't treat them as if they were fools, and don't take away their dignity.

It is extremely important to remember that simply because a person has advanced in years doesn't mean that he or she is infirm or no longer able to think or be physically active. Most adults remain physically and mentally active until the time of their deaths. Old age doesn't have to mean dependency. It is, rather, a sign of wisdom.

---

8. *Discuss this statement: "You reveal your true faith in God by the way you value and care for the sick, the elderly, and the helpless."*

9. *Why are many youth afraid of spending time with the elderly? How can one overcome these fears?*

10. *How has your character been influenced by an elderly relative? What qualities do you most admire in that person?*

Living a Moral Life: Gifted and Growing

Most older adults lead active lives, sharing their gifts with others. This man reads the newspaper over the radio to people unable to read it for themselves.

Summary

- The fourth commandment promises blessings to those who respect elders.

- Christian obedience involves compassion and understanding between those who command and those who obey.

- Parents need understanding and acceptance from their children.

- Improved communication skills can effect a deeper relationship between children and parents.

- Recall the basic communication skills: 1) Show respect; 2) Avoid accusations; 3) Listen; 4) Confront the Issue; 5) Touch; 6) Plan ahead; 7) Be open; 8) Resolve anger.

- Honor the elderly and learn from their wealth of experience. They offer many insights into the purpose of life.

SECTION 1
Checkpoint!

■ Review

1. How does Christian obedience differ from obedience in general?

2. Why might communication between parents and their children be difficult?

3. Use a concrete example to illustrate each of the eight basic skills in communicating.

4. What contributions can the elderly make to society? To the lives of people your age?

5. Words to Know: obedience, accusations, isolation, sarcasm, customs, ethnic values.

■ In Your World

1. How does American society view old age? What are the predominant attitudes towards growing old? Support your answers with examples from television and other media.

2. How much do you know about your parents' childhood, their personal problems, their goals, or their favorite things? Ask them about any one of these topics. In your journal, write what you learn from this inquiry.

■ Cases

Agnes was always quick-witted. She enjoyed writing children's stories and spending time with her grandchildren. Often she would take them for long walks on the beach, telling stories of the sea and those who had the courage to explore unknown waters.

At 65, she suffered a debilitating stroke. She lost some of her speaking ability, and found her mobility restricted, too, but she never gave up. After two months of therapy she began to show signs of improvement. She wanted to go back home to her apartment and live as she had lived before—spending time with her kids and grandchildren. They were her life. At first she managed, but the daily chores began to take their toll. Each day became increasingly difficult.

Some of her children suggested she live in a nursing home. She refused—saying the workers were uncaring. Her children, however, had to work and couldn't take time off from their jobs. They needed to make a decision within a week because of her weakening condition. The grandchildren felt that she should move in with them. What do you think?

Living a Moral Life: Gifted and Growing

SECTION 2
Authority Protects Freedom

Jesus' own life is the best teaching available on parent/child relationships, and shows the positive effects of obedience. Saint Luke tells us that Jesus "went down with them, and came to Nazareth, and was obedient to them. And Jesus advanced in wisdom and age and favor before God and man" (Luke 2:51-52).

Real Independence

About one hundred high school students were asked these questions: Who or what helps you most to be a morally good person?; Who or what is the greatest obstacle in being a morally good person? Almost every answer to the first question included "parents," and several said "Parents and good friends." Almost every answer to the second was "peer pressure." One girl responded, "When my friends are morally good, I find it easier to be good. If my friends don't care, I will pretend that I don't either. When the people you hang around with aren't morally good, but they still are your friends, it's hard to say you think something is wrong and risk losing their friendship."

Some teens think that when they don't listen to their parents anymore and do what their friends want, they are free and adult. They're wrong. They have taken one step to adulthood, but they are still not free. They are being influenced by their peers, by the media, by advertising, and by their own inner fears of rejection. In fact, many teens are more afraid of going against the group than they ever were of going against their parents.

A person is truly free when he or she can follow the values from within his or her own heart, no matter what

Saint Paul encourages parents to raise their children lovingly.

parents, friends, or peer groups say or think. The truly free person knows that God supports him or her even if rejected by friends.

All Authority Comes from God

What about people who are a strong influence on others even without official authority? Friends with attractive personalities and the gift of natural leadership can be good guides, but a person is not obligated to follow them. If there is a conflict between a person with official authority, such as a teacher, and someone with personal influence, our obligation is to obey the one with official authority.

Whenever possible, those in authority should use persuasion. They should appeal to the intelligence and goodwill of others, listen to their ideas, and adapt to their limitations. If a good thing must be done and persuasion fails, authority may use force and impose penalties. An example of persuasion is the variety of state programs that encourage citizens to clean up litter. An example of force and penalties is the number of stiff litter laws and fines to punish offenders.

Creative Obedience

Being obedient doesn't mean being a robot or a slave. It should mean that we do what is expected of us in our own way, using our creative ideas whenever possible. Creative obedience requires listening and talking. As we move out of childhood we talk to our parents more often about our life—both its day-to-day happenings and the larger decisions concerning our future. Part of adult living is asking for reasons behind commands and using our creativity to carry out these commands. Life-giving obedience has most or all of these qualities:

- *It is careful to understand the command and to carry it out correctly.*

- *It is questioning in the sense of asking for reasons; trying to understand in light of our goals.*

- *It is creative in that we use our personal gifts and initiative to carry out the command in our own style.*

Living a Moral Life: Gifted and Growing

- It is cooperative in that we work with authority to achieve a goal.

- It is responsible for seeing a command through to the end and for correcting any mistakes.

- It is reasonable in accepting the limitations of those in authority and in not demanding that they be perfect before we will obey them.

- It is respectful by not insulting the person in authority or mocking the command.

---

11. List five or six qualities that would make a parent a ''person of influence'' at home.

12. Describe several conflicts a student might encounter between a person with influence and one with authority.

13. Which of the above qualities seem hardest for teenagers to maintain in their relationships with their parent.

14. List some of the reasons why people lie to their parents. What evils are built into this habit?

''Doing what I want'' is not necessarily a sign of independence or maturity.

Forgive and Be Forgiven

How do you feel when you are rejected because of your differences from other people? Do you reject your parents because their values and decisions are different from yours? How do you feel when you are not forgiven even though you're sorry? Do you keep a grudge against your parents even if they are sorry for hurting you?

Forgiveness is one of the most difficult forms of compassion, but it is absolutely demanded by Jesus. ''If you forgive others their transgressions, your heavenly Father will forgive you. But if you do not forgive others, neither will your Father forgive your transgressions'' (Matthew 6:14-5). You may still feel the hurt of the offense, but you have to let the other person know that you hold no grudge and will not seek revenge.

Chapter 7   A Long Life

The perfect parents probably do not exist. Every family's circumstances and personalities practically guarantee that there will be at least occasional arguments between parents and teenagers. Both can benefit from having a general idea of what teenagers want and need from parents. In this way, parents can better address those needs and adolescents can establish realistic expectations. The following is a list of some often mentioned expectations youth have of their parents. See if you agree.

- *Teenagers want parents to take an interest in their activities and to be available when they need support.*

- *Parents should always try to understand their teenager's point of view.*

- *Parents should exchange ideas with their teenagers, talking with them, not at them.*

- *Parents should love and accept adolescents as they are. Often, teenagers feel worthless because they cannot meet their parents high expectations.*

- *Parents should respect their children's privacy. Teenagers resent when their parents eavesdrop on their phone conversations, or open their mail.*

- *Parents should allow their children to learn to be independent by giving them leeway in the choice of friends, clothes, or music. Teenagers want to be allowed to prove that they can handle this autonomy.*

- *Parents need to be consistent in enforcing family rules.*

- *Parents should do their best to provide a positive emotional environment at home.*

- *Parents should "practice what they preach" and not be afraid to admit mistakes when they are wrong. (Adapted from F. P. Rice, The Adolescent: Development, Relationships, and Culture, 2nd edition, Boston: Allyn and Bacon, 1978.)*

PRAYER FOCUS

Philippians 2:14-16 offers us Saint Paul's comments on the importance of obedience. Read this passage several times, quietly to yourself, and see how it speaks to your own life. Use this passage as a starting point for a meditative prayer.

"Do everything that you may be blameless and innocent, children of God without blemish in the midst of a crooked and perverse generation, among whom you shine like lights in the world, as you hold on to the word of life, so that my boast for the day of Christ may be that I did not run in vain or labor in vain."

Because you are human, you will make mistakes. It isn't easy to admit you're wrong, and it doesn't get any easier as you grow older. If you first forgive yourself and try to learn from your mistakes, you will find it easier to admit your mistakes to others and forgive others for their mistakes.

---

15. *Give two examples of what you think of as unfair or extreme parental expectations. Discuss them in class.*

16. *How old do you think a person is before he or she shakes free of peer pressure? Or doesn't it depend on age? Explain.*

17. *If a parent really abuses a child, where can the child go for protection and advice?*

18. *Share with the class some creative ways to show forgiveness.*

Summary

■ Honoring your parents includes providing financial assistance, offering personal services, and giving respect.

■ Adult obedience entails asking for reasons behind commands and using creativity in carrying out those requests.

■ Remember that parents need to be treated with the same compassion and understanding that you would expect from them.

■ Know the qualities of true obedience: it is questioning, creative, cooperative, responsible, reasonable, and respectful.

Autonomy: self-directed behavior or moral independence.

SECTION 2
Checkpoint!

■ Review

1. How are you to show honor to your parents?

2. What are the characteristics of true obedience? Use an example to illustrate each characteristic.

3. How should people in authority exercise their power?

4. What is the creative aspect to being obedient?

5. List three of the influences that fool teens into thinking they are truly independent?

6. Why is forgiveness an essential component in any strong parent/child relationship?

7. Words to Know: honor, obedience, independence, forgiveness, autonomy.

■ In Your World

1. When a parent dies or divorces and the other remarries, sometimes the children resent the new father or mother. Discuss some ways to reduce this resentment.

2. Explain what Jesus meant when he said, "The scribes and Pharisees have taken their seat on the chair of Moses. Therefore, do and observe all things whatsoever they tell you, but do not follow their example. For they preach but do not practice" (Matthew 23:2-3).

3. Write a skit in which a parent and a teen son or daughter talk over a parental rule. Include some of the qualities of obedience, but omit a few. Let the class decide which qualities are lacking. Redo the skit using all of the qualities of obedience. What difference does that make in the outcome of the discussion?

■ Cases

Kristin's boy friend's family is going away for the weekend, and he asked her to go along. Kristin's parents aren't very trusting of her, especially after Kristin lied to them about going to the library, and instead met her boy friend for a pizza. Kristin will be with her boy friend's parents the whole time so nothing will happen that is morally wrong.

■ Role play a scene with Kristin and her boy friend's parents after she tells them her parents refused. Discuss ways Kristin might be able to convince her parents to let her go.

Living a Moral Life: Gifted and Growing

Family Problems

Families in today's world face many challenges unknown to past generations. The practically perfect nuclear family of the 50s, idealized in "Father Knows Best" and "Leave It To Beaver" never really existed in real life. Single parent families (caused by death or divorce) and blended families (a spouse with children from one marriage with a spouse and children from a different marriage) make up more than half the households in America. Add the problems of alcohol and chemical addiction, both parents working outside the home, and the high cost of living, and you have some idea of the problems families face today.

Marriage and Divorce

People who enter a marriage usually don't plan for it to end in divorce. Instead, they plan to love each other faithfully until death parts them. The Church teaches that the sacrament of Marriage binds a couple for life. However, the reality and frequency of divorce suggest that this is not an ideal world. Divorce was once a forbidden word in Catholic households. Today, approximately one in three Catholic marriages end in divorce.

Several answers have been offered as to why so many marriages today fail.

- *Lack of commitment to permanence and fidelity in taking the vow;*

- *Mobility of society;*

- *Media images;*

- *Poor social and psychological preparation for married life.*

Chapter 7   A Long Life

Research into marriage and divorce shows that people who marry someone of the same religious faith, someone with shared common values, a person they have known for some time, or a person who is past the age of twenty-five tend to have marriages that last. Marriages with the highest failure rates are those among teens, among people who don't communicate well, who have not known each other long, who have few common values, and those where the couple has lived together in an intimate relationship prior to marriage.

 Values for Life

"Blessed are the merciful, for they shall be shown mercy" (Matthew 5:7). It is understandable that a person who experiences the painful effects of a divorce or alcoholism might harbor some resentment toward parents or family members. Such feelings must be overcome before one can lead a fulfilling and productive life. Accepting the faults and weaknesses of loved ones is a good start. It is lifegiving not to blame parents; learn from them and support them. Mercy is one way to extend support. Children who act mercifully toward their parents relieve them of the burden of guilt and become catalysts for healing.

Conflict of Loyalty

For teens who come from divorced homes, what are some of the problems that they face? One of the most common problems for children of divorced parents is a conflict of loyalty. Which parent deserves their trust, their love, and their support? Both do, of course.

Gloria finds herself torn. She feels that she generally agrees with her father more often than she agrees with her mother. Gloria knows, however, that there will be less hurt for everyone if she can remain neutral. Sometimes Gloria's father wants her to reveal the faults of her mother. Gloria has learned to say, "If you want to know what Mom is doing, you will have to ask her." This seemingly hard answer has kept Gloria out of the middle during her parents' conflicts. Another thing Gloria has learned from experience is that if she wants one of her parents to know something about the other parent, it's better to speak when both parents are present.

Realizing that it is unfair to spend Christmas day with just one parent, Gloria has decided to spend Christmas day with her grandparents. Thus, she can avoid feeling disloyal toward either parent.

After a divorce, one parent may want to limit a child's contact with the other parent. Both parents need their children's love, even though it must now be given separately. Loving both parents is difficult when there is pain.

Living a Moral Life: Gifted and Growing

Children of every age suffer when their parents divorce.

Remarriage can create a renewed conflict of loyalty. Even though the new stepmother or stepfather can never replace the biological parent, he or she is, nevertheless, a unique person who deserves compassion. Children should allow this new parent to share his or her special gifts.

Love and loyalty are high values. In divorce, these values are severely tested, and may not always be lived out perfectly. The challenge for children in a divorce situation is to maintain their love and loyalty without destroying themselves. This takes creative thinking and prayer.

Who's to Blame?

Everyone in a divorce situation feels badly. Parents feel guilty for not being able to make their marriage work and for "betraying" their children. Relatives feel ashamed about a divorce in their family. Children feel guilty about being the cause of the family breakup. It is important to remember that children do not cause a divorce. It is the parents' choice and there are always many complex factors involved which they cannot explain to their children.

A teen need not feel guilty about parental problems such as alcoholism or gambling. Adults are responsible for their own decisions. Feelings of guilt on the teenager's part have no foundation in reality. Children are not to blame for their parents' decisions, just as parents are not to blame for their children's decisions.

For this reason, children should not feel guilty about confiding to someone else their family troubles. Even if a child has promised not to speak of problems outside the home, the promise is not binding. Promises and commands are binding only if they do not cause harm or violate God's law. Children who need help to survive difficulties at home, should ask for it. It is important to choose a trustworthy adult who can keep the matter confidential. This kind of communication is neither disloyal nor immoral and a priest in the sacrament of Penance is always a good person to trust.

In times of family strife, it's important to have a trusted person with whom you can confide.

Living a Moral Life: Gifted and Growing

Parents always need to know that they are loved by their children, especially during times of pain, such as during a divorce.

During a period of parental conflict, children need compassionate support from outside the family. Troubled parents are often too preoccupied with their own problems to guide their children. Within families, older children can support younger ones. Good sibling relationships can develop, and the older children can benefit from having someone to care for. A friend, or perhaps someone who has gone through a divorce, can be a great help. Relatives and warm, outgoing families are good stand-bys, often supplying the togetherness the family of origin lacks. A school club, a prayer group, or a church organization can also provide needed personal and moral bolstering.

Anger Can Be Good

Anger and resentment are natural in children whose parents have divorced or separated. It is helpful for anger to be expressed and its energy channeled constructively. A drama group, the school newspaper or band, or a community or church youth group can also offer outlets for angry feelings by introducing teens to friends and adults who will support them through a family crisis. Keeping a diary or journal and expressing feelings in poetry or songs are other healthy ways of releasing anger and other emotions.

One girl redirected her anger when her parents divorced. She became an expert handball player. Exercise and games of any kind are good ways to release anger in a legitimate way.

Types of Families

Though young people long for independence and desire to get out on their own, they often experience fears and uncertainties about becoming adults. Many worry about failing in the world. Parents also worry about their child's ability to cope with the "harsh realities of life." The way in which adolescents resolve conflicts about becoming adults depends in large part on their relationship with their parents. There are various styles of family relationships.

- **The Authoritarian Family**—*Parents behave as "bosses." They feel no need to explain their actions or demands. Such parents act as if their son or daughter has no right to question parental decisions.*

- **The Democratic Family**—*In this family style the adolescents participate in decisions affecting their lives by discussion and negotiation. Parents listen to their children's reasons for wanting to go somewhere or do something and make an effort to explain their rules and expectations. Though adolescents are given a voice in the decisions that affect them, parents retain final say in all matters.*

- **The Permissive Family**—*In this family style the children exercise total freedom in all matters that affect their lives. The parents may attempt to guide the adolescents, but give in when the children insist on having their own way. Parents may give up their parental responsibilities altogether, setting no rules for behavior, making no demands, and voicing no expectations.*

Of the three styles of family governance, studies have shown that adolescents raised in the democratic style have more confidence in their values and goals than young people raised in the other two styles.

New Life

In a divorce, something precious dies. A person shouldn't feel obliged to deny this loss or pretend that the marriage will suddenly revive. Divorce is always painful. It will take time for wounds to heal. How we respond to the pain of divorce will hasten or lengthen our healing process.

A divorce can make ties with other relatives stronger. A grandmother, an uncle, or a cousin may became a prominent friend and an influential guide during the transition. Teens may find that they can finally develop good relationships with each parent now that the parents' marital conflicts no longer stand in the way.

A new sense of personal strength and maturity can come to a teen after the experience of a divorce. Gradually, feelings of loss are replaced by other, more positive experiences. The discovery that even the most trusted

As the family situation changes because of the loss of a parent, it's important for older teens to be supportive of younger siblings.

human relationships sometimes fail can bring young people to a new and deeper relationship with Christ. It is just in these times of crisis that people discover for themselves that Christ will not fail them.

---

19. *What are some negative ways to express anger?*

20. *After a divorce, a parent may expect too much from a teenage son or daughter. Mom or dad may put a teen in charge of the house, for example, or constantly expect advice. What can a teen do when he or she is asked to do too much?*

21. *Sometimes children of divorced parents fear that they have inherited their parents' faults. Judging from your knowledge of human character, how realistic is this fear?*

22. *How can you help a friend overcome the shame that he or she feels about having divorced parents? What other practical help can you offer?*

Alcoholism in the Family

One of the major causes of divorce in the United States is the disease of alcoholism. In addition to the immediate family, alcoholism affects grandchildren, great grandchildren and in-laws. Some of the problems that teens experience in relating to their parents may result from alcoholic grandparents or other relatives. Each subsequent generation suffers the effects of the previous generation's behavior.

Adult children of alcoholics explain that they learned three rules in early childhood: 1. Don't talk. 2. Don't trust. 3. Don't feel. These rules, while destructive to personal growth, were necessary for survival when parents showed unpredictable anger, violence or withdrawal. Children who followed these rules and never learned another way to live, may, as adults, treat their own children as they were treated.

Living a Moral Life: Gifted and Growing

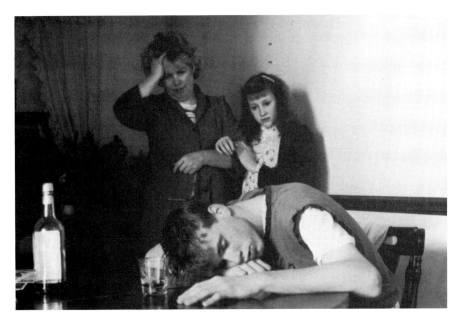

Alcoholism is a leading cause of family problems.

Other families with serious problems, like unemployment, sexual abuse, long-term illness, and death or divorce, find that the rules against talking, trusting, and feeling are their means of survival as well. These perversions of God's design for family life often lead to physical, emotional or sexual abuse. Under abuse, it becomes extremely difficult for children to love, respect and obey these parents. If you find yourself in one of these family situations, talk to a school counselor or a trustworthy adult. You can get help. Other sources of support are Alanon, Alateen and Adult Children of Alcoholics (ACA) groups, whose phone numbers are in every phone book. Even though you don't think your family's problem is linked to alcohol, these adults can help you express your feelings and learn skills of family communication. Your first duty is to love and care for yourself—your safety and your physical and emotional well-being. You may not be able to feel love or respect for your parents until you are able to love yourself as being good, capable, and gifted.

23. *What are some of the effects that alcoholism can have on a family? How is each family member affected?*

24. *Debate this statement: "The best cure for alcoholics is to refuse to clean up after them and to cut ties with them until they accept responsibility for their own lives."*

Summary

- Divorce and other family problems can create conflicts of loyalty and feelings of guilt in the children.

- Adults are responsible for their own decisions. Teens should not blame themselves for family problems.

- Anger can be released by channeling the energy into some constructive activity.

- Alcoholics and family members of alcoholics can seek help from local agencies, such as Alcoholics Anonymous, Adult Children of Alcoholics, and Alanon.

■ Review

1. How can a divorce challenge the relationship between a child and his or her parents?

2. Describe the three family styles and the one which is most effective for producing autonomous adults. Explain your answer.

3. What are some of the potential conflicts that can arise in a divorced family? How can one resolve these conflicts?

4. How can anger be turned into a positive force? Use an example to illustrate your answer.

5. How can a teen develop strength and maturity after the experience of a divorce?

6. What are the three rules learned by children of alcoholics? How can these "rules" affect their adult life? Where can they seek help?

7. Words to Know: resentment, anger, alcoholism, loyalty.

■ In Your World

Interview a peer from a divorced family. Ask him or her what is the most difficult part of his or her parents' separation. Report the content of the interview to the class without revealing the identity of the person interviewed.

■ Cases

Lawrence was eighteen when his parents decided to divorce. The decision came as a complete surprise to him, as well as to his younger brother and sister. "Mom and dad never fought nor showed any sign of anger toward each other," he recalled. The experience of the separation drew the three closer—so much so, that they would often refer to themselves as the "sub-family." The children, though upset at the separation, learned from the experience. All three managed to pay their way through college and to develop relatively happy dating relationships. But, in spite of these achievements, each has a fear of settling down permanently with a single partner.

■ What positive things did the children learn from the experience of a divorce? What were some of the long-term negative effects? How did the experience affect their ability to enter into trusting friendships?

CHAPTER

7 Review

■ Study

1. Why is it important to show respect toward all elderly persons now?

2. Give an example of an "I-message" that begins a conversation.

3. Define the eight basic skills in communicating. Why is each important?

4. Give an example of a parent appreciating the differences between two of their children. Give an example of a child appreciating the difference between a mother and a father.

5. How does obedience to God lead to freedom?

6. Why should you obey a teacher you do not personally respect?

7. Give an example of creative obedience.

8. What is true independence? Explain.

9. What factors are necessary in a strong parent/child relationship? Explain.

10. Explain an effective way to exercise authority.

11. Give one example of a destructive outlet for anger and one example of a constructive one.

12. What are some of the effects of being raised in an alcoholic family?

13. How should you respond to the problem of alcoholism in your family? Where can you go to for help?

14. What is autonomy? How does the family contribute to working toward autonomy?

- *Second, he says that we can know how much we love God by looking at how we care for other people.*

- *Third, we need to show love for and cooperation with not just blood relatives, but every person.*

- *Lastly, Jesus promises that he will live with us through his Spirit. We will then have the power to keep working at compassion.*

If you look closely now at the Great Commandment, you will see that you begin by loving yourself. Even Jesus loved himself. He took care of his health, tried to balance preaching and healing with prayer and parties. He wasn't afraid to accept praise from God and spoke with the certainty of a person who knew who he was. Your love, too, starts with a healthy respect for yourself as a child of God and practical care for your own well-being.

Christ is often found in the words and actions of the people we come into contact with each day. The compassion Jesus showed for others can shine through in the way people treat each other. The following stories are examples of Jesus' compassion taking flesh in the actions of people.

Jesus in the Flesh

Looking in antique stores for a crucifix, a man found one with the Christ-figure badly broken: one leg and one arm were missing and the face had almost been chipped away. Even though it looked ugly, the man bought it and took it home. That night he held the cross and found himself saying, "Jesus, who did this to you?" A voice answered him, "Quiet. It doesn't matter how I got this way. But why are you so concerned about a statue? It is a much greater sin to disfigure my image in the living—men and women and children. Let my missing arm remind you to help those who are exploited. Let my disfigured face urge you to treat the faceless people without rights with dignity and respect. Let your love touch me in people who are suffering."

Compassion for a Trespasser

Mike Suarez caught a young man robbing his mother's home and chased the thief onto a nearby pier. The thief jumped into the water, but couldn't swim. Suarez used a

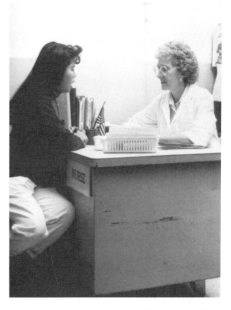

It all starts with caring for yourself.

"You must be my hands and feet."

nearby rowboat to haul in the thief. Later Suarez said, "Sure, I was angry with him, but when I heard his cries, I had to help him—no matter what harm he had done me."

Appearances Can Be Deceiving

In a small village lived a very rich man who never gave money to the poor. One day a beggar made the mistake of going to his door for some food. "Don't you know by now I don't give things away?" the rich man said gruffly. Everyone in the village called the man "the Miser." They didn't even use his name. In contrast, there was a simple shoemaker who was very generous and never turned anyone away. Everyone loved him and called him a saint. When "the Miser" died, no one walked in his funeral procession. He was buried at the edge of the cemetery, away from the other graves.

Soon after his death, a strange thing happened. The shoemaker no longer gave money or food to the poor. He told people he had nothing to give. It was so unlike him that the rabbi asked him why he had changed so. The shoemaker explained, "Many years ago the man you called 'the Miser' entrusted me with the task of distributing his money to the poor. I was not to reveal this until his death.

Living a Moral Life: Gifted and Growing

Each month he secretly gave me more money. You people never questioned how I, a poor shoemaker, could have so much to give away."

The rabbi was deeply ashamed. He called the villagers together. " 'The Miser' lived by the Scriptures and gave alms in secret," he said. "We sinned by condemning an innocent man." When the rabbi died, he wanted to be buried next to the man called "the Miser."

1. *Describe a situation where you may have misjudged someone's generosity and compassion. How did you realize your mistake in judgment?*

2. *How can you show compassion toward someone who has offended or hurt you? How can our nation demonstrate compassion toward other nations?*

3. *Name some people who show compassion toward others. What motivates these people to act as they do?*

Physical and Emotional Well-Being

Saint Paul says that our body is a temple of the Holy Spirit and that we should present our body as a living sacrifice, holy and pleasing to God (1 Corinthians 6:19; Romans 12:1). Any neglect of our body is a violation of the fifth commandment. We have a duty to protect our life.

As a teen, you are more capable of independent decisions, like caring for your own health. It is no longer your parents' responsibility to see that you eat balanced meals. Only you can control what you eat and the amount of sleep you get. Sleep is very important, because it is during sleep that the body grows and repairs itself. Exercise and periodic medical examinations can also contribute to physical well-being.

A healthy person has an emotional balance, which involves many things. Three essentials for this balance are the expression of feelings, emotional control, and our relationship with God. It is important to remember that emotions are neither good nor bad. They are simply a natural part of being human.

The Expression of Feelings

A feeling contains energy that must somehow be released. If it isn't released or expressed, it will trigger bodily reactions that eventually damage a person's mental and physical health. Unexpressed feelings don't just go away after a time; instead, they remain alive and accumulate deep within. Emotions that have accumulated over months or years often will erupt in ulcers, depression, or violence toward others or against oneself.

Emotional Control

Negative feelings such as hate and anger need to be controlled in order to prevent violence. Otherwise, if these emotions get out of hand, you may find yourself acting from hate or anger. Other emotions, such as affection, are pleasant and attract you to engage in desirable behavior. Even affection, if left to go out of control, can lead to serious problems.

Human beings have long-range needs and goals that require years of preparation and work. Some of these goals might be to achieve a balanced Christian character or to live a rewarding married life. In order to achieve these goals you sometimes need to restrain the emotions that draw you to immediate and often temporary pleasures.

God's Help

You may hear people say, "My feelings got the best of me; I couldn't control them." If your power of self-control is weak, often you can't control your feelings. This is especially the case with such basic and powerful passions as anger and sexual desire. Yet the picture isn't as dark as it first might appear. Jesus offers help in time of need. His presence strengthens your will-power so that you can direct

Learning to control your emotions is an important step toward moral maturity.

For Example

To achieve the goal of a productive, healthy life, you may need to restrain your immediate desire for a dangerous thrill like drinking or smoking.

Living a Moral Life: Gifted and Growing

Using drugs can cause irreversible damage to your body or even kill you.

Drugs

There is no way to use drugs recreationally and temperately. In most cases narcotic or hallucinogenic drugs do serious damage to the body on the first use. Even drugs like marijuana, which are not physically addictive, can become psychologically addictive.

Many drugs which are illegal may be used legally under the care of a physician. The pain killing power of morphine—a heroin derivative—is legendary. It is also highly addictive, even when prescribed with care. Marijuana has been used experimentally with success in organ transplant and cancer patients. Marijuana also deadens the mind, confuses judgment, and often leads to harder drugs.

The recreational use of these drugs—outside of a doctor's care—is considered immoral because of the physical, emotional and mental damage that they do. Recreational uses include overdosing with cough syrup and sniffing glue, correction fluid, or any other chemicals to get a high.

Tobacco Products

Whether cigarette smoking is immoral or not is a point of debate among theologians. Cigarettes are addictive, they are known to cause cancer and lung disease. In addition to the detrimental effects on the smoker, the smoke from cigarettes has been shown to harm non-smokers.

Temperance: the virtue of using moderation in action, thought, or feelings.

What are some of the reasons teens smoke?

The leading cause of death in the world today is tobacco products. Even the smokeless tobacco so popular among teens has been linked to gum cancer and death. Pregnant women who smoke increase their babies chances of being born with a low birth weight and decreased brain activity. Using temperance with smoking is difficult because tobacco is so addictive that quitting is extremely painful. The easiest way to stop is not to start.

8. Why is drinking so popular among young teens and even preteens? How about cigarettes or smokeless tobacco?

9. Why does civil law prohibit the possession and sale of alcohol to minors? What is your moral duty with regards to obeying alcohol laws? Explain.

10. Some parents are glad to see their children drink or smoke at home but not "behind their backs." Is this a responsible approach to the situation? Why or why not?

Spiritual Well-Being

Your spiritual well-being hinges on your personal relationship with Jesus Christ. Since you are changing in so many ways, your relationship with him is bound to change. It should be growing more personal, more realistic.

The sacraments, especially the Eucharist and the sacrament of Penance, are powerful ways for Christ to touch and transform you into an integrated man or woman. The Eucharist should mean something different to you now than it did when you were a child. Christ strengthens your character positively by healing you in all areas of your life. Penance is a sacrament of healing. This sacrament heals you even when you have not committed serious sin.

Living a Moral Life: Gifted and Growing

During adolescence many teens drift away from the sacraments at a time when the benefits of the sacraments can be most helpful. Often their faith is challenged by peers: Celebrating the Eucharist at Sunday liturgy is not an acceptable thing to do to be part of the in-group. Adolescence is also a time when teens are most likely to be sensitive to their own faults and weaknesses. The idea of confessing faults or failures to a priest, even a sympathetic one, is just too embarrassing. But turning to Jesus, in personal prayer and through the Church, is a valuable asset that the Catholic teen can readily make use of in times of difficulty. The challenge is to control fears and emotions and act in one's best interest.

11. *Explain Cardinal Bernardin's statement, "Right to life and quality of life complement each other in domestic social policy." On a personal level, how does this statement apply to living a "heroic social ethic"?*

12. *In addition to abortion, what other contemporary moral issues would fall under this "consistent ethic of life"? Why?*

13. *What does the Eucharist mean in your life now?*

14. *How does the sacrament of Penance help spiritual well-being?*

Summary

- Christ's new commandment calls us to show compassion toward all people, not just friends or relatives.

- Take good care of your body, your mind, and your feelings because you are good and can bring God's love to others.

- The fifth commandment states that all life is sacred and that human beings must work to build a compassionate society.

■ Review

1. What is the meaning of love as it is used in Jesus' commandment to "love your neighbor"? Explain.

2. What are four aspects of Jesus' new commandment?

3. How do we usually meet Christ? Explain.

4. Why does the fifth commandment require that we protect our physical well-being?

5. What harmful results come from not expressing emotions?

6. Give two reasons why drunkenness is morally wrong.

7. Explain the meaning of having a "consistent ethic of life."

8. How do the sacraments of Eucharist and Penance contribute to your spiritual well-being?

9. Words to Know: compassion, murder, temperance, emotions.

■ In Your World

1. Describe a situation when you felt that your emotions were "out of control." How did you release those feelings? How could you have better dealt with those emotions? Explain.

2. What are the drugs readily available in your school or neighborhood? Who uses these drugs? What is the attraction of these drugs? What can you do to stop drug usage in your school or neighborhood? How can you help the drug users get off drugs?

■ Cases

My sister was always trying to fix me. She thought I was hopelessly backward. Some would call me a borderline nerd. But the natural desire to be like my big sister, to be liked by her, won out. My brother believed I was destined to weirdness, too. In the end, though, I decided, "Yeah, that's right—I am different from you." I began to cultivate the difference.

- In what ways could Stephanie's brother and sister have shown compassion for her? Explain.

- How can you learn to work through the pain of criticism towards self-acceptance?

SECTION 2
Compassion for Others

Conflicts are a normal part of life, for each person has different needs, ideas, and levels of maturity. Some people fear facing a conflict, because to them, conflict means fighting, and fighting means violence.

But conflict can be a good, healthy, nonviolent struggle. It can force opponents to cooperate, even when they disagree. This partnership of opponents may be one meaning behind these words of Jesus: "For if you love those who love you, what right have you to claim any credit? And if you save your greetings for your brothers, are you doing anything exceptional?" (Matthew 5:46). At times even a brother or sister can be "the enemy," and that's when you prove your love.

Conflict without Violence

How can you be a partner to your opponent in a fight? What do the two of you have in common? Often both sides in a conflict possess partial truth. How can you meet your opponent half-way, present your truth, and listen to the other without destroying him or her. Each must respect the other as a bearer of truth.

Struggling to blend the particular truth both people possess will lead to the resolution of the conflict. It will take time, but in the end, both people will be changed by becoming stronger, more open, more compassionate, and better able to settle future conflicts without violence.

A Method of Conflict Resolution

When you are in conflict with someone and need to talk, try to make eye contact in order to communicate a positive, spirit of acceptance. Begin with an honest statement of your own feelings about the other's behavior. Do not accuse the other or presume to know their motives. Allow plenty of time first to listen and then to allow negative reactions to be spoken calmly.

- **Define and limit the conflict.** *Talk about only one issue and be sure both parties know the issue. Raising past hurts only paralyzes the process.*

- **Identify the problem.** *Listen to all parties until the real problem surfaces. It may be much deeper than the immediate conflict and require farther-reaching solutions.*

- **Examine the problem.** *Know each other's point of view. Ask each party to state the problem as the other person sees it. The other person must agree that the restatement is, indeed, his or her point. This step forces both parties to verbalize the other's truth and accept it as a valid position.*

- **Survey alternatives.** *Examining three or four alternatives usually insures that neither party will be forced to accept a one-sided solution. If help is needed to come up with new alternatives, stop the process for a few days and then resume.*

- **Find a solution.** *Construct a solution that benefits both parties. The solution itself need not be perfect. Both sides should agree to try it for a specific length of time and meet again to evaluate it.*

- **Remain open.** *If no agreement can be reached, agree to disagree, and maintain the relationship. Rather than one party giving in or both giving up, determine to get a third party to help or both do more fact-finding; or wait until changed circumstances make a solution possible.*

One great danger among friends is the put-down. A "put-down" is a remark or series of cruel comments that cut down the dignity of another person. Those making the put-downs may do so to feel better about themselves. In reality, they are showing their jealousy and fear of not being noticed. The only way they can come out "on top" is to step on somebody else. Among teens, this seems to work, for a time; the victims are really hurt. Put-downs are morally wrong; they are detrimental to friendships by destroying trust.

19. *Describe some ways you can correct the behavior of a friend or peer without alienating him or her.*

20. *What kinds of put-downs are the most painful? Why? Why are students who get good grades often put down or teased?*

Younger Children

Often the people most in need of our compassion are younger children. Because adults and other children often take advantage of them, they are likely to be victims of anger or frustration. Showing compassion to children helps teens develop problem solving skills. They also experience the satisfaction of having positive influence on the next generation.

Children are impressionable, vulnerable, and, for the most part, unable to defend themselves or express their troubles. Thus, every family member is responsible for protecting them and encouraging their growth.

Because children have little sense of danger, they need physical protection. Everyone has a serious obligation to avoid putting children at risk of harm. Children also need the physical contact and reinforcement of gentle people who hug and kiss them, pat them on the head, and put an arm around their shoulders. Brothers and sisters can satisfy this need as well as parents.

Children also have strong emotional needs. Many may feel inferior or totally unwanted. They need older people to spend time with them, talk to them about their interests, and treat them with respect. They should never be manipulated like pets or servants. We can help children appreciate themselves by complimenting them and encouraging their creativity. Since labels like "Our Star Player" and "The Brain" tend to make children feel that their worth is in their successful performance, such labels should be avoided. One child's label can easily make a less gifted brother or sister feel unloved.

Children have a keen desire for moral heroes and heroines, and possess an innocence that makes them trust all adults. They tend to accept whatever they observe in adults and in older brothers and sisters as correct behavior. Because we may be someone's hero or heroine without knowing it, we have the responsibility to be a good model. Actions that may be proper among our own age group may be harmful to children.

Bribing children with candy or money to keep them from reporting something they saw us do, teaches them dishonesty. If we break promises or lie to them, we teach them to be untruthful. Jesus strongly condemns the person who steers a child toward immoral living: "Whoever causes one of these little ones who believe in me to sin, it would be better for him to have a great millstone hung around his neck and to be drowned in the depths of the sea" (Matthew 18:6).

Children need to be corrected firmly but gently. We are guilty of teaching immoral behavior if we allow a child to do something wrong without correction. Besides notification of the misdemeanor, a child needs to know the reasons for its unacceptability. But we should be careful not to destroy a child's self-concept in the process of correction. Instead of saying "You are bad," it is better to say, "You are a good person, but this is a bad thing to do because..." It is detrimental—embarrassing and humiliating—to punish a child in the presence of other children.

Living a Moral Life: Gifted and Growing

21. *Share with the class some personal observations of the care brothers and sisters can give to younger children in their family. What gifts do these children give to their brothers and sisters in return?*

22. *How can you express anger caused by something a child has done without physically or emotionally abusing the child?*

Summary

- Conflicts are a part of life. Try to use your mind and gifts to resolve all conflicts peacefully.

- A commitment to nonviolent resistance often takes more courage than acts of physical violence.

- Exploitation and prejudice are ways in which we don't show compassion to other human beings.

- Don't be afraid to give moral guidance to friends, peers, or especially, young children.

SECTION 2
Checkpoint!

■ Review

1. Must all conflicts include violence? Why or why not?

2. What were Gandhi's views on conflict resolution? Explain.

3. Why is nonviolent resistance not a form of cowardice? What is the goal of nonviolent resistance? Explain.

4. What are the six steps in conflict resolution? Explain each one.

5. How should you provide moral guidance to children?

6. Explain this statement: "A true friend would confront you on a moral problem he or she recognizes in you."

7. Words to Know: nonviolent resistance, boycott, scandal, putdown, exploitation, prejudice, discrimination.

■ In Your World

1. Identify a current social or moral problem. Plan a course of nonviolent resistance to confront that problem. Present your resolution to the class and how you would propose to put your resolution into action.

2. Describe a recent confrontation you had with a friend or peer. How did you resolve the conflict? What steps, if any, were missing from the method of resolution presented in this section? Explain.

3. How would each of the following threaten friendship and thus violate the fifth commandment?
   1. Daring another person to do a dangerous thing.
   2. Rejecting someone who is different.
   3. Getting revenge on a friend or peer.

■ Cases

Frank and Lisa are members of a racial minority in a large high school. There is a teacher in the school who is extremely prejudiced against their race. Now Frank and Lisa have been suspended as a result of a conflict that began when the teacher called them an offensive name.

■ How would you organize a plan of nonviolent resistance? What nonviolent tactics could you employ to have the students reinstated?

■ What options are open to the students? Which of these options would promote a peaceful resolution to the problem? Which would not?

Living a Moral Life: Gifted and Growing

23. *Who is the person you would go to if you needed support during a very difficult emotional situation? Why?*

24. *Who would you contact if a friend of yours talked about attempting suicide?*

Abortion

Abortion is the termination and removal of the human life growing inside the womb. An abortion may occur naturally, (spontaneous abortion), when for some unknown reason the body rejects the growth of this new life, or when, through medical complications or for unexplained reasons, the fetus dies in the mother's womb. A spontaneous abortion occurs, usually within the first three months of pregnancy. When an abortion is caused by human intervention, the intention is a conscious termination of the life of the fetus.

The fight against abortion continues on the legal front, through peaceful demonstrations, and through passive resistance at abortion clinics.

Fetus: an unborn infant.

As Catholics we believe that life itself is God's greatest gift to us. We also believe that life begins at conception (Psalm 139). Since the growing life inside the woman is human, it deserves the utmost protection and respect. Our faith reminds us that the "first right of the human person is the right to life" (*"Declaration on Abortion,"* Sacred Congregation for the Doctrine of the Faith, 1974, #11). Thus, the Catholic Church condemns abortion as the taking of an innocent life. Pope John Paul II reminds us that: "Every human person—no matter how vulnerable or helpless, no matter how young or old, no matter how healthy or handicapped or sick, no matter how useful or productive for society—is a being of inestimable worth created in the image and likeness of God" (John Paul II—Address in Detroit, September, 1987).

Prior to 1973, abortion was illegal in the United States. In 1973, the Supreme Court considered the case entitled *Roe v. Wade*. By a 7-2 decision, the court held that the fetus is not a person in the legal sense of the term and that a woman has the right to terminate her pregnancy until the time in which a fetus is capable of existing outside of the mother's womb. The court determined that it was possible for a fetus to survive outside of the mother's womb after the sixth month of pregnancy. Because the Supreme Court ruled that a fetus was not a person during the first six months of pregnancy, it concluded that the mother had a right to have an abortion anytime during her first six months of pregnancy. The father had no legal say in the matter of an abortion.

Roe v. Wade stood for sixteen years as the single most important case regarding the legalization of abortion until July 3, 1989 when the Supreme Court, in the case of *Webster v. Reproductive Health Services,* ruled five to four that each state has the option of considering more restrictive laws on abortion. Such a ruling means that the citizens of all states can have a much greater role in deciding the limits on abortion for their states. Now the question of abortion is out of the hands of the court and in the hands of elected state lawmakers.

Since we now have a voice in the abortion debate, it is urgent that we be informed about the issue. As Catholics we also have the obligation of understanding what our Catholic faith has to say about abortion.

Living a Moral Life: Gifted and Growing

The Catholic Church condemns abortion, whether or not it is declared legal by the state. If a Catholic decides to have an abortion, she, and anyone directly assisting her, faces automatic excommunication, that is, the offender is considered to have left the church's communion and requires absolution for reconciliation with the Church before receiving the sacraments.

---

25. *What would you say to a friend who is considering an abortion? Would you feel or act differently toward her?*

Euthanasia

Euthanasia is a willful act to end a person's life because of incurable illness or old age. It can be carried out by the persons themselves (a form of suicide) or by another person.

Central to the issue of euthanasia is the question of the quality and value of human life. Supporters of euthanasia say that it is a humane alternative to suffering, whereas opponents argue that euthanasia is a rejection of hope. What is important is that the dignity of the human person must be upheld, regardless of the person's condition. Life is a gift from God. To take it at will is to deny the purpose and value of that gift. The Catholic Church teaches that euthanasia, or mercy killing, violates the dignity of the human person and usurps the authority of God who alone is master of life and death.

An argument for euthanasia is that it is not humane to force a person to live in extreme pain and suffering when there is no hope of a cure. When there is no hope of improving a person's condition, the Catholic Church teaches that extraordinary means should not be used to sustain a person's life. Extraordinary means is any attempt to sustain the body when it would otherwise expire naturally. In such cases, the Church permits the removal of any life sustaining machine. This is referred to as "dying with dignity" and is not the same as directly causing someone's death — euthanasia.

For Example

If the body is being kept alive by a respirator, while the brain has ceased to function, it is permissible to remove the machine, allowing the person to die naturally with dignity.

Absolution: the confessor's act by which he removes the guilt of sin in Christ's name.

Euthanasia: to cause the death of a person who is suffering greatly, or who is very old. Also called mercy killing.

Who has the right to remove life support systems? When does such action become euthanasia?

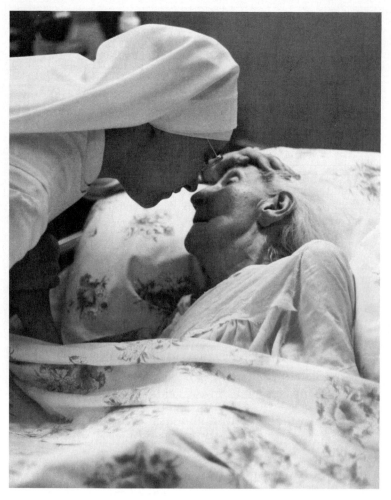

In 1990, the Supreme Court, in a case concerning the Permanent Vegetative State (PVS), decided that without a clear statement of consent from the patient, the state could continue to keep him or her alive through intravenous feedings. Such feedings are not considered extraordinary means by the Church. In another case, a doctor invented a machine that could be used by patients to take their own lives. This "suicide machine" was condemned by the Church.

Another moral concern is living-wills—instructions from a patient setting out his or her wishes in case he or she becomes comatose. There is much debate in the area of moral theology on this matter. As long as the person does not request euthanasia or suicide, theologians would generally support the idea of a living will.

Living a Moral Life: Gifted and Growing

■ Review

1. Give an original example of exploitation.

2. What is the single greatest way to prevent suicide?

3. How can a woman be physically and emotionally damaged by an abortion?

4. Under what conditions can a Christian justifiably fight in a war? Explain. What legitimate alternative is there to fighting? Explain this viewpoint.

5. What is the difference between euthanasia and allowing someone to "die with dignity"?

6. Words to Know: euthanasia, abortion, conscientious objector, pacifism, Just War Theory.

■ In Your World

1. There is food enough for everyone, yet people starve. Research the reasons for this phenomenon. Present your findings to the class. Decide on a course of action that could be taken by the class to discourage waste and promote generosity overseas and within your local community.

2. Many groups exist to fight hunger and oppression in the world. Some, like Amnesty International, Catholic Relief Services, and Oxfam America have organized activities that groups can participate in to help other human beings in need. Contact one of these groups and see what you can do to help change these oppressive situations.

■ Cases

Charles tells his story: "My older brother is always chewing tobacco, smoking, drinking, and experimenting with drugs. He pressures me into doing these things. If I don't follow him he says, 'I remember when we were good brothers.' This statement hurts my feelings. I don't want to do these things, but I want to be a good brother and share some activities with him." What are Charles' options? Use the OPTION ARROW to determine the choice Charles should make.

8 Review

■ Study

1. What does Jesus mean by "love your neighbor"?

2. What is the message of the fifth commandment? How does it apply to your physical and emotional well-being?

3. Why is it necessary to control your emotions?

4. Discuss whether the following is true or not: "Temperance is the virtue of abstaining from alcohol." Explain your answer.

5. List the various dangers of alcohol consumption.

6. Explain the "seamless garment" ethic.

7. What are the six steps in conflict resolution? Explain each.

8. How can nonviolent resistance effect a change in the opposition? How does suffering contribute to this change?

9. How should you provide moral guidance to friends? children?

10. How does exploitation harm other people?

11. Give three examples of prejudice.

12. What are the signs of someone who is considering suicide?

13. Why is abortion a moral evil? How can an abortion hurt the woman?

14. What arguments does the conscientious objector use to support his or her position on war?

15. What conditions must be fulfilled in order for a Christian to justifiably fight in a war? Explain each.

16. Why is euthanasia considered to be morally wrong? What alternative is there to "mercy killing"?

■ Action

1. Visit a hospice or home for the terminally ill. Spend some time talking to the patients, comforting them.

2. Have a panel discussion on the types of exploitation that are aimed at children and teenagers, and the ways in which teens exploit others. Be sure to research your topic thoroughly.

3. Report on recent statistics in these areas: child abuse, crimes resulting from alcoholism and drug abuse, the destructive capacity of nuclear weapons, the exploitation of the poor, racist or hate groups, and abortion. Present your findings as a group or individually to the class.

4. Organize a food drive for the poor and hungry in your area.

5. Collect clippings from the paper which describe the debate over your state's pending abortion legislation. Write an elected state official and offer your opinion on abortion legislation.

■ Prayer

1. As a group, write a "Prayer for True Friendship." Then use these prayers at the beginning of class.

2. Call on the Holy Spirit to assist you in your work for a more compassionate world. Copy these words down, and carry them with you. Say them when you feel alone in a struggle:

   "Come, Holy Spirit, fill the hearts of your faithful. Enkindle in them the fire of your love. Send forth your Spirit and we shall be created, and you shall renew the face of the earth."

Sexuality and Relationships

OBJECTIVES

In this Chapter you will

- Identify intimate exchanges in the natural world.

- Understand the differences between love and infatuation.

- Learn how extra-marital sexual intercourse can hinder the growth toward wholeness of a young person.

- Recognize the reasons why people reach sexual maturity before they reach emotional maturity.

- Consider the many purposes of sexual relations.

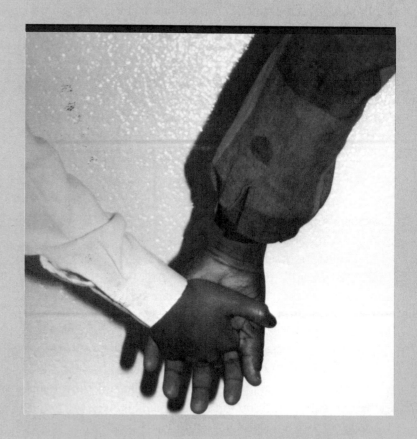

I came so that they might have life and have it more abundantly.
—John 10:10

The Life-Giving Exchange: Sexuality

Think for a moment of the life-giving exchanges continuously going on in nature. Leaves fall from trees and fertilize the soil. Soil feeds plants that exchange oxygen with animals and humans. Animals eat plants and then fertilize the soil with their bodies. Heat evaporates water into the air, and the air returns it in the form of rain. The universe is an intricate system of life-giving interchanges, and the universe reflects its Creator. God is a mysterious exchange of life and love, never holding on but always giving and receiving. God made us in the divine image, ''male and female he created them'' (Genesis 1:27). We are either one sex or the other, each one needing the other for an exchange of life and love.

Human beings grow through exchange, whether of air, ideas, friendly embraces, meaningful glances, or even angry words. All human exchanges have one thing in common: they all involve the body. The sixth and ninth commandments offer you guidance in responding to the demands of your body. You are to be faithful and responsible to yourself and to others. You must also learn to control your desires.

Harmony and Balance

A basic Chinese symbol is the *Tai Chi* (pronounced tie-chee). It is a circle separated into two halves with a curving line. One half of the circle is black; the other half is white. The symbol represents the mystery of how opposing forces provide balance in nature. The dark side refers to *yin* qualities in nature: passive, quieter, cooler qualities in

Finding harmony and balance between our masculine and feminine sides is a challenge for most people.

nature. *Yang* qualities, by contrast, are the active, bright, warm qualities in nature. In order for there to be harmony in nature or society, there must be a balance between these opposing forces. Each side complements the other side, forming a union of opposites. Moreover, one side cannot exist apart from the other. The concept of light needs the concept of darkness in order to make sense. The idea of masculine doesn't really make sense apart from the idea of feminine. Warmth is appreciated by experiencing cold. So, opposite forces in nature define each other and form a whole.

In addition, the Tai Chi symbol has a dot of the opposite within each side which represents the fact that a little bit of the opposite is found in each thing. Rarely is a room completely black; usually it will have some light present. Women are sometimes said to have ''masculine'' qualities, such as aggression or drive. Men are said to demonstrate ''feminine'' qualities when they act with compassion, or tend to the welfare of the young or ill. In order to be whole, a person needs to develop his or her opposite self.

Becoming Sexually Mature

Not every human being has a flawless figure, perfect grooming, or muscular physique. Television performers and models spend hours hiding their natural imperfections from the camera. The development of our body, emotions, and character into a whole, mature man or woman will be slow and uneven. Our appearance will always have some flaws, but it is, nonetheless, natural and good.

When we become impatient or frustrated with our changing self, or want to do foolish things to hurry up the process of maturing, it helps to remember that these changing qualities are all normal and necessary aspects of every life. ''I give you thanks that I am fearfully, wonderfully made'' (Psalm 139:14).

Living a Moral Life: Gifted and Growing

Physical Development

Puberty is a dramatic stage of physical development after birth. It is then that increased levels of hormones signal the body to develop to maturity. Boys' voices deepen, their muscle mass increases, beards begin to grow and sperm are produced. Girls begin to menstruate and develop breasts and rounded hips. But sexual development begins long before puberty; it begins at the moment of conception. The first few months of prenatal life establish the pattern for everything that will happen in puberty.

To appreciate the wonder of human sexuality, we need to know that we are male or female in five ways. First, gender is determined by genes: every woman has female sex chromosomes in every cell of her body; every man has male chromosomes in every cell. The chromosomes from the father determine the child's gender. Second, gender is indicated by genitals, the reproductive organs of the body. In the first month of development, all fetuses are genitally female. During the second month the male fetus develops a penis, testes, and connecting tubes.

Third, gender is identified through the secondary sex characteristics: low voice, beard, and muscular body in males; higher voice, breasts, and rounded body in females. Fourth, during the third and fourth month of pregnancy, a complex combination of chemicals works on different parts of the brain for males and females, "programming" these parts so that the person feels attracted to the opposite sex when puberty begins. The brain, then, is a major sex organ.

Men and women differ in many ways, but those differences cannot be equated as better or worse. They are just different.

Chapter 9   Sexuality and Relationships

Not So Fast

(From *"Zorba the Greek"*)
Not so fast, not so fast
Let it grow, let it last.
Nature knows when and why the butterfly
I remember one morning when I saw a cocoon in the back
of a tree. I remember, I marveled that imprisoned inside was
a butterfly, waiting to be free.
Not so fast.
I was very impatient and so I warmed the cocoon with the
breath of my sigh.
The butterfly trembled and began to emerge like a miracle,
right before my eyes
Not so fast
All at once I discovered that its delicate wings were all
crumbled and torn
That he still was not ready—I had made him be born
But the wonder of life and death of its plan
So he died in my hand, by the will not of God
But of man
Every man has a moment and I'm waiting for life,
when I am finally free
I must not be hurried—Give me life give me time,
like a butterfly, a butterfly
Not so fast.

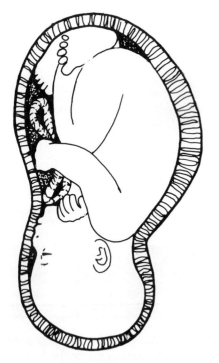

Our sexual identity developed while we were in the womb.

Fifth and finally, we are different in gender by behavior. Men interact with women differently from the way they interact with other men. The same is true of women. Sex-typical behavior is programmed into the brain starting with the fifth and sixth months of development. While not controlling the way people choose to act, it influences people's mannerisms and attitudes.

The wonder of God's creative power comes clear as we begin to understand the extreme complexity of our development from the first moment of conception. Within the newly-formed cells of a new human being are all the programs needed to develop not only arms and legs but also genitals and secondary sex characteristics. The development begins even before a mother knows she is carrying new life!

Because prenatal development is so delicate and complex, foreign chemicals in the mother's body can upset it. Drugs, including alcohol and marijuana, are known to disrupt fetal development. It is very important, then, that any woman who has a possibility of being pregnant not drink alcohol or use pot. It's in the first weeks of pregnancy that the greatest possibility for irreversible damage to the unborn child exists.

---

3. *Bring to class snapshots of yourself, one taken two years ago and one taken within the past six months. How has your face changed over time?*

Emotional Development

Social and cultural expectations as well as body chemistry shape the emotional differences between men and women. What we think of as natural behavior may in fact be the result of cultural conditioning. Culturally, a woman is allowed to express her deeply felt moods and feelings. She can cry without embarrassment, reveal her need to be liked, and care for others. Often, she can easily discuss her feelings with her friends when she feels the pain of awkwardness, rejection, and failure.

A Woman's Attitude Toward Herself

Our culture can give a woman the message that her body and emotions are her real self. She may be expected to be gentle in her speech and controlled in her actions. If she feels hurt, she can usually cry without fear of disapproval.

A woman's attitude about herself affects how she enjoys herself.

She may also see other women expressing their religious faith and feelings with freedom.

But a woman indoctrinated in this way can be carried away by her emotions just because she needs to be cared for and feels rejection so easily. To this woman, any personal attention is interpreted as a sign that she is liked as a person, and she will invest her whole person in her return gestures. This woman needs to understand that she is not obligated to conform to the stereotypes that society places upon her. She would benefit from seeing women she admires in roles of strength and control.

A woman's emotions are somewhat influenced, but never completely controlled, by her ovulation cycle. On days close to ovulation, a woman tends to feel good about herself, optimistic, and desirous of affection. This is natural because these are the days when sexual intercourse can result in conception. On the days close to and during menstruation, she often feels anxious and less self-confident. A woman should know when her moods are related to ovulation. This will help her understand her increased desire for men on these days.

A Man's Attitude Toward Himself

Caring for children is a very "manly" thing to do.

A man's emotions, a deep and important element in his personality, develop under different social and cultural influences. Since a man lives in a highly competitive society that rates people on measurable results, he may fear being labeled "unmasculine" if he cannot produce athletically, mechanically, and sexually. Men feel the pressure of being unable to live up to the impossible image, the same as women do. A man often hesitates to talk about his feelings. He may have picked up wrong messages: a man should always be tough, put mind over matter, not let his emotions affect him. These are erroneous cultural lessons that need to be unlearned.

Our culture tends to identify a man's mind as the center of his true self. A man brought up to believe this may think he has to keep his emotions buried by the force of his will. The extreme of this belief is the macho man who cannot express his feelings. If a man receives the message that his

Living a Moral Life: Gifted and Growing

body is a thing to be used, it then becomes his status symbol. He will fear any hint of weakness or loss of control. He will think tears are not acceptable, and that his body should function like a well-run machine, never breaking down. But thinking that the body is separate from the mind, heart, and feelings is harmful. This man may have difficulty expressing religious beliefs with his body or his emotions. No matter how deeply he believes, it may be hard to let those beliefs flow freely. This man needs to see men he respects expressing themselves religiously and sincerely, showing emotion and being vulnerable.

Sexual feelings are wonderful gifts from God. They can, however, be misused or abused.

---

4. *Describe a TV commercial that shows a lack of awareness of the need to be patient with one's physical and emotional changes. How do advertisers want you to respond to this ad?*

5. *What are some similar and different ways women and men express feelings?*

Sexual Feelings

The sense of warmth and excitement that a person feels in his or her body, sometimes most strongly in the area of the sexual organs, is natural and not in any way sinful. A woman may be aroused when a man touches her or smiles at her. A man may become aroused when he reads a romantic passage in a story or watches a love scene, or when he thinks about romance. It may also come without any specific cause or stimulation, especially when he or she is relaxed before sleep.

Spontaneous sexual feelings occur when we feel happy and comfortable about our bodies. We can be aroused at the sight of a certain woman or man. These are all innocent pleasures related to our sexuality and are intended by God. This spontaneous sexual pleasure is natural and good.

Sexual feelings can also be stimulated through intentional fantasies, self-arousal (masturbation), petting, passionate kissing, or pornography. Deliberately indulging in any of

Menstruation: a woman's monthly blood flow that occurs when an egg has not been fertilized. The blood and tissue are the lining that the womb produces in preparation for a fertilized egg.

Ovulation: the process in which a ripe egg is released from an ovary.

these activities inappropriately could be sinful. The key words here are "deliberately" and "inappropriately." The seriousness of such arousal depends upon psychological factors and a person's emotional state.

Making A Moral World

No truly loving relationship can survive without a commitment from both persons. Commitment means giving fully of one's self without reservation. In a commitment we are bonded with the other person. This usually happens fully only after much prayer and reflection. Quick decisions do not lead to real commitments. In fact, commitments are grown into, not merely chosen. Once made, commitments are not easily broken. The life-giving power of sexuality makes the need for a true commitment all the more obvious. Without this sense of responsibility, sexual intercourse lacks significance and is reduced to a mere biological act.

You Belong to Christ's Community

Some very basic truths, carried to their logical conclusions, can change your whole way of thinking about yourself. For example, God made you, and whatever God makes is good in every way. The Son of God became a man and thus is fully human. In your effort to honor Jesus as the Son of God, you may sometimes forget how human he was. He experienced every human emotion, including those related to sexuality. Being male, he went through all the normal stages of masculine development. All the bodily functions were a normal part of his life, along with all human feelings. "For we do not have a high priest who is unable to sympathize with our weaknesses, but one who has similarly been tested in every way, yet without sin" (Hebrews 4:15). His death and resurrection conquered sin. We will not be conquered by sin if we maintain a close relationship with him. Everyone baptized into Christ comes alive with the energy of the resurrection. "So whoever is in Christ is a new creation" (2 Corinthians 5:17).

All the powers and processes of human nature are good. The process of growth, with its ups and downs and periods of pain, is intended by God and is blessed. The power to enjoy pleasure is a gift God wants you to have. Curiosity, a mental process, is good, and the knowledge you gain about yourself through curiosity is also good. These powers and processes have been given to you not just for your private fulfillment but for sharing with others as part of your mission.

As you develop physically and emotionally, the faith community encourages a deeper personal friendship with Christ and a fuller sharing of yourself and your talents with others. The sacrament of Confirmation strengthens this sense of mission. As a member of the Catholic community, you share a wisdom that blesses and celebrates human life.

Living a Moral Life: Gifted and Growing

Why do we become physically mature and feel the urge for sexual intercourse so many years before we are ready to marry? The acceptable age for marriage is determined by culture. In Asia, Africa, and Latin America today, couples still marry very early. In the United States, the gap between physical maturity and marriage is greater. Time and experience are required to master all the aspects of living as an adult in our culture. Despite the difficulties these years cause, there are some wonderful advantages in them.

One advantage is that the years between sexual maturity and marriage provide you with the time you need to integrate your sexual powers within your personality, to feel them, and to gradually learn to control them before experiencing sexual intimacy with another person.

A second advantage is that sexual maturity draws you to desire friendship with members of the opposite sex. The years before marriage assure the time you need to develop deep emotional and spiritual relationships.

A third advantage is that you have time to consider choosing either marriage, the lifestyle of a single person, or the consecrated life of a priest or religious. You can slowly come to know just how you are being called to use your sexuality. And then you need time to experiment in directing your sexual powers toward deep—but not exclusive—friendships, and toward other forms of creativity.

Summary

- Sexuality reflects the life-giving exchange in nature, balancing opposing forces which creates harmony.

- Physical and emotional development both take years of growth before maturing.

- Cultural expectations influence the attitudes that men and women have towards one another.

- Sexual feelings are good and are a normal part of maturation.

- Every truly loving relationship cannot survive without a commitment from both persons.

Although people in many countries marry when they reach sexual maturity, marriage in the United States usually takes place when the couple is much older and ready to enter the work force.

■ Review

1. Point out two basic differences between a woman's and a man's adolescent development.

2. What are some messages women can pick up from our culture?

3. What are some messages that men can pick up from our culture?

4. Describe five ways in which genders differ. Explain each.

5. Give one advantage and one disadvantage of the gap between physical maturity and emotional social maturity.

6. Words to Know: gender, sexuality, puberty, menstruation, chromosomes, ovulation, conception.

■ In Your World

1. Describe ways the media and advertisers present the sexually "mature" individual. How do they address the emotional aspect of maturity? Why do they focus mostly on physical appearance and performance?

2. Make a list of the ways in which men seem to differ from women. Compare your list with a list made by a person of the opposite sex. Discuss how your lists agree and disagree.

■ Cases

One-half of the class should make a list of the difficulties teens experience in our culture because they are physically mature almost fifteen years before they may be ready to marry. Be specific about sources of the difficulties. The other half of the class should list all the ways teens have today to help them remain chaste—ways their grandparents didn't have or need. Use these lists to consider how society has changed in the last 50 years concerning sexual maturity.

Developing Intimate Relationships

Developing a balanced, complete relationship requires skills most people find difficult: talking honestly, expressing feelings honestly, and admitting ideals honestly. Understanding when and how to use these skills takes serious study and many hours of practice.

Two Friendships

■ *Juanita still didn't know why she liked him. Her dream-idea of a boy friend was someone tall, athletic, very good-looking, and generous in giving her expensive gifts. Rick was none of these things. She didn't even like something about his face—it reminded her of a boy in grade school that she had hated. And Rick wore platform shoes to make himself look taller. She thought that was a little silly. What did one inch more matter to her?*

Maybe she liked him because he didn't have any of those dreamy qualities. He was real. He smiled at her in the morning in a way that showed he was really glad to see her. Sometimes he asked her advice about his problems with his family. He liked to be at her house and even seemed interested in her father's collection of old cameras.

There definitely wasn't anything exciting about Rick. Because he was plain, she felt comfortable and at ease with him. It was strange. Was this love? Juanita couldn't answer that. She knew she had a lot to learn.

■ *Billy Joe ached inside. It had happened again and was even more painful than the last time. His girl friend had broken up with him. Do girls realize how much that hurts? What had he done wrong? He thought he had been on his best behavior. Had he overdone it, sounding like a phony? He had expected this relationship to last, but maybe he had expected too much, forced too much too fast.*

Billy Joe realized at least one thing. He had to let her go. He wouldn't bother her. Maybe that would prove his love for her more than anything—letting her be free. But why did love have to be so painful? Can you love by not loving? It didn't make sense. He would have to do more thinking.

---

6. *What qualities of friendship are illustrated by these two relationships?*

7. *Why does real friendship take so long to develop? Why is there always some pain?*

8. *Write out the thoughts of Rick, Juanita's friend, or the thoughts of the girl who just broke up with Billy Joe.*

Friendship without Romance

Human beings can live happily without physical sex, but they cannot live happily without intimacy. Intimacy is personal closeness based on trust and sharing. We are not intimate with many people, but we need to be intimate with a few people all through life. Intimacy satisfies some of our hunger to be known and cared for. "Bear one another's burdens, and so you will fulfill the law of Christ" (Galatians 6:2).

Time, effort, and patience are required to develop intimacy. Two people need to learn how to talk together, listen carefully, enjoy leisure time together, be silent, celebrate, work, cry, support each other, suffer, and share ideas about God, death, sex, and life's meaning. When you begin to learn how to talk to another about your ideas, to

Living a Moral Life: Gifted and Growing

Dancing is an enjoyable way for friends to have fun.

ask about his or her feelings, and to share a spiritual vision of life, you are learning how to be a totally sexual person. For most people it is easier to begin to learn this kind of sharing with friends of the same sex first.

Touching

Touching between members of the opposite sex can be misinterpreted. Both the man and the woman should be honest with themselves about what they want to communicate. Touches can carry sexual messages, but not necessarily. The meaning of a touch is not based on how much emotion it contains or how much body contact is made. It depends upon the intent of the people touching.

It is a general misconception that a romantic relationship can be kept alive only with progressive physical contact. Personal intimacy is achieved more by talking, listening, observing, reflecting, and then talking some more. This is the way couples find out if they are really compatible.

Love or Infatuation?

Falling in love with someone is not the same as really loving someone. Falling in love is a feeling of physical and emotional attraction for another. It can happen at any age.

Chapter 9   Sexuality and Relationships

Even the most mundane task is enjoyable when done with the person you love.

The process of infatuation (falling in love) is good and is blessed by God. Although it is not truly love, an infatuation draws you to the opposite sex and can help your emotions mature.

These feelings are good because they teach us about our emotions, they help us get to know the opposite sex, and they can serve to hold people together as they develop a loving commitment. But the experience of falling in love does not always lead to a stable relationship. It cannot, by itself, support the demands of a long sexual relationship or the stresses of marriage and children.

What Is Love?

People use the single word "love" for just about every relationship they have with anything that strongly appeals to them: "I love my dog;" "I love my mom;" "I love chocolate ice cream;" "I love, I love, I love."

The word "love" is used so loosely that it can have many different meanings. It's easy to see why people get so confused when someone says, "I love you." Does this mean that you like me? Does it mean that you think I'm pretty? Does it mean that you want to get closer? Does it mean that you care for me and want a lasting relationship?

Living a Moral Life: Gifted and Growing

Signs of Infatuation and Love

Here are ten signs that distinguish infatuation from love.

1. **Infatuation** seems to happen all at once and disappears quickly. **Love** grows slowly.

2. **Infatuation** is jealous, mistrusting and uncertain. **Love** is trusting and secure.

3. **Infatuation** is in a hurry. The couple can't wait—for sex, to go steady, or even for marriage. **Love** is patient. Waiting for what is right is easy.

4. **Infatuation** is very often sex-centered. **Love** cares for the other and is not selfish.

5. **Infatuation** might lead a person to do things he or she doesn't really think are right, just to keep the other person interested. **Love** makes a person more likely than ever to do what he or she knows is right.

6. **Infatuation** tends to make one willing to sacrifice good relationships in order to spend all available time with this other person. **Love** enhances all of the other good relationships.

7. **Infatuation** is a ride on an emotional roller coaster, depending on warm feelings to sustain it. **Love** is a steady and unshakeable attitude.

8. **Infatuation** can demand that the partner think, look, and act as the other person wants. **Love** is honest. One's deepest self can be shown.

9. **Infatuation** often makes a person feel trapped, chained, or confined, as though he or she is missing out on other activities. **Love** encourages freedom and reaching out to others.

10. **Infatuation** often overlooks faults that need to be addressed in the relationship because the other person is "the only one that matters." **Love** won't ask a person to compromise the things and people that are valuable. Love can grow only in a climate of mutual respect.

> **Infatuation:** a sudden, strong, emotional attraction, sometimes called romantic love.

The Greeks realized that sexual love needed to build upon the strong foundation of friendship and love.

Does it mean that you feel sexually turned on and want me mostly as a means of physical release right now?

"Love" can mean any and all of these things. To help clear up the confusion, it can help to describe the various kinds of experiences called love. Centuries ago, the Greek thinkers used different words to express different love feelings and relationships between people. *Eros* was the word they used for what people would probably call "falling in love" with someone, including sexual attraction. *Philia* was the word they used to show friendship. Finally, *agape* was used to mean the kind of love—the respect and justice—people are to show every person as a fellow human being. In brief:

- **Eros** *means "I'm in love with you."*
- **Philia** *means "I like you as my friend."*
- **Agape** *means "I wish for your welfare, whether I like you or am in love with you or not."*

When Jesus says to "love your neighbor," some persons respond that it is impossible for them to like everyone. These people should know that the intended meaning of "love" in this passage is *agape*. Thus, each person is to treat every other person with respect and compassion—to do good to one's fellow human being whatever his or her emotions.

It is important to realize that all three forms of love must be present if an intimate relationship with another is going to last. The deepest love between a man and a woman requires: that they care about each other's well being *(agape)*; that they like each other, enjoy each other's personality *(philia)*; and, finally, that they are sexually attracted to each other *(eros)*.

It's simple. You can't really love somebody if you don't genuinely care about him or her. And you can't really love the other person if you aren't also good friends. Perhaps this is why so many marriages fail. There wasn't first a strong foundation of caring *(agape)* and friendship *(philia)*, before the two acted on romantic feelings *(eros)*. For this reason, love might be described as a triangular structure. If there is no foundation of caring *(agape)*, there can be no friendship *(philia)*. And without these two, the highest expression of

Living a Moral Life: Gifted and Growing

love (eros) will crumble and fall apart. And just as a triangle narrows toward its pinnacle, the various expressions of love move from the lesser intimacy shown to all to the greatest intimacy, shown to one other person.

---

9. *Share the list of ten signs of love and infatuation with a married adult and ask him or her to comment on them from experience. Share your findings with the class.*

10. *Read 1 Corinthians 13. In what ways do you agree with Saint Paul, and in what ways do you differ?*

Dating

Dating is a means of getting to know people. It doesn't have to mean that the people are romantically interested in each other. In fact, any time we arrange to meet someone of either gender, we are planning a date. Dates involving men and women may begin gradually with group activities like skating parties. Even college students group date by meeting friends at the local pub or going to a film as a large group of friends. Group dating can be planned by either women or men just as easily, can be inexpensive and can prevent you from falling into some common dating traps.

Spotting the Date Traps

An experience that should be enjoyable and helpful toward maturity can actually become a trap that takes away freedom and leaves a person feeling used or betrayed.

■ ***Power-Dating Trap***—*Some people date in order to have power over others rather than to develop friendship. They give just enough attention or affection to keep the other thinking there is some love, but the other person always feels a little frustrated. The power date usually gets angry and jealous if the other person begins to be interested in a third party because that means a loss of power. If you sense that someone is* controlling you by this kind of dating, it may be time to free yourself from the relationship.

- ***One-Date-Going-Steady Trap**—There is a widespread myth that one date means a couple is going steady and belong exclusively to each other. It makes just as much sense as thinking that one admiring look at a car is the same as making the final payment of ownership.* Teens often get caught in this trap and fear talking to another guy or girl after they've had a date. It is actually healthier for teens to date several people at one time. It helps them learn how to act socially and how to make friends with different types of personalities. Young adults are not afraid to date more than one person until they are pretty sure they have found a lifetime companion. Don't be afraid to tell a date, "I'm just not ready to get exclusive. I wouldn't get mad if you went out with somebody else."

  Exclusive dating can lead to a sense of security, knowing there will always be that other person to go out with. But the longer the exclusive relationship lasts, the deeper the hurt and loneliness when it ends, and the easier it is to fall into the next trap.

- ***Can't-Break-Up Trap**—It is terribly hard to break up, even when there is no interest in dating the other person anymore. It may be that the other one is getting very serious, or has different values.* Feeling

Dates don't have to be for romance. Dates can be more fun when friends enjoy each other's company.

Living a Moral Life: Gifted and Growing

more and more uncomfortable around her or his other friends is another sign. A break up is definitely in order if the other uses physical or verbal abuse. The person may be afraid of revenge, such as the other spreading stories, or of never having another date.

Everyone has these feelings. They are a part of every experience of loss or death. But every death allows for new life. Use the OPTION ARROW to figure out if breaking up is the choice to make. If it is, tell the other person simply, clearly, and definitely that you want to stop dating. You don't have to give any reasons other than that you need some time and space away from the other. Use gentle words to ease the other's pain. It is more loving to be honest than to continue pretending you like the other. Read again the feelings of Billy Joe at the beginning of this chapter.

- **_Dating-Only-For-Romance Trap_**—_Some people think they have to be sexually attracted to each other to date. Then a date seems to be a failure if it doesn't lead to deeper and deeper romances._ Many good friends are made through dating wisely; by accepting dates from guys who don't seem too attractive or by seeking out interesting girls who are not the most popular. It's possible to meet another person through dating someone casually who could end up being your spouse. Dating for friendship also helps a person to keep sexual feelings in perspective and teaches skills in relating to the opposite sex without the pressure of getting too passionate, too soon.

- **_You're-Weird-If-You-Don't-Date Trap_**—_There is no correct age to begin dating. Teens, though, seem to think that if people their age aren't going out with the opposite sex, they are strange._ This is not true and can cause deep hurt. It may cause people to be labeled if they aren't romantically attracted to the opposite sex, but they need to be assured that this is normal. They should not be pressured into dating. Rather, they would benefit from joining activities where both sexes mix, like skating, volunteer work, music groups, or some club of specialized interest. Being part of a group helps a person to develop social skills and to be comfortable with the opposite sex without having to get romantic. It also eases the pressure from peers. A final observation is that people who accuse others of being ''weird'' are often doing so only because they are insecure and feel superior only when they put others down.

■ **Dating-Has-To-Lead-To-Sex Trap**—*If you learned about dating only from television and films, you would conclude that after a few dates (and sometimes after only one) it's time for sexual intimacy.* It's the generic date: man meets woman, man and woman go to a show or go walking or to a party, man buys woman a few drinks, man or woman asks, "Your place or mine or the car?" Man puts on some romantic music and woman turns out the lights, man and woman undress each other—instant love. The generic date is the product of television shows and movies—a date not based in reality, depicted with little imagination.

Avoiding the Traps

To avoid these traps, it's important to be creative. Below are listed a few creative ideas for what to do on a date. They may sound strange at first because television or movies infrequently include them as possibilities. But television need not control your life or limit your fun. On your next date:

1. Take a bus tour of your city.
2. Plan a surprise picnic lunch for your date.
3. Take a stroll along the beach or take a hike in a wooded area.
4. Serve a meal together at a hunger center.

There are many creative things to do on a date. Both the man and woman are responsible for deciding where to go and how expenses will be paid.

5. Go to a public spot and watch the people.
6. Visit an art museum.
7. Play miniature golf.
8. Visit three historic spots in your city that you've always wanted to see.
9. Window shop in the most exclusive area you can find and observe what kinds of people actually make purchases.
10. Make a special meal together and invite friends to share it.

An interesting class project would be to work to expand this list into fifty activities. Have several student volunteers actually use these ideas on dates. An article for the school newspaper, inviting other students to come up with fifty more, could be a class challenge.

---

11. *List the advantages and disadvantages of spectator dates (going to a show or watching a game on TV) and of participation dates (playing a game, cooking).*

12. *Give some reasons why people your age may not choose to date. List some other supports a person who doesn't date may be able to find.*

13. *Ask your parents and one other person if they dated for other than romantic reasons. Share stories with the class.*

Summary

- Be patient and allow intimate relationships to develop slowly. Remember: lasting relationships require not just romantic feelings, but an attitude of genuine care for the other person.

- Dating can be an opportunity for personal growth. Be wary of any situation that compromises your values or self-worth.

- The survival of romantic love first requires a foundation of friendship and caring between the couple.

SECTION 2
Checkpoint!

■ Review

1. Why is intimacy necessary for happiness?

2. When dating, what are some signs that a person should step back from physical closeness?

3. Give several ways to distinguish love from infatuation. Is infatuation an unhealthy experience? Why or why not?

4. Explain at least three date traps.

5. What are the various forms of "love"? What did Jesus mean when he said, "Love your neighbor"?

6. Words to Know: infatuation, love, intimacy.

■ In Your World

1. What do women expect from men on dates? What do men expect from women?

2. What is the best way to end a relationship without intentionally hurting the other person? Discuss the effects of these wrong ways of breaking up:
   ■ Using the silent treatment;
   ■ Starting a fight;
   ■ Giving dishonest reasons for breaking up;
   ■ Making the other feel guilty about the end of the relationship.
   What are some healthy ways of breaking up?

■ Cases

Todd hasn't had a sexual experience yet and he's confused. He's heard so many things about sex from so many different people. Maybe everybody's confused, he thinks. Being a healthy, inquisitive male, he'd like to experiment and find out for himself. But also being an intelligent guy, he knows that he should consider the consequences, even of experiments. Being a person who tries to sort things out, he reads of a way to "un-confuse" the message coming to him.

■ In pairs or groups of three, with one person being Todd, fill out a chart according to the columns below. The first column can have as many entries as you can think of.

Column 1. Person or groups saying something about sex.
Column 2. Their message to Todd about sex.
Column 3. Their knowledge of who Todd is as a person.
Column 4. Their personal care about Todd's development.
Column 5. What they will gain if Todd follows their advice.
Column 6. The amount of trust Todd should put in this group.

Living a Moral Life: Gifted and Growing

Becoming Sexually Responsible

Our goal as Christians is to grow into healthy, happy, balanced adults with mature faith. We have received gifts and guidance, intelligence, creativity, friends, and moral principles to help us achieve that goal. God is close as we struggle to grow. God doesn't throw down constant "rules," threats or punishments to keep us from having fun! That image of God is false. Any one who speaks about God that way is promoting an unbalanced view of God.

Years to Grow

Imagine yourself an inventor who has invested all your life savings and fifteen years of constant labor into your creation. You know you will need another fifteen years and are ready to dedicate the time, energy, and money you need to carry on your work. One day you meet someone who is casually interested in your project and offers to help you. Being a trusting person, you bring this new acquaintance to your workshop. The visitor is amazed at your progress but then begins to turn one wheel and adjust another lever—it happens so fast—and before you know what is happening, the whole invention is destroyed—in fifteen minutes. Fifteen years gone in fifteen minutes. And then the stranger says "so long" and disappears.

After fifteen or so years of growth, it takes only fifteen minutes or so to have sexual intercourse and possibly become a parent of a child. The girl then faces nine months of pregnancy. It is estimated that it costs more than $200,000 to raise a child today. The girl, usually, must also set aside her own educational and social life. All for fifteen minutes of intimacy? popularity? power? It hardly seems worth the cost!

Our brother, Jesus, encourages you to take it easy; let yourself grow slowly, naturally. Moral rules are there to guide growth, not destroy fun. There are thousands of ways to enjoy opposite-sex friends besides the one way that you are cautioned to wait for—sexual intercourse. God wants you to use good sense and not destroy your life project in fifteen minutes.

An Intimate Exchange

Genital sex is an intimate exchange between human beings. When it is given and received in marriage, it builds the couple into a community of life and love. It is an exchange of love in a special, vulnerable embrace, an embrace that can be the beginning of a human life. Sex is meant for marriage because that lifelong commitment "for better or for worse, in sickness and in health" protects people from being used as objects by others, either for pleasure or for power.

We hurt ourselves when we separate the body, mind, and soul into compartments. When we treat our bodies as if they were something we own, we pull ourselves apart. If we admire someone only because of his or her mind, or make fun of someone else only because he or she looks different or has unusual ideas, then we are separating a part of the person from the whole person. But then we also wound ourselves. Whenever we act in a manner that separates a part of us from the whole, we sin. Sin is any divisive action that hurts our relationships with others and our relationship with God.

When sex is separated from the marriage commitment, it tends to separate the body from the person as a unity.

Sexual intercourse is most properly the response by a married couple to the love that they share for each other.

Living a Moral Life: Gifted and Growing

Sexual intercourse should be the gift of one's whole self to another person. It should not be used merely for the short-term experience of pleasure which is part of sexual intercourse. If a woman, for example, has sexual intercourse with a man because he bought her dinner or has been dating her a few times, then sexual intimacy becomes a cheap thing to be purchased. However, when sexual intercourse is part of a lifetime commitment of love and fidelity, its value is beyond price.

Sin weakens our ability to give love as fully as we receive it. We want to hold on for security. We don't want to risk losing anything to another. We sometimes grab more than we need at the expense of others. Selfishness, fear, guilt, or the painful experiences from the past are all obstacles to the free, loving exchange that God meant sex to be.

Things to Consider

In the real world, many other qualities are important for happy, enriching relationships: humor, compassion, patience, honesty, generosity, and self-control, just to name a few. It's not good sex that makes a great relationship, but a great relationship that makes good sex.

One of the most important life skills for anyone is the ability to work with different kinds of people and to socialize in a variety of ways. Experience gradually teaches us how to relax with quiet people, how to laugh with outgoing people, how to listen to and learn from wise people. It teaches us how to give to and receive from the disabled, and how to be ourselves even with the rich and popular. We need the freedom from sexual pressures to be able to mix with the wonderful variety of human beings, and we have that freedom and the time to use it while in high school.

Most people at some time in their lives feel that they don't like themselves. They think either their body is ugly or their personality is terrible or they are simply unlovable, or bad. These feelings poison spiritual growth. Sexual intercourse can't cure those feelings. In fact, sex can make them worse because it can give a person the false sense of being really loved. When a sexually active relationship ends after only a few months, the person is left with a deeper sense of rejection and self-hatred than before the sexual experience.

For Example

There are hundreds of ways to exchange love other than sexual intercourse: embraces, looks, letters, songs, dance, conversation, gifts, messages sent through friends, prayers, time spent together, and even kissing after a fight.

Why Wait Until Marriage?

Why, then, should sexual intercourse wait until marriage? Just because God said so? No. The reason God said so is because it's good for your growth, for the growth of the person you love, and for the growth of your children. It is also good for the world. Society needs the gifts and talents of youth to be well developed.

Sexual intercourse between people still developing emotionally or psychologically can be hazardous in so many ways. It can severely damage people emotionally, especially women who may invest more emotion into a relationship and may need more emotional tenderness out of it. When a woman gives herself sexually, she may expect emotional fulfillment in return. With sex outside of marriage, she might receive, instead, rejection or a casual brush-off. Afterward, she may be afraid to receive love for a long time.

Adolescence is a time to think and to share feelings, but only in ways that will help a person grow.

Living a Moral Life: Gifted and Growing

Many men are also very sensitive to loving feelings and deeply scarred by premarital sex, but are afraid to tell anyone because it doesn't seem the "masculine" thing to do. Premarital sex can easily become a using of the other for selfish pleasure.

People who think every friendship necessarily leads to sex will tend to limit friends to those who have "sex appeal," which is usually restricted to physical attractiveness. Adolescence is the time to explore relationships, not to get locked into one level. People also can experience a deep sense of guilt because they know sexual intercourse belongs only with a marriage relationship. Of course, forgiveness is freely given by God, but people carrying guilt often find it hard to ask for it, feeling that they are unworthy.

Lastly, sexual intercourse outside marriage is a threat even to your physical well-being. Sexually transmitted diseases, including the deadly HIV/AIDS virus, can be passed on through one single sexual encounter. For anyone not living in a monogamous marriage, the only guaranteed protection is abstinence. Other sexually transmitted diseases (STDs) are passed to sexual partners easily and can cause serious illness, sterility, and mental retardation in one's future children.

Benefits of Waiting

On the positive side, an adolescence and young adulthood without sexual intercourse leaves one free to develop many love-making skills: conversation, reading body language, sharing ideals and dreams, creative gift-giving, and expressing feelings honestly. The benefit of a good reputation, even though called "weird" by kids who think sex alone proves that someone is normal, is worth the effort. Being lonely from time to time may be the price required to protect a personal life project with sixty or more years of happiness to enjoy.

Only you can control your choices. After thinking about why you should wait until marriage for sex (or choose secondary virginity—choosing to remain sexually chaste from now until sex for marriage), only you can decide to do it. Once you have decided within yourself, you can develop more and better ways to stick to your values.

Answering a Line

Develop your own short, firm response to the persuasive "lines" people use to urge another into sex. Here are a few possible responses to familiar lines.

- ■ **Everyone is doing it.** *Then it won't be hard for you to find another partner.*

- ■ **I'll show you how much I love you.** *Show me by buying a pizza.*

- ■ **Let me show you how to be a woman.** *If my father says you can make me a woman in one night, I'll do it. Let's go home and ask him.*

- ■ **What's wrong with you? Are you gay?** *If you think only sexually active people are normal, I can give you a list of normal (girls, guys) to call. You don't want me.*

- ■ **Don't tell me you're so old-fashioned.** *I'd rather be free and old-fashioned than modern and somebody's slave.*

- ■ **You've led me on this far and now you have to go all the way—I can't stop.** *Sorry, but you can choose to stop any time. If you can't stop, there is something wrong with you. You'd better see a doctor.*

- ■ **You've been asking for it all evening—don't back out now.** *You have misread me and that's your problem. You need a course in communication. I have a phone number you can call—at home.*

- ■ **If you don't, that's the end of our relationship.** *If that's what you want, then that's the end. I can't be forced by threats.*

- ■ **If you love me, you can prove it in one way.** *No, I can prove it in a hundred other ways if you really want my kind of love.*

The most important help is the love and support from the people who are important to you. You have the assurance of support from Jesus, but to strengthen your reliance on his support, you need to talk to him every day and express your need in prayer.

You also need at least one person your own age, of either sex, who shares your values. A trustworthy adult at school may be able to tell you the name of a classmate who is also looking for a friend like yourself. Find an adult with whom you can talk frankly about all your feelings and choices. There are some things a peer cannot help you get through because she or he is as inexperienced as you are. Ideally, you should be able to share problems with a parent, but if that isn't the case, find another adult.

---

14. *What are some of the ways men encourage women to sleep with them? Likewise, how do women persuade men?*

15. *How might teens feel pressured into having sexual intercourse before marriage? What are some common, unhealthy reasons people give for having sexual intercourse before marriage? Is self-esteem at issue here? Explain.*

Some Further Tips

Alcohol weakens human thought processes and will power. When on a date or at a party, don't drink. Your partner does not need reasons why you won't drink or have sex. Say simply and firmly, "I'm not interested." If the other asks "Why?" respond, "I don't give my reasons." The danger in trying to explain is that the other may make fun of your reasons and make you feel ashamed or childish. Then when you run out of reasons, the other may say, "Okay, you don't have any good reason to say no—so you have to say yes." Hold onto your reasons and character.

If the other person is really pressuring you, get away as quickly as you can, even if you have to make up a story like "I feel sick and I'm going to vomit." Use a drugstore or a gas station, on the pretext of having to buy aspirin or use the wash room, then call home or call the police. You know you should get away when you begin to feel afraid and wish you were home. Trust your feelings, say a quick prayer for an idea, and act. Don't worry about what the other person might think.

Rape

Women who are raped (forced into sex against their consent) are often afraid to report it, especially when they are raped by a person they know. Their feelings of guilt, shame, abuse, and depression are worse than if they had been attacked by a stranger. Many rape victims are at least acquainted with the rapists. This person may even be a friend. Women who are four years or more younger than their partners are easy victims of date rape because they tend to trust and be impressed by older men's attentions. Rape is immoral and criminal. It is a crime against women, an abuse of sexuality, and an abuse of human dignity and freedom.

The term date rape is applied to situations where a woman (usually) is forced to have sexual intimacy (not just intercourse) with her date against her will. Several college students have been recently thrown out of school because they took sexual liberties (deep kissing, groping, pulling off clothing) with a date or someone they met at a party. Such behavior is a violation of both the woman and the man. No one, no matter how much money he or she has spent on a date, has the right to sexual favors. You have a right to say **"NO"** at any time, and have that "no" respected by the other person.

Date rape, when it involves sexual intercourse, is a crime and should be reported to the police. If you are forced at any time into sexual activity against your will, fight it. Scream, yell, kick as hard as you can in strategic places (groin, knees, face), scratch and bite. If you feel troubled by something that has happened on a date, talk to your parents, a priest, or a trusted advisor or teacher.

Living a Moral Life: Gifted and Growing

Forcing a person to participate in a sexual act against his or her will is the crime of rape.

16. *What kinds of situations could easily lead to date rape? Why is this form of sexual abuse so common today among young people?*

17. *What would be your first thought if you heard that a woman you know was forced into sex by a guy you know?*

18. *What should a woman do if she is a victim of date rape?*

19. *List some things a woman needs to know and needs to do so that she will not be a victim of date rape.*

Forgiving Yourself

Many people have a morbid fear of the guilt of sexual sins. Some of it is caused by labeling these sins as the only "dirty" or "immoral" ones. You cannot change this fear in others, but you can relieve yourself of the paralyzing shame and guilt that keeps you from the prayer, forgiveness, healing, and strength God wants to give you. No sin is unforgivable, unless you refuse to "come home" to God. In sinning, you turn away from God; to come back, all that is needed is the desire to do so. "If we acknowledge our sins, he is faithful and just and will forgive our sins and cleanse us from every wrongdoing" (1 John 1:9).

You may be very sorry for a sexual experience and yet admit that it was pleasurable and maybe even an act of love. God understands that. God also understands that you are just learning the power of sexual passion and can get carried away with it almost before you realize what is happening. Since strong emotion lessens the guilt of sin, sex is often a lesser evil than cold, calculated exploitation of others by powerful and greedy people.

20. *Why might a sexual sin be a lesser evil than the exploitation of others? Explain.*

21. *How can one free him- or herself from the feeling of guilt associated with sexual sins?*

 Values for Life

"Blessed are the meek, for they will inherit the land" (Matthew 5:5). The meek person lives a life of humility—recognizing and affirming the truth about oneself and sharing that truth with others. Meekness means being willing to share your true feelings, thoughts and weaknesses with your loved one. Only then can true intimacy be achieved. It also implies that a person is gentle with all they meet, accepting everything with great understanding.

Summary

■ Make a pledge to yourself to talk to a trusted adult if you have any fears, confusion, or guilt about any aspect of sexuality.

■ A responsible person will not jeopardize his or her future or the future of another by abusing their sexuality.

■ No person has a right to sexual intimacy. Forcing a person to engage in sexual contact is a form of rape.

282

Living a Moral Life: Gifted and Growing

■ Review

1. Give three common-sense reasons for waiting until marriage for genital sex.

2. How can engaging in genital sexual activity stunt the personal growth of a young person?

3. Why is alcohol a dangerous thing to have on a date?

4. Why are young women frequent victims of date rape?

5. What are some ways to "put off" the verbal and physical advances of another? What can you say and do? Use examples.

6. Words to Know: rape, AIDS, STDs, sex appeal, date rape, meekness.

■ In Your World

1. Where do Catholic teens go for help when they have questions concerning dating and sexual activity? Make a list of these people or places and discuss the type of answer the teen is likely to get at this place.

2. What can the Church do to help teens with questions concerning their bodies and their sexuality? Develop a plan for your high school to implement that will provide a place for teens to go to get honest, factual answers.

3. What questions do teens have about sexuality? Do a survey and find out what people in your school want to know. Publish your findings in the school newspaper.

■ Cases

Heather and her best friend Nicole have been carrying on a three-day marathon conversation about life. They have been discussing things like how to tell if a person is mature, how honest you really have to be, and if you can really prove there is a God. Heather told Nicole that she broke up with her boy friend in college because he was getting very serious about marriage and sex. But now Heather hasn't any dates because she was going with Brian for so long. She regrets breaking up with him. Maybe she should invite him to a party and start up their romance again.

■ In pairs, work through the OPTION ARROW as Heather and Nicole might do.

▪ Study

1. Describe how the Tai Chi symbol of yin and yang represents the life-giving forces in nature.

2. How are women typically taught to behave in society?

3. What are a few typical attitudes males have about themselves?

4. What can we learn from the fact that people reach sexual maturity long before emotional maturity?

5. How does infatuation differ from love? Explain. How can infatuation be a good experience?

6. Explain at least three date traps.

7. When should physical activity be stopped by unmarried couples?

8. How does touching reflect the degree of how committed you are to another person?

9. How can premarital sex harm a person's ability to develop positive relationships?

10. What are some ways to say "no" to the sexual advances of another person?

11. What is date rape and how does it affect the victim? Explain.

12. What are some healthy activities for dating? List a few examples.

13. What are the dangers of alcohol consumption with respect to dating?

14. How can sexual fantasies become harmful to one's personal development?

15. What are the three forms of love? Describe each and how they build on one another.

■ Action

1. Have women make a list of things they would like men to remember when they deal with women. Have men make a similar list for women. Prepare to discuss these lists in class.

2. Offer a backrub to different members of your family. Note the different reactions both to the offer and to the backrub.

3. In our culture, parents stop cuddling their sons much sooner than their daughters, and in general, boys are hugged and touched less and less. Give some reasons for this.

4. Find out about one of these famous friendships and share your findings with the class: Saint John of the Cross and Saint Teresa of Avila, Saint Francis of Assisi and Saint Clare, Saint John Bosco and Saint Dominic Savio, Saint Ignatius of Loyola and Saint Francis Xavier, Saint Perpetua and Saint Felicitas.

5. Ask a person who has been married at least ten years: "What other exchanges between married partners are as important as the exchange of sex?" Share the responses with the class.

■ Prayer

1. Write a prayer of thanksgiving about a close friend. Share that prayer with him or her.

2. Spend a few moments each day praying for your friends and family by name. If you pray for a boy friend or girl friend, ask Jesus for the insight to help strengthen that relationship.

3. Praise God every day for the complex development of your maturing self. Ask God to bless your emotional and physical growth.

4. Spend some time observing the life-giving exchanges found in nature and in your own life. Thank God for these gifts of life.

CHAPTER

10

Issues in Sexuality

OBJECTIVES

In this Chapter you will

- Recognize the harmful effects of sexism and prejudice.

- Consider the dangers of premarital sex.

- Understand the differences between natural and artificial forms of birth control.

- Learn the importance of living a chaste life.

- Recognize the message of Jesus' command to love the sinner, not to judge him or her.

Be merciful, just as [also] your Father is merciful.
—Luke 6:36

Respecting Differences

Whether intentional or not, human beings tend to make judgments concerning other people because of their gender or their sexual orientation. Understanding how this happens, as well as understanding your own attitudes towards others, can help you learn to treat each individual with the dignity they have as a creature of God.

Sexuality and Prejudice

A whole person is someone who is able to recognize and achieve a balance within him- or herself. A whole person is able to affirm the so-called feminine and masculine sides to one's personality. For example, the competitive spirit always to win or to challenge others must be tempered with a spirit of cooperation and compassion. Acting on behalf of justice must also include acting on behalf of mercy. Each of us shares qualities which are recognized within society as typically masculine or feminine. Often, society will encourage the judgment or prejudice of a person, based on his or her own gender or sexual orientation. The Gospels, however, clearly challenge these and all forms of injustice.

Sexism: A Social Injustice

Sexism is a form of prejudice that results in discrimination against a person because of his or her gender. A woman who holds negative or suspicious feelings about her own masculine side and then projects these feelings onto men is acting in a sexist way. She may either idealize men and expect them all to be mechanically skilled, decisive, and protective, or she may hate men and say such things as "all men want only one thing—a woman's body." A man who holds negative or suspicious feelings about his own feminine side and then projects these feelings onto women is acting in a sexist manner. He may either idealize women, expecting them all to be sweet, tender, and sexually naive or attack them as being seductive, weak, stupid, and emotionally unstable.

In society as a whole, sexism can be found in the attitudes and practices that deprive one gender, usually the female, of human rights. For centuries, many societies have assumed that men are superior to and more fully human than women. Men have treated one another as if they were more intelligent, powerful, wise, and more trustworthy than women, and therefore, men have controlled women's lives and used women like property. Many states in this country still have laws that discriminate against women. Some laws limit married women's rights, while other laws allow wages to be higher for men than for women doing equal work.

Sexism has deprived women of their rights throughout the world.

Living a Moral Life: Gifted and Growing

Men do not experience this form of sexism as often as women because the prejudice is in their favor, but injustice has been noted. Before 1980, for example, judges in divorce cases presumed that the father was less capable of rearing children than the mother. Successful single fathers today prove that such a presumption is unfounded. It is especially important for Christians to be aware of sexism and to work for just treatment of women and men in every area of life.

Sex Stereotyping

Masculinity and femininity are parts of every person. Women are capable of so-called ''masculine'' traits and men are capable of what we label ''feminine'' traits. A whole person accepts his or her whole range of responses and qualities.

Men may be embarrassed to take a cooking course. Women may sometimes hesitate to sign up for metal shop or electronics classes. This embarrassment and hesitancy are the effects of another kind of sexism — sex stereotyping. This is the injustice of judging that certain human traits belong only to men and others only to women.

How can you break out of the prison of stereotypes? One simple way is to meet the challenge of each new situation with whatever powers you possess. If an adult needs help carrying something, offer your assistance. It doesn't matter whether the adult is male or female or whether you are male or female. When a younger student accidentally falls, help him or her to get up, whether you are younger or older, the same for the opposite sex. There is a person who needs help, and you are a person who can give it. If a teacher asks for someone to head a committee and you have the skill, volunteer for it. If you let life draw out the wide variety of your qualities, you will be developing into a free, responsible Christian, adequate to meet life's challenges.

Sexual stereotypes should not prevent you from doing things that you enjoy doing.

1. *List four examples of sexism that you have personally experienced. How did they make you feel?*

2. *Ask a parent or a working friend what rules they have on the job concerning sexism.*

3. *Stereotyping has been called a "prison without walls." How does it lock up people who stereotype others? people who are stereotyped? Give some specific examples.*

4. *What qualities considered feminine are men often afraid to show? Can you tell why? What masculine qualities do women often hide, especially around men? Why?*

Homosexuality

Homosexuals are first and foremost people—children of our loving God. They are truly human persons with complete personalities and varied gifts, interests, and needs. They are novelists, poets, composers, dancers, artists, priests, sisters, physicians, athletes, lawyers, professors. They like running, singing, playing cards, having pets, caring for gardens, going to movies, listening to music, and having supper with their families.

There are two meanings of the word "homosexuality": one refers to homosexual orientation and the other to homosexual activity. Homosexual orientation is the preference for the companionship, affection, and intimacy of a person of one's own gender. Homosexual activity is engaging in genital pleasure with a person of the same gender.

A person who has a homosexual orientation may be said to be "gay" or to be a "lesbian." A gay person is someone who accepts his or her homosexuality even though he or she may not express it in genital activity. The term gay is more often applied to men. Women who are homosexuals are called lesbians. Researchers have not come to agreement on what factors cause homosexual orientation.

Living a Moral Life: Gifted and Growing

Dispelling Some Myths

There are a number of myths about homosexuality that are factually unfounded and have caused people to be treated unjustly.

- **Homosexuality is contagious.** *No one can "catch" it from another person or cause it in another.*

- **Homosexuals look different.** *Some homosexual men may have more feminine-type behaviors or appearance and some homosexual women may look more masculine. However, this reversal in appearance can also be present in fully heterosexual men and women.*

- **Homosexual genital activity is a sign that a person is a homosexual.** *Physical genital activity with someone of the same sex is not a sign of being a homosexual nor can it make someone become one. Research shows that many men and some women have had homosexual genital experiences, especially in adolescence, and have developed healthy opposite-sex relationships without a preference for same-sex activity.*

- **Homosexuals are sick and can be cured if they want to be.** *Homosexuality is not a disease. A homosexual preference says nothing about the person's health, intelligence, or emotional balance.*

- **Homosexual orientation is a sin.** *This statement is as false as saying that heterosexual orientation is saintly. There is no moral significance in being born with either orientation. A person sins only by deliberately misusing his or her sexuality.*

- **Homosexuals are attracted to everyone of the same sex and place too much emphasis on sexual activity.** *Sexual activity is only one facet in anyone's life and is no more an obsession of every homosexual than it is of heterosexuals. They are not attracted to everyone of their sex any more than a heterosexual is attracted to everyone of the opposite sex.*

People who are homosexual are to be treated with dignity and respect. Genital homosexual activity, however, is always immoral.

Making A Moral World

As Christians, we are clearly called to work for the common good. We can promote the common good in two ways: first, we must work to preserve and protect human dignity while guaranteeing the rights of all; secondly, we must care for all who need help and cannot help themselves. Prejudice, ignorance and hatred are destructive forces in the world—undermining the goal of social justice. Choose to be informed on issues before you act, then your contributions will be more effective in helping to promote the good of others.

What Do We Know?

Although the causes are still unknown, some things are fairly certain. Homosexuality and heterosexuality are not neat, clear-cut categories into which we can place people. Imagine a line on the floor through the center of the room. One end represents strong opposite-gender attraction and exclusive opposite-gender activity. The other end represents strong same-gender attraction and exclusive same-gender genital activity. There are degrees of sexual attraction and activity all along the line, with differing numbers of men and women in each segment of the line.

Exclusive Homosexual Activity _____ Exclusive Heterosexual Activity

Living a Moral Life: Gifted and Growing

There are people who fit along all segments of the continuum, not just at either end. There seems to be a continuum of behavior and preference. Many people have strong preferences for persons of the opposite sex and have never had a homosexual experience. Some people, referred to as bisexuals, are interested equally in homosexual and heterosexual experiences. It is estimated that less than 10% of the U.S. population is exclusively homosexual in orientation. Whatever the percentage, it is generally understood that the percentage of male homosexuals is twice that of females.

Homosexuality is not considered something a person chooses but, rather, something he or she discovers during adolescence or later. Because it can make the individual feel so different from family and friends, the person usually fears to reveal this secret, leading to feelings of guilt, fear, and self-hatred. Feelings of homosexuality need not cause a person to feel guilt, shame or fear. Hating one's self or withdrawing from friends and family cannot improve the situation. Sharing fears and feelings with a trustworthy counselor or friend is the best way to find support and inner peace. Lastly, a strong homosexual orientation is difficult to reverse, no matter how much the person may want to be heterosexual.

The Catholic Church teaches that sexual orientation does not diminish our rights and dignity. A person who is homosexual is to be treated with the dignity and justice which is rightfully his or hers.

Homosexual activity—that is physical genital relations—always lacks the element of being open to new life, no matter how personally loving or permanent a homosexual relationship may be. Homosexual activity, therefore, is always objectively wrong. The homosexual person has just as much a need for sexual control as any person, but also just as much or more need for support and real love. The answer is not bias, but understanding. It is not for us to judge another person. If two men or two women are living together, no one has the right to condemn them as sinners. The condemnation may be a more serious sin than any activity that may actually be happening.

People who knowingly condemn homosexuals and deny them their human rights are the sinners in this case. Jesus himself teaches: "Be merciful, just as [also] your Father is merciful. Stop judging and you will not be judged. Stop condemning and you will not be condemned...For the measure with which you measure will in return be measured out to you" (Luke 6:36-38).

Jesus spent much of his time socializing with people considered sinners in his day. He accepted them as persons deserving respect, friendship and, if they needed it, forgiveness and healing. If Jesus came in human form today to our country, he would probably spend a lot of time in gay neighborhoods, caring for AIDS patients, visiting prisons, or sharing a sandwich with a bag lady on a street corner.

What's the Christian Thing to Do?

A disciple of Jesus will ask, "What is the caring thing to do? What attitudes and behaviors will be life-giving?" The most basic attitude is acceptance of everyone as a person, loved by God, called to be a brother or sister, and worthy of respect and just treatment. A Christian doesn't label people or stereotype their behavior or values. No matter how people differ from you, there are still a thousand more ways you are like them than the one way you may be different from them. The Christian thing to do, then, is to show respect for others as equals and friends, not pity, fear, or rejection.

If a friend, classmate, or member of your family tells you he or she may be homosexual, you may feel shocked, fearful, and helpless. Feelings are neither right nor wrong. It's better to be honest about those feelings than to repress them. You might say something like, "Thank you for trusting me enough to tell me. I don't know how to react. I feel a little scared (or afraid or helpless) but I want to do what is really good for you. What do you need from me? How can I be your friend?"

Living a Moral Life: Gifted and Growing

Jesus befriended the outcasts of his day.

5. *What other generalizations have you heard about homosexual persons?*

6. *Why is there so much fear associated with homosexuality?*

7. *Think of a time when you felt different from people all around you. What emotions were aroused in you? What behavior from others helped you feel good again?*

Summary

■ Sexism is a form of prejudice that undermines God's plan for a just society.

■ You can avoid stereotypes and their use by encountering every new situation with an open mind.

■ Homosexuals are people, children of God. Stereotypes concerning them are false or misleading.

Checkpoint!

■ Review

1. Give three examples of sexism.

2. How do sexual stereotypes harm social harmony? Explain.

3. How can a person overcome the use of sexual stereotypes? Explain.

4. How does homosexual orientation differ from homosexual activity?

5. List and explain four of the myths about homosexual persons.

6. What is the Christian response to the homosexual person?

7. Words to Know: sexism, sexual stereotyping, homosexuality, heterosexuality, gay, lesbian.

■ In Your World

Imagine yourself in a situation that calls for a quality usually associated with the opposite gender. You are the only person around to help. See yourself answering the need and feeling good about being capable of it. Then picture yourself with a group of friends. The same situation that you imagined above comes up but none of your friends moves to help. You do. Is it harder to imagine yourself helping when your friends are around? Why or why not? Share your feelings with the class.

■ Cases

There is a popular image of the "real" man. He is strong, willful, rugged, able to take charge of a situation, and enjoys competitive sports. But what about a man's "feminine" qualities? Are women attracted to men who enjoy using their "feminine" side? What about men who become nurses? Are these qualities culturally or naturally part of gender? Share your opinions.

Clothing which is modest at the beach or pool will usually not be considered modest elsewhere.

others. Immodest dress or behavior may invite another to think that you are open to the idea of genital sex even when that is the farthest thing from your mind.

It is impossible to develop a list of what would be immodest clothing. Cultural habits and community standards differ between countries, states, and towns. For example, it is considered modest, in some parts of Africa, for women to wear only a skirt. In the United States, a person dressed in this way would probably be put in jail for indecent exposure. A swimsuit which may be modest at the beach would be immodest at a dance. Parents, schools, and other authorities usually establish their own standards, which teens often find limiting. The best idea is for you to understand what your dress communicates to others, and then dress accordingly.

Sexual teasing is one of the cruelest forms of immodesty. It means deliberately arousing someone sexually and then deliberately rejecting him or her. Because it is cruel and dehumanizing, it is unChristian, even when it seems to be done in fun.

8. *What is the difference between flirting and being immodest?*

The Second Vatican Council speaks very forcefully on the importance of married life. "The intimate partnership of life and the love which constitutes the married state has been established by the creator...It is an institution...receiving its stability...from the human act by which the partners mutually surrender themselves to each other...For God himself is the author of marriage and has endowed it with various benefits and with various ends in view...The intimate union of marriage, as a mutual giving of two persons, and the good of children demand total fidelity from the spouses and requires an unbreakable unity between them" *("Pastoral Constitution on the Church in the Modern World," #48).*

Sexual pleasures are reserved only for marriage because those joys are connected with the giving of one's whole self to another and with that, the responsibility of caring for the other and for the new life that may come. The love found in a married relationship "leads the partners to a free and mutual giving of self, experienced in tenderness and action, and permeates their whole lives; besides, this love is actually developed and increased by the exercise of it. This is a far cry from mere erotic attraction, which is pursued in selfishness and soon fades away in wretchedness" *("Church in Modern World," #49).*

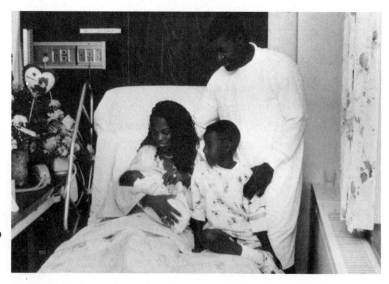

Children are the natural response to married love.

Loving sexual activity between a couple is gentle, supportive, and life giving. Marriages where one or the other partner is selfish, childish, or manipulative with regards to sexual intimacy often end in divorce. Sexual intimacy is a gift shared by each person within a marriage. Neither partner ever has a right to demand or take sexual favors from his or her partner. Such behavior violates the gift of sexuality, along with the dignity and worth of each partner.

As part of the marriage ceremony, the couple promises to accept children lovingly from God. However, even in marriage, sexual responsibility is necessary. Few couples today are physically, emotionally, or financially capable of rearing a large family. A couple, by following their conscience, may responsibly limit the number of children they have and when they have them through family planning. A combination of mutual love, patience, self-control, and a woman's periods of infertility make it possible for any couple to be responsible parents.

The Natural Method

The Church teaches that every act of sexual intercourse must be open to the possibility of procreation. According to the Pope Paul VI's letter *"Humanae Vitae,"* only a method which works with a woman's natural fertility cycle meets that requirement.

Natural Family Planning (NFP) is based on the wife's natural cycle of fertile and infertile days between menstrual periods, working from the signals within a woman's body that indicate the day when her ovary releases an egg, and she can therefore become pregnant. These signals include body temperature, location of the cervix, and changes in vaginal mucus. When a couple learn how to interpret these signals, they can tell when they should abstain from intercourse if they wish not to have a child or have intercourse if they are trying to conceive. The period of fertility lasts about eight to twelve days, but may be longer. If a couple does not want another pregnancy, they refrain from genital activity. During the days of fertility, they make love in other, non-genital ways.

A woman can understand her fertility cycle by keeping track of her morning temperature daily.

No method of contraception—the preventing of pregnancy—is 100% effective, except abstinence. Natural Family Planning, when used properly, is 98% effective in preventing conception. As an added bonus, it is also effective in helping couples who want to conceive. Instead of refraining from intercourse on the fertile days, they plan to have intercourse. No other method offers this advantage.

Some people mistakenly think that NFP is just like the rhythm method of the 1950s. Rhythm relied only on counting days between periods, each woman using the same number of days. Because every woman's cycle is different, and because most women will have differing numbers of days in their cycle from month to month, the rhythm method had a high rate of failure. NFP, because it allows a couple to plot the fertile days, shapes to fit the woman's body.

Natural Family Planning works when the the love-making and life-giving powers of sex in marriage are united. A couple must be in agreement as to the nature of sexual intimacy in their relationship at all times. Where sex is used selfishly, or as a weapon, NFP is less effective.

NFP is ecologically sound, medically safe, as inexpensive as the initial training course to learn, and helps couples discover other creative ways to show their love to each other. Some couples find it difficult to abstain from sexual intercourse during the fertile days. Many couples find it helpful to talk about their feelings and find support from other NFP couples. But NFP is not just another means of birth control: it is a whole way of living the commitment of marriage.

Artificial Means of Birth Control

Other methods of birth regulation are called artificial because they introduce foreign elements into the body or require a frustration of the act of intercourse. For various reasons, each has been rejected by the Church's teaching authority (magisterium) as being an immoral means for birth regulation because they don't meet the requirement that every act of intercourse be open to the possibility of conception. The following methods of contraception are listed for your understanding.

Two methods of contraception are withdrawal and the use of a condom. They work by preventing semen from entering the woman's vagina. In withdrawal, the man tries to withdraw the penis from the woman's body before ejaculation—the release of semen during orgasm. Not only is it extremely difficult to withdraw before orgasm, this unnatural act is a highly ineffective means of contraception. Semen is released in small amounts throughout sexual arousal. Even one drop of semen in the vagina can result in the conception of new life.

A condom is a rubber, balloonlike covering which traps semen. It is placed over the erect penis before genital contact is made. Both withdrawal and the use of a condom are rejected by the Church because they interfere with the natural result of sexual intercourse.

There are mechanical devices which are used in the woman's body. The diaphragm is a shield placed at the opening of the womb (uterus) to close up the entrance. It must be used with a sperm killing chemical jelly to be effective. The diaphragm must fit perfectly, so it requires a

Orgasm: the peak of sexual pleasure at which the male releases semen and the female feels a release of pressure.

prescription and initial insertion by a physician. It is inserted prior to intercourse and removed afterwards by the woman. The IUD (intrauterine device) is a small plastic coil or loop that a doctor places inside the uterus. It remains there until removed by a physician. How the IUD works is unclear, but it does prevent pregnancy. One theory is that it causes an abortion by preventing the newly fertilized egg from implanting itself in the uterine lining. The IUD has been known to cause bleeding, cervical infection, permanent infertility, and even death among women users.

Surgical birth prevention is called sterilization. In a woman, the fallopian tubes can be cut (tubal ligation) so that the egg cannot travel to the uterus. In a man, the tubes leading from the testes can be cut (vasectomy), preventing sperm from mixing with the semen. These methods are very reliable, but can permanently destroy one of life's greatest gifts, the power to bring forth new life. People who have been surgically sterilized and later regret it sometimes seek the reattachment of the tubes. This reverse surgery is very delicate and not always successful.

Chemical contraception—the pill—was hailed as the perfect solution to unwanted pregnancies at first. But its many dangerous side effects have made both doctors and women more and more reluctant to use it. Oral contraceptives cause the body to produce hormones artificially and so fake a pregnancy condition. As a result the ovaries do not release eggs, and no conception is possible.

Tampering with the woman's hormonal balance can cause blood clotting, cancer, strokes, and even death. Smoking is especially dangerous to women on the pill. A doctor's prescription is required for each woman, since age, body weight, and personal health affect how the pill will work.

A new discovery is the drug called RU-486. Developed in France, this drug works by causing the fetus to be aborted prior to the seventh week of pregnancy. It requires no surgery and so provides a much simpler way to procure an abortion. Not yet available in this country, this pill has been condemned by the Church.

Humanae Vitae

In July of 1968, the encyclical *"Humanae Vitae"* (On the Regulation of Birth) was presented to the Church by Pope Paul VI. The encyclical addresses the questions of natural and artificial birth control, and the sacredness and purpose of marriage. Above all, the letter affirms the sacredness and dignity of every human life.

The teaching states that marriage "is a very special form of personal friendship, in which husband and wife generously share everything, without undue reservations or selfish calculations" (*"Humanae Vitae,"* #9). The purpose of marriage is "the begetting and educating of children. Children are really the supreme gift of marriage" (ibid.). This is why the act of sexual intercourse is sacred and is proper only within marriage. Responsible parenthood is the real purpose of marriage and implies therefore, "that husband and wife recognize fully their own duties towards God, towards themselves, towards the family and towards society" (*"Humanae Vitae,"* #10). Following the teachings of *"Humanae Vitae,"* in short, means allowing God to work through you by being open as a couple to the possibility of new life—God's design—within the context of marriage.

It is the purpose of marriage to bring forth children. For this reason, artificial means of birth control are not allowed by the Catholic Church because they endanger a healthy moral attitude towards sexuality. One must consider the consequences of widespread use of artificial birth control. It is feared that individuals, growing used to the employment of contraceptive practices, may finally lose respect for the other person and, no longer caring for his or her physical and psychological health, may come to the point of considering his or her partner as a mere instrument of selfish enjoyment, and no longer as his or her respected and beloved companion (*"Humanae Vitae,"* #17).

With the legal availability of abortion, some women have turned to it as a form of birth control. Abortion in any form is morally evil. To use abortion as a form of birth control is an even greater tragedy.

---

9. *What would you say to a mother who told you she had the doctor prescribe the pill to her daughter?*

Solutions?

Many adult groups are offering a variety of solutions to the increasing rate of teen pregnancies. Below, in alphabetical order, are the six which are strongly advocated in some groups.

1. **The Abortion Solution:** Provide low-cost abortions for teen mothers without requiring parental knowledge or consent.

Its Appeal: It removes the problems connected with teen mothers and the unwanted child permanently and completely.

Its Problems: It is a serious objective moral evil against human life and often causes deep moral guilt. It can leave feelings of revulsion for sexual contact, damage reproductive organs, and cause severe emotional shock. It ignores the rights and responsibilities of the father and encourages teens to hide problems from their parents. It offers a medical solution to a spiritual and emotional issue. It is the least acceptable solution, even by those who want abortion provided, because it offers a short-term answer that causes long-term harm.

2. **The Contraceptive Solution:** Make contraceptives easily available to all teens who are sexually active.

Its appeal: It is easy to accomplish, and it offers scientific efficiency. It can be funded by tax dollars and

Living a Moral Life: Gifted and Growing

bypass parental permission. Some contraceptives may also provide some—but not total—protection against sexually transmitted diseases.

Its problems: No contraceptive is 100 percent effective even if used carefully. Couples often want spontaneity and romance in sex and many tend to be careless. Contraceptives require a certain degree of education as to their proper use. So often, teens misuse contraceptives and then are unwilling, or unable, to accept the consequences of the resulting pregnancy. Contraceptive use can reflect an indifferent or noncommittal attitude on the part of the man and woman toward the relationship. In other words, contraceptives offer sexual pleasure without responsibility toward the other person. Pregnancies resulting from contraceptive failure can reinforce the double standard that only the woman can get hurt.

3. **The Family-Bond Solution:** Strengthen family bonds by improving communication and by encouraging family sharing and physical expressions of affection among family members.

Its appeal: Many groups support this no-cost, no-risk solution. It centers sexuality within the family and supports the parental responsibility to inform the children on sexual matters. It provides teens with an avenue to express their emotions, and assists them in overcoming social pressures to be sexually active. This approach builds self-confidence in the teens while teaching them to act responsibly.

Its problems: Family bonding is a slow process, requiring much love and patience. Today's families are widely scattered. Some parents are afraid to set definite guidelines and are reluctant to discuss sensitive issues with their teenage children. Television and busy, conflicting schedules often leave little time for family bonding.

4. **Friendship Solution:** Teach teens how to be personal friends with one another without entering into a physical relationship.

Its appeal: All groups, except for those profiting from teen sexual activities, support this solution. It helps teens share feelings and ideals, allows for a natural sexual development, and removes peer pressure and the fear of rejection if one has had no sexual experience. It gives skill in forming close, nonexploitative relationships and supplies what teens want most—friendship and peer acceptance.

Its problems: Many teens are insecure and doubt that they can form a lasting friendship without sex. Advertising teaches teens they must be physically attractive and athletically successful to be popular. Friendship requires patience and fidelity, both of which are difficult for young people.

5. **The Sex-Education Solution:** Teach teens the facts about sexual development and pregnancy.

Its appeal: Knowledge will lead to the wise choices needed for basic health. Teens like being trusted to make their own choices. Sex education teaches them respect for the beauty and complexity of human sexuality and can teach the skill of saying no without losing friends.

Its problems: Along with the facts, teens also need to learn the moral value of using their sexual powers as God directs. One needs to respond to the facts with a strong sense of values and responsibility. Ideally, sex education belongs in the family, but many parents feel afraid and unprepared to talk about sex. Some parents, without valid reason, fear that sex education will encourage teens to experiment.

Sex education is an important tool to prevent teen pregnancies when it is taught along with faith and morality.

Living a Moral Life: Gifted and Growing

6. **The Value-Challenge Solution:** Develop in teens a sense of personal worth, responsibility, and self-control. Encourage them to keep their high ideals and live their values.

Its appeal: It is supported by all who live by moral values. It appeals to teen's high idealism, their need to be treated as adults, and their sense of self-worth and character. It flows from the Biblical command to love God and love your neighbor as yourself.

Its problems: Not too many adults speak to teens about values. There is often a conflict or contradiction between one's chosen values and society's values. Profit-minded groups exploit teen desires for pleasure and excitement. Many people cannot truly appreciate certain life-giving values because they have not yet learned that pain is a part of life and that moral growth is a slow process.

---

10. *Which solution is most unappealing to you? Why?*

11. *Which solution(s) would you want your parents to support? Your friends? Which ones are consistent with Christian values? Why? Ask your parents which solutions they think would work.*

New Questions

With modern technology come not only ways to prevent conception or end fetal life, but also many new questions about helping couples overcome natural obstacles to conceive new life. While conception is a blessing and a gift, not every answer provided by science is morally acceptable.

According to the document *"Instruction on Respect for Human Life in its Origin and on the Dignity of Procreation"* (Congregation for the Doctrine of the Faith, 1987), the Church provides the following directions:

- *Prenatal diagnosis and assistance is acceptable if done for the best interest of the individual fetus. "Medical research must refrain from operations on live embryos, unless there is a moral certainty of not causing harm to the life or integrity of the unborn child and the mother, on condition that the parents have given their free and informed consent to the procedure...If the embryos are living, whether viable or not, they must be respected just like any other human person; experimentation on embryos which is not directly therapeutic is illicit" (Section 1, #4).*

- *"The freezing of embryos...constitutes an offence against the respect due to human beings...Certain attempts to influence chromosomal or genetic inheritance are not therapeutic, but are aimed at producing human beings selected according to sex or other predetermined qualities. These manipulations are contrary to the personal dignity of the human being and his or her integrity and identity" (Section I, #6). Replacing deformed genes may be morally acceptable.*

Children can be sources of great joy. Appropriately used, technology can assist a couple in having a child.

■ *Test tube fertilization using sperm or eggs from a partner other than the marriage partner is not acceptable morally, nor is use of a "surrogate" mother. If technology does not substitute for sexual intercourse, but "serves to facilitate and to help so that the act attains its natural purpose" it can be morally acceptable (Section II, #6).*

Medical technology in this field is changing daily. The moral understanding of these technologies is developing just as fast. The important constant to remember is that the Church sees the preservation of the embryonic fetus and the preservation of the marital union as essential. Children are a gift, not a right. A couple may desire a child so greatly that they will want to do anything to get one. The Church understands that there are moral limits which must be followed.

Summary

■ Use your sexuality responsibly. Virginity, chastity, and modesty can help prepare you for the lasting commitment of marriage.

■ Sexual intercourse plays an important role in God's plan by allowing married couples to participate in the creation of new life. For this reason, sexual intercourse is appropriate only within marriage.

■ Unwanted teen pregnancies are best avoided by strengthening family bonds with love and by a Christian, value-centered education.

Illicit: not permitted.

Embryos: early stage of fetal development.

Chromosomes: Chemical make up of cells, passed on to children through the Genes—that which controls heredity.

Surrogate mother: a woman who is paid to have another couple's child.

■ Review

1. How does chastity differ from purity?

2. What is the difference between virginity and secondary virginity?

3. Why is the act of sexual intercourse appropriate only within marriage?

4. What form of birth control is permitted by the Catholic Church? Why?

5. List three forms of artificial birth control and the potential risks to the user from each.

6. List six solutions to the problem of teen pregnancy. Include risks and appeals for each. Which ones are morally permissible?

7. Words to Know: virginity, modesty, purity, Natural Family Planning, artificial birth control, condoms, IUD, sterilization, contraception, RU-486.

■ In Your World

1. What values would be transmitted to the student body at high school which freely and confidentially distributes contraceptives to students? What would be the moral dangers of instituting such a school policy? What alternatives are there to this solution to the problem of teen pregnancies?

2. Depending on which studies you read either more than 70% of teens or fewer than 25% of teens are genitally sexually active by the time they finish high school. Do a confidential survey of your school. Have five males and five females answer whether they have ever engaged in genital sex, how often, and the number of partners. Be sure to find out ages. Discuss your findings.

■ Cases

Laura has a bad reputation because she has had several intimate sexual relationships. During the summer between sophomore and junior year, she meets a couple of older teenage women who are not sexually active. Gradually, she learns how free they are and admires their strength. She would like to be chaste—secondary virginity they call it—but how can she change her reputation? Also, how can she approach those who know her past reputation? Should she quit school and get a job outside the neighborhood? Use the OPTION ARROW as if you were one of Laura's friends working through it with her.

SECTION 3
Issues for Decision Making

There are many issues in sexuality that are controversial and require our close attention. As Christians, we are called to treat one another as Jesus treated us. This means that we care for others, regardless of what they say, think, or do. If the person is acting in an immoral manner, we may challenge the person to act otherwise, but we must challenge in a spirit of compassion and love. So, we can judge the act, but not the person who is committing the act. This is the unique Christian response.

Sexual Fantasies

Imagination is a very good and necessary power that helps us to plan our future, to form our ideals, and to provide a harmless escape from life's pressures. Thoughts or pictures in the imagination (fantasies) are in themselves neither good nor bad.

We have only limited control over the fantasies that come into our minds. It seems that men, more often than woman, will find images of the opposite sex, of sexual organs, or sexual activity suddenly appearing in their imaginations without outside stimulation or inner desire. This is especially true during puberty. This may happen every day or several times a day. Connected with these thoughts may be the natural desire for sexual pleasure.

No matter how often they arise or how intense they seem to be, these involuntary, unstimulated thoughts and desires are not sinful. Only when sexual fantasies are deliberately stimulated and held in the mind for the purpose of arousing selfish genital pleasure are they morally wrong.

Pornography

Sexual fantasies are often aided by pictures or the written word. Pictures of a mother nursing a child may cause sexual fantasies in a male. Reading a romantic novel may stimulate sexual feelings in a female. But along with innocent material, we are also tempted by pornography.

Pornography presents sex as a purely physical act separate from personal commitment and love. It teaches that human beings are mere animals and that the highest value in life is immediate pleasure. It is another example of pulling apart what is meant to be connected, damaging our human wholeness. Also, pornography often illustrates distorted forms of sexual experience, including violence.

Pornography harms young people whose attitude toward their own sexuality and the opposite sex are still developing. Young persons with a steady diet of porn might assume that these distortions are a normal part of a sexual relationship.

Literature or art which excites sexual feelings is not necessarily pornographic. Pornography has a workable legal definition used by the United States Supreme Court. A work is pornographic if it appeals predominantly to prurient interests, if it is clearly offensive in depicting sexual conduct, and if it lacks serious literary, artistic, political, or scientific value.

Pornography is a form of exploitation. Sexual exploitation has two forms. Exploitation for sex means using people for one's own sexual pleasure. Exploitation through sex means manipulating others to gain their money or service by appealing to their sexual desires and fears. Pornographic material abuses everyone involved—from the person who produces the material, to the men and women used in the process, to the people who consume it. Pornography generally degrades women, equating them with sexual objects to be used and abused. Child pornography portrays children in the same light.

Besides sexual degradation of the other, pornography can also lead to sexual perversion. It can lead to voyeurism (sexual satisfaction from watching others), rape, and violence.

---

13. *What advice would you give to someone who habitually and purposely views pornography? How would you encourage him or her to seek healthier activities?*

Pornography is degrading to everyone involved in producing or using it.

Masturbation

Masturbation is the self-stimulation of the genitals to arousal causing physical pleasure and possibly orgasm. A common experience in the early stages of the sexual development of boys, masturbation occurs less frequently in young women. Women who masturbate usually begin to do so in their twenties and thirties.

Masturbation releases sexual tension, provides experiences of pleasure, and causes no physical harm. Yet, because masturbation is selfish, it is immoral. It is basically an incomplete sexual experience and that is why Catholic morality considers masturbation objectively wrong. Even when done with another, called mutual masturbation, it remains a selfish act done for one's own pleasure, not life-giving as the gift of sexuality is intended to be. It can be a symptom of problems at home, work, or school, or of social difficulties for which one hasn't found help or is not facing honestly. It then acts as a temporary escape from inner pain.

It is morally wrong to continue to deliberately masturbate once a person realizes the implications of his or her actions. The seriousness of the act and the degree of personal guilt in each case has to be determined. A positive way of determining the seriousness of masturbation is through a conversation with a priest in the sacrament of Penance.

Prurient: appealing to or arousing sexual desires.

14. *What social pressures might influence a person's decision to seek sexual release through masturbation? Explain.*

Incest

Incest is sexual intercourse or marriage between close family members. Almost every society—primitive, ancient, and modern—has prohibited incest, especially between father and daughter, mother and son, and between sister and brother. This also applies to grandparents, aunts, uncles, and first cousins. Incest is not considered natural or normal sexual behavior. Children born from incestuous relationships are often born with birth defects and retardation. In most cases incest is a form of rape. A parent or other older relative will force a person to engage in sexual intimacy. The adults in these situations are mentally ill and need care. The victim of incest almost always needs psychological assistance to overcome the emotional pain caused by the violation.

A person who feels pressure from a relative to be sexually intimate—from simple kissing which becomes a little too intense to touching genital areas—or who has already been an incest victim can find help. Through a priest, a counselor, or a child-abuse agency, he or she can learn to deal with the trauma of incest, and prevent it from happening again.

Prostitution

Prostitution is the offering of one's body for sexual intercourse in exchange for payment. Though practiced by women most often, there are also male prostitutes. Many teenagers are trapped into prostitution as soon as they arrive in a strange city after running away from home. Prostitution has risen considerably as prostitutes sell their bodies to support their drug addiction, especially to crack—a form of cocaine.

Values for Life

"Blessed are the clean of heart, for they will see God" (Matthew 5:8). The clean of heart are those who act for the good of others, without seeking reward or selfish gain. They value openness to others, and to God's will in their lives. The clean of heart love unconditionally, showing that love in situations many would choose to avoid, either because of prejudice or fear. Purity of heart requires courage and a commitment to one's beliefs.

Living a Moral Life: Gifted and Growing

Teenagers who run away from home are often forced into prostitution to survive.

Jesus teaches the right attitude toward prostitution. When he was asked to condemn a woman caught in the act of adultery, he forgave her and told her to sin no more (John 8:1-11). He was not embarrassed when a prostitute washed his feet with her tears (Luke 7:37-39). He even announced that the prostitutes would enter the kingdom of God before the chief priests because these women opened their hearts to God's Word (Matthew 21:31-32). Jesus saw prostitution as a social evil, an exploitation of women, but he never condemned the prostitutes themselves. His most telling action was to give a former prostitute, Mary of Magdala, the mission of announcing the news of his resurrection to Peter and the other disciples (John 20:11-19).

It should be clear that using a prostitute is a serious moral evil. Paying for the use of a man or woman's body makes that person an object, separating the person's body from his or her whole self. In addition, it is an abuse of one's sexual power, casually throwing away that which should be an expression of love and an avenue of life.

Prostitution is immoral not simply because it involves paid sex. It is also immoral because it takes advantage of people, using them, forcing them into a way of life which is reprehensible. Men and women who become prostitutes generally have low opinions of themselves. Often victims of sexual abuse as children, these people have poor family relationships and few educational or job opportunities. Helping these women and men find meaningful work and warm friendships can remove some of the pressures that lead them into prostitution. Supporting agencies that provide havens for teen runaways help men and women toward a life of love and dignity.

---

15. *How does Jesus' attitude towards prostitutes apply to how we should treat all people who are labeled "sinners"?*

Sexually Transmitted Diseases

Sexually transmitted diseases (STD), or venereal diseases (VD), are highly contagious diseases which cause serious and sometimes permanent damage to the reproductive system. They are passed from one person to another by intercourse or by some other intimate sexual contact. More than 13 million people in the United States are infected with over twenty types of sexually transmitted diseases.

The only way to be infected is through close body contact with someone who has a disease. The symptoms are not always visible, so you may not know who is infected. The syphilis germ enters the body through the moist skin of the mouth or the genitals. Therefore, even tongue kissing with a person infected with a STD can pass the germ through a break in the skin of the other person. This is unlikely, but it is possible.

Sexually transmitted diseases are often difficult to detect. Mild at first, the symptoms disappear quickly, but the disease continues to spread through the body. Symptoms include burning sensations around the genitals, pus or a rash in the genital area, swelling and abdominal pain. Untreated syphilis can cause blindness, deafness, paralysis, insanity, and death. Gonorrhea damages the reproductive organs and can result in blindness, sterility, and death.

Living a Moral Life: Gifted and Growing

Helpful Hints

Here is some practical advice about masturbation:

- *If a person is concerned about masturbation, he or she can speak to an understanding and skilled counselor.*

- *Keep a positive, joyful attitude about sex and work at developing responsible self-control.*

- *By developing a healthy friendship with Christ through prayer, the sacraments, and practical charity, any problem can be overcome.*

- *Don't get overly worried about masturbation. Charity and honesty are much more important issues for concern and effort.*

- *Don't get discouraged. Have patience.*

- *Don't expect instant success. All growth and change takes place slowly.*

- *Keep a sense of humor.*

- *The sacrament of Penance can provide peace and strength.*

- *Spend time with friends pursuing hobbies and subjects of personal interest.*

- *Don't dwell on the sexual images which lead to masturbation.*

◆

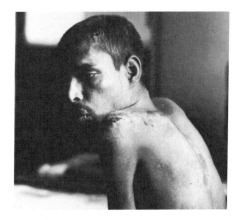

Some forms of STD's infect the unborn children of infected mothers causing birth defects and even death.

People who experience these symptoms need to receive immediate medical treatment to prevent further damage to their bodies. Most strains of STD can be cured if detected early. Unfortunately, too many people are embarrassed to admit their sexual behavior and fail to seek treatment. This

Sexually transmitted diseases can lead to disfigurement, blindness, or even death.

behavior is as foolish as the activity that caused the problem. It is better to seek help from a physician than to suffer further harm to one's self and others. Condoms offer only limited protection from acquiring VD or STDs through sexual intercourse. The only sure way to prevent an STD is to refrain from all genital sexual activity. Remaining chaste until marriage and faithful after marriage are the best ways of avoiding these sexually acquired diseases.

---

16. *What advice would you give to a friend who is sexually involved with many partners? Do you think you have a right to give such advice? Why or why not?*

AIDS

AIDS (Acquired Immune Deficiency Syndrome) is an especially dangerous disease. It is caused by the human immunodeficiency virus (HIV). There is no known treatment or cure, and those afflicted with it usually die painful deaths. HIV is transmitted through the exchange of body fluids during sexual intercourse of any type, by contaminated blood transfusions and by using drug needles already used by someone with HIV. The virus can be transmitted to a newborn at birth or through breast feeding if the mother is infected with it.

Condoms have been presented as a way to prevent a person engaged in "at risk" sexual contact—sexual intercourse with several different partners, with intravenous drug users, and homosexual intercourse—from catching the disease. The Surgeon General of the United States has said that a person engaging in such sexual behavior is better protected by condoms then if nothing at all is used, but that the only really effective way to prevent the transmission of AIDS during intercourse is abstinence. In their document *"Called to Compassion and Responsibility: A Response to the HIV/AIDS Crisis"* (November 1989) the American bishops say: "The 'safe-sex' approach to preventing HIV/AIDS, though frequently advocated, compromises human sexuality and can lead to promiscuous sexual behavior. We regard this as one of those 'quick fixes' which the report of

Living a Moral Life: Gifted and Growing

the presidential commission says foster 'a false sense of security and actually lead to a greater spread of the disease.'...The use of prophylactics to prevent the spread of HIV is technically unreliable. Moreover, advocating this approach means in effect promoting behavior which is morally unacceptable...It is not condom use which is the solution to this health problem, but appropriate attitudes and corresponding behavior regarding human sexuality, integrity and dignity" *(Section IV, #3)*. The Church then considers the use of condoms immoral and, with the Surgeon General, encourages abstinence and chaste behavior.

What about the condemnation and rejection that some people with AIDS have experienced? Are there "innocent" people who have contracted AIDS through transfusions and some "guilty" ones who are being punished for their homosexual activity? No! God neither punishes someone with sickness nor reward another with good health. All people with HIV/AIDS, no matter how they acquired the disease, should receive assistance. By "preserving and protecting human dignity while guaranteeing the rights of all...(and) caring for all who need help and cannot help themselves...we discover Christ in them and they in turn are able to encounter Christ in us" *(Section V, #7; Section VI, #1)*.

Here is how one person with AIDS expressed his feelings, ten days before he died at age 33:

"Whether a person with AIDS is an I-V drug user, or contracted it in the womb, or is a mother who contracted it from a husband, or is a gay man, doesn't matter. That we make this matter tells us something about ourselves, not about the person suffering from AIDS. We will, I hope, be mindful of the kind of compassion that's needed for anyone who is suffering."

AIDS is not a homosexual disease. Anyone coming in contact with the semen, blood, or other bodily fluids of a person infected with the virus is at risk.

---

17. *Do you think it is moral for public health agencies to distribute "clean" hypodermic needles to I-V drug users to prevent the spread of AIDS? Is this supporting the habit of drug use? Is this moral? Why or why not?*

Promiscuous: sexual behavior with frequent partners.

Prophylactics: something used in prevention, a condom.

A wise person knows that responsibility means using things for their proper purpose while at the same time respecting all other basic life values. Now that you are experiencing the power and pleasure of your own sexuality, it is important to keep in mind its purpose. It is in the giving and receiving of physical, emotional, and spiritual love between a man and a wife, remaining open to the new life that might come, that sexuality is fully understood. Decisions to engage in genital sex outside of marriage are irresponsible and, therefore, immoral.

You may hear people say, "By using contraceptives to protect against pregnancy, anyone can enjoy sexual intercourse responsibly." Preventing two immature people from becoming parents does not make their sexual activity responsible. Sexual exchange is a total gift of one person to another. It is meant to seal a lifelong commitment to marriage. When teens use contraceptives, this purpose of sexuality is frustrated. Only in marriage can sexual powers be used responsibly.

18. *What does it usually take for a person to realize that he or she is acting irresponsibly? Give an example to support your view.*

19. *Are using contraceptives a sign of sexual responsibility? Why or why not?*

Summary

■ Sexual abuses, such as prostitution, pornography, and incest, demoralize the human spirit by exploiting the victims as objects of selfish pleasure.

■ Share sexual struggles with someone you trust and who will offer reasonable advice.

■ Educate yourself on the dangers of sexually transmitted diseases, but show Christian compassion to those who are sick.

Living a Moral Life: Gifted and Growing

■ Review

1. When are sexual fantasies immoral? Explain.

2. How does pornography harm young people?

3. Why is masturbation selfish?

4. What was Jesus' attitude toward prostitution? Explain.

5. Why is prostitution a serious moral evil? Give two reasons.

6. Give two types of STDs and how they physically harm people. What is the surest way to avoid contracting an STD?

7. Give three ways AIDS is transmitted to others.

8. Words to Know: pornography, prurient, incest, prostitution, STD, VD, HIV, AIDS.

■ In Your World

1. List the many ways people use each other. What groups may be exploiting you through your sexual desires or fears? How can you resist these groups or influences?

2. Do a class study on AIDs. Divide into several groups, with each group being assigned a particular aspect of the disease. Answer these questions: How does the disease work? How is it transmitted? Who are most at risk? How can it be prevented? What happens when you get the disease? How is it treated? How are people infected with the disease treated? Teach others what you have learned.

■ Cases

Mrs. Kulek is cleaning out her oldest son's room at his request, since he is now living in an apartment. She finds a stack of old pornographic magazines which she throws in the trash. Jim, her fifteen-year-old son, finds them there and sells them to some junior high boys for a dollar each. Jim needs the money for new track shoes.

■ Was Mrs. Kulek wise in her actions?

■ Is Jim guilty of any wrongdoing?

■ If Mrs. Kulek discovers what Jim has done, what should she and her husband do?

C H A P T E R
10   Review

■ Study

1. Give one sexist practice that deprives women of their human rights.

2. Give an example of sexual stereotyping.

3. How should a Christian approach the issue of homosexuality? Explain.

4. List four stereotypes about homosexuals. Explain how each is a myth.

5. What is secondary virginity?

6. What is the physical basis for Natural Family Planning?

7. Why does the Catholic Church consider artificial means of birth control morally inappropriate?

8. Name three artificial means of birth control and how they work.

9. What are two moral, healthy ways to prevent teen pregnancies? Explain.

10. What forms of assisted conception are considered immoral. Why?

11. How are sexual fantasies considered a normal part of sexual maturation? Explain.

12. How does pornography demoralize the human being?

13. Why is masturbation considered an incomplete sexual act and therefore immoral?

14. How do STDs harm people? How do they spread? What is the best way to avoid catching these diseases?

15. What are the myths associated with AIDS? What are the most common ways that it is passed from one person to another?

16. What is the appropriate Christian response to the AIDS patient? Explain.

- *the victim;*
- *the victim's other relationships;*
- *the liar's character;*
- *the liar's other relationships;*
- *society as a whole.*

The evilness of lying goes beyond the misuse of language. It attacks basic human dignity by limiting the victim's freedom. Without knowing it, deceived persons lose their freedom of choice. False information steers them away from the best options or deprives them of alternatives. And if they discover the deception, they feel cut down, disgraced, and cheated. For example, a store might carry several items of equal quality. The clerk, however, shows a customer only the most expensive item, saying it is the only kind available. While this may result in the most profit for the store, it denies the customer true freedom to choose. While not directly lying, the clerk is engaging in deception — suggesting that this is the only item available by his or her action.

Cases of Deception

The following cases offer ways in which people deceive or are deceived.

A. To prevent Scott from fearing that he might still have cancer, his parents never told him that he had a cancerous kidney removed in infancy. When Scott asked why he was not permitted to play football in high school, his parents said that he had fallen off a swing while his sister, then six, was taking care of him. They blamed his lost kidney on that accident. Scott's sister was told the same story, but she did not remember the fall.

B. Two girls tell their mothers that they are going to a show on Saturday night. Instead they crash a party. They are having a good time until a fight starts. When the police arrive, both girls are arrested along with everyone else. The mothers are shocked, hurt, and angry because their daughters' lies put them in such danger. One girl's father blamed the mother for not checking out the girl's story more carefully. The other father grounded his daughter for a week.

Lies can quickly sour the relationship between you and your parents.

Falsehood: a statement that is not true.

Making A Moral World

Vaclav Havel, Czech playwright and essayist, spoke out against the lies of an oppressive government, criticizing the Communist government of Czechoslovakia for denying individual freedom and failing to support human dignity. For his ideas, Vaclav was sent to prison. He writes, "When I speak of living in the truth, I naturally do not have in mind only products of conceptual thought, such as a protest or a letter written by a group of intellectuals. It can be any means by which a person or a group revolts against manipulation: anything from a letter by intellectuals to a workers' strike, from a rock concert to a student demonstration, from refusing to vote in the farcical elections, to making an open speech at some official congress, or even a hunger strike for instance." (*Living in Truth*, Vaclav Havel) Eventually the Communist government fell and Havel was elected president of Czechoslovakia in 1989.

C. A giant electric utility announces to its consumers that their monthly bill will increase significantly to absorb the multi-million dollar cost of a nuclear power plant. Then the media discovers a confidential report kept on file in the corporation that lists dozens of structural defects in the plant, whose corrections are the source of the multi-million dollar deficit.

D. The President of the United States spoke on at least three occasions about his involvement in the Iran-Contra Affair. On March 4, 1987, Ronald Reagan said that he was angry about the activities undertaken without his knowledge, but after just one month he admitted, "There's no question about my being informed...I was definitely involved in the decisions about support to the freedom fighters—my idea to begin with." Finally, a short time later he said, "Well, I wasn't giving those orders, because no one had asked or had told me what was truly happening there."

---

3. *State the underlying reasons why people lied in cases A, B, C, D. What possible motives could they have had?*

4. *One of the evils of lying is that one lie breeds another. Why is this so? Find other examples where one lie led to many others.*

Excuses for Deceptive Speech

Excuses for not telling the truth, whether occasionally or habitually, fall into six categories: 1) fear, 2) greed, 3) competition, 4) public protection, 5) popularity, and 6) revenge.

Fear

When afraid of losing something precious or of facing something bad, a person may feel that protection is a higher value than truthfulness. Some young people think that lying is their only weapon against those who deliberately limit

A lot of popular magazines and newspapers play upon people's curiosity, fear, and greed.

their freedom or fun. While they may also believe that they can wait until adulthood to build an honest character, they couldn't be more mistaken. Every choice they make determines the direction of their adult life. Teens who cannot accept reality will have greater difficulty accepting it later when their honesty will be tested for bigger stakes.

Greed

Greed is an uncontrolled desire for what you do not have. Not content with what is yours, you may be tempted to steal money, possessions, pleasures, power, or even the freedom that will eventually come with adulthood. Because our society stresses the importance of wealth, greedy people are seemingly rewarded as long as they are clever enough to cheat without getting caught. Once caught, society treats them as criminals. However, greed always affects people negatively. Michael Milken, who orchestrated the "junk bond" scandal of the 1980s, went to jail for his greed.

For Example

Terrie, student government president and captain of the basketball team, was afraid to admit that she had been drinking liquor in the park. She knew it would embarrass her family, shame her office, and keep her from at least one game. She did admit it, however. The team won the district championship, and in June, Terrie received the "Woman of the Year" Award for strength of character.

Success

The goal in any competition is to win the prize. This third category includes all the excuses people give when they want to win dishonestly. What can you do when competitors cheat? You have four choices: cheat more cleverly than the rest and pretend it is good; cheat, but do it as a compromise and regret it; be honest and settle for limited success and rejection; or leave the race and aim for your own goals based on your own values.

One of the greatest heroes of honesty is John the Baptizer. He began to preach before Jesus arrived and won a sizable following. Many people were sure John was the Messiah. He could have been jealous when Jesus started attracting his disciples, but recognized something about his character. He knew exactly who he was, and he spoke it with assurance: "You yourselves can testify that I said [that] I am not the Messiah, but that I was sent before him" (John 3:28). These powerful words constitute wise advice to guide everyone's drive to success.

Public Protection or Massive Social Good

When there is a specific threat to a specific victim, the case for or against justifying a lie is clear-cut. But when the threat is vague and the victim is "the general public," justification becomes more difficult. For example, are teachers justified in deceiving students as part of a lesson on deception?

One danger inherent in a person's drive for success is the temptation to do anything to guarantee a victory.

Living a Moral Life: Gifted and Growing

Academic Dishonesty

Cheating in school is widespread occurrence, even in scholastic institutions with strong safeguards against it. Consider the following case.

In March, 1976, the entire junior class of West Point, 823 cadets, were given the same take-home exam in electrical engineering. When the tests were handed in, the instructor found that 117 papers had suspiciously similar phrasing and matching misspellings. Upon investigation, 202 cadets seemed to have "collaborated." The penalty for any cadet found guilty of cheating was immediate dismissal, with a requirement of two years enlisted service before being considered for readmission.

Army Secretary Martin R. Hoffman reduced the penalty for those found guilty to a one year dismissal, with readmission after only one year because of the large numbers of men involved. In the end fewer than ten cadets were finally found guilty.

- *The honor code of West Point states that "a cadet will not lie, cheat or steal or tolerate those who do." Cadets are obliged to report others who break the code. As a result of the widespread dishonesty, the practice of take-home tests was eliminated and all tests will be supervised.*

- *One editorial written about this case stated, "Trust is the essential ingredient of leadership. If these cadets cannot be trusted in such mundane matters as take-home examinations, how will they perform in the real tests of life?"*

What are some of the reasons people give for cheating on tests?

The deceivers would argue that their aim is the public good, either by increasing our knowledge of human behavior, by exposing lawbreakers, or by preventing public panic. But in these cases, the threat to public welfare is not always immediate, and the harm to public trust may be greater than the good achieved. It is government's responsibility to represent the people, not deceive it. When members of the executive branch of government lie to Congress, as happened in the Watergate and Iran-Contra scandals, the damage done to the nation cannot be easily calculated.

Popularity and Social Life

An important value to young people is popularity, either in groups or in male-female relationships. Young people may tell lies to gain friends and to avoid parental restrictions so that they can go out. None of these reasons justify lying, and often the lies backfire. The damage done to parental trust and the teen's falsified relationship with his or her parents can be irreparable.

Revenge

This is another common moral evil that uses lies as a weapon. Some people use lies to get revenge on someone who has hurt them. Because backbiters don't consider the long-term consequences of their innuendoes, innocent people are often hurt for life. Some people relish the "good feeling" of hurting someone who hurt them. Jesus proposed an ideal diametrically opposed to revenge: "love your enemies, and pray for those who persecute you" (Matthew 5:44).

---

5. *How does lying for popularity eventually harm one's reputation? Give an example.*

6. *Sandra, twenty-two, allowed her eighteen-year-old sister, Nancy, to use her name to get a legal drivers license so Nancy could go to bars and drink. What is Nancy greedy for? Are both girls morally guilty? Which is more at fault? Explain your answers.*

Living a Moral Life: Gifted and Growing

7. *Give original examples of pressures a teen might feel to lie or cheat for success.*

Cheating

Cheating is deception by trickery. It is a lie made through one's actions rather than with one's words. But the harmful consequences and the intention of deceit are the same. Cheating is so prevalent in our society that when someone speaks out against it or refuses to be a part of it, he or she is often laughed at as a fool. Yet the person who speaks out against cheating possesses real strength of character. Cheating is no less evil because "everybody does it." Such an attitude merely multiplies the distrust which eats away at society.

8. *Do you believe that high school students are too influenced by peer pressure to assist the faculty in controlling cheating? Why or why not?*

9. *Would you support a high school "honor system" in which students are left alone during an exam but are expected to report any cheating they see? Give reasons.*

10. *In the West Point case, if you were a trustee, would you vote for keeping the part of the code that requires personal honesty, but dropping the part that requires reporting cheaters? Why or why not? Should a co-pilot report that the pilot of a passenger jet is intoxicated?*

Summary

- Avoid deceptions of all kinds because it weakens you as a person and damages trust among people.

- Cheating is a form of deception.

■ Review

1. What is the most important level of truthfulness? Why?

2. Why do people lie to themselves so often?

3. List the six categories of excuses for deceptive speech. Explain each.

4. In what five directions does the damage of lying spread?

5. Give two reasons that show lying is an unwise reaction when one is afraid.

6. Why are liars poor judges of whether their lies are necessary?

7. Words to Know: deception, detraction, lie, veiled speech.

■ In Your World

1. Share the story of someone's revenge that took the form of a lie or gossip. What are the short-term and long-term consequences of this type of revenge?

2. Give examples of the lies that little children tell their parents; that students tell teachers; that merchants tell customers; that doctors tell patients; that government leaders tell the public; that employees tell employers; and that spouses tell each other. What motivates these lies?

■ Cases

Jerry, president of his class, was responsible for organizing the dance committee. It was important that this dance be financially successful. In the process, he showed aspects of a conceited and dishonest character: He took all of the credit while doing little of the work, bossed other members around, and refused to consider any idea that was not his own. The faculty moderator decided to tell him what his weaknesses were and how to correct them.

■ How will truth-telling strengthen Jerry?

■ How will it free him?

■ In what way is the exposure a compliment to Jerry?

■ How will it affect Jerry's other relationships?

■ How will it affect the moderator's other relationships?

Combating Dishonesty

As the public becomes more aware of deceptive practices, it begins to apply more pressure on legislators to enact laws that protect the truth. Professional organizations are also beginning to stress honesty in their codes of ethics. The American Medical Association's Principles of Medical Ethics, Section 4, states that physicians "should expose, without hesitation, illegal or unethical conduct of fellow members of the profession." In 1975, the Department of Health, Education, and Welfare published a regulation requiring the informed consent of any person agreeing to take part in a medical experiment. The Federal Communications Commission monitors commercials and prohibits the airing of those that make obviously false claims or imply falsehoods about a competitive product. These types of activities are all steps in the right direction.

A Valid Reason

The one and only valid reason for telling a falsehood is to save a higher value that is being threatened. Telling the truth is an essential building block to human trust. Our relationship with God and with others is based upon telling the truth. But just as human life may be taken for a greater good in an extreme case, so truthfulness may need to be sacrificed to preserve a greater good.

The necessity of telling a falsehood to save a greater good does not, however, make the falsehood morally good in itself. It only makes the deceptive speech the lesser of two evils. And it is never justified if an honest means will save the threatened value. Catholic theology sometimes calls justified falsehood "veiled speech" to distinguish it from unjustified lying.

> **Code of ethics:** a pact made by members of a profession to act morally in their work.

For Example

If a very angry person, intending physical harm, wants to know where your friend is, you are under no obligation to reveal your friend's true location.

Great caution is necessary when judging whether veiled speech is really justified, because often the speaker will be prejudiced in favor of what he or she wants. All of the following conditions should be present before you can clearly use such deception without moral guilt:

- *A high value is threatened. Values higher than, or equal to, truthfulness include human life, bodily integrity, national security, and material goods of very high value.*

- *The threat must be real, extreme, and immediate. The danger may be a physical threat as with an attacker, a long-term threat as with an enemy occupation, or a moral threat as with a gossiping person sure to cause harm. The danger is extreme if it threatens to destroy a higher value.*

- *There is no honest alternative. Even if the honest alternative would require the sacrifice of a lesser value such as money, time, or convenience, it must be chosen.*

- *The good effects of the deception must outweigh the evil ones. You must choose the course of action that will save the highest values and bring about the least evil.*

- *The person or persons being deceived have no right to the truthful information or would use it for evil.*

If a case is determined to justify the use of veiled speech, then the consequences must be weighed and damage prevented before veiled speech may be used. Some listeners, especially little children, may not know when a person is speaking an untruth to save a higher value. We have the responsibility to explain our actions as soon as possible to innocent persons.

---

11. *Give an original example where the use of veiled speech would be justified. Provide reasons for your example. When would it not be justified?*

12. *How does lying for popularity eventually harm one's reputation? Give an example.*

Living a Moral Life: Gifted and Growing

Twelve Steps

The twelve steps of Alcoholics Anonymous (AA) can be applied to anyone who seeks personal growth. The twelve steps below have been modified from the twelve steps of AA.

- **Step One**—*We admit we are powerless over the problem—that our lives have become unmanageable.*

- **Step Two**—*Believe that a Power greater than ourselves can restore us to health.*

- **Step Three**—*Turn our problems over to the care of God. This requires humility.*

- **Step Four**—*Make a searching and fearless moral inventory of ourselves.*

- **Step Five**—*Admit to God, to ourselves, and to another human being the exact nature of our problems.*

- **Step Six**—*Next, have God remove all these defects of character.*

- **Step Seven**—*Humbly ask God to remove our shortcomings and resolve our problems.*

- **Step Eight**—*Make a list of all persons we have harmed or with whom we have problems and begin to make amends with them.*

- **Step Nine**—*Make direct amends to such people whenever possible. Stay with it, be kind and consistent.*

- **Step Ten**—*Continue to observe ourselves and how our behavior affects others.*

- **Step Eleven**—*Seek to improve our conscious contact with God through prayer and meditation.*

- **Step Twelve**—*Carry the message of how God helps us overcome personal problems. Share this truth with others as a way of assisting God's will on earth.*

(Adapted from Al-Anon Twelve Steps)

Bring evidence of dishonesty to public attention as soon as you can.

Bodily integrity: the health of the body is threatened.

Personal Pressure

Your personal efforts to encourage honesty are very important. As an individual, you can exert pressure—on family and team members, or members of groups and clubs to which you belong—to eliminate deception and reward honesty.

If you feel caught in a system that forces people to be dishonest to accomplish goals, you can present alternatives for action to someone in authority. When doing something deceptive is suggested "just for fun," the simple solution is not to go along with the idea. Instead, you can encourage the group to come up with a clever, but honest alternative. You do not give up your responsibility to act morally just because you are a member of a larger group. A single person's influence can be strong enough to prevent the deception.

Don't hesitate to report evidence of dishonest practices to the organization responsible for the actions, or to the local newspaper editor. To protect other citizens, report shoddy business practices to the Better Business Bureau. Alone, you won't be able to change the whole world, but that personal commitment to truthfulness will influence many others.

---

13. *In what other ways can an individual work for a climate of greater truthfulness in society?*

14. *Which step in the Twelve Step program do you find most challenging? Why? Which do you find most appealing? Why?*

Alternatives to Lying

It takes cleverness, creativity, and a compassionate heart to be honest and yet not hurt people unnecessarily. Practicing the following six alternatives to lying will help a person develop these qualities.

PRAYER FOCUS

Christians believe in the teaching that the Holy Spirit dwells within each person. If you truly believe this, then it follows that to know God more intimately is to understand and accept the truth about yourself. When you try to be something you are not, you obscure the picture or truth of yourself, and therefore, distance yourself from the living God. In effect, you live a lie. But when you accept the truth of yourself, you accept the truth of God's plan on earth.

Praying to the Holy Spirit for guidance can help you be an honest person. Here is a prayer to the Holy Spirit.

"Come Holy Spirit, take hold of my life, guard me in your loving way. Guide me in love, preserve me in truth, Spirit come."

Living a Moral Life: Gifted and Growing

The eighth commandment is not limited to protecting truthfulness alone. It also promotes the values of fidelity and honor. Honor is the harmony between your thoughts and your words. Fidelity is the harmony between your words and your deeds. You are faithful when you "keep your word" or "stand up for your beliefs."

Keeping Promises and Secrets

Keeping promises and secrets is one of the basic obligations of human beings to one another. When you confide something personal to another, you entrust something of yourself to his or her safekeeping. It's important to keep secrets if a person's reputation is at stake. It is not necessary to promise directly to protect a reputation. You are obliged by justice to do so.

Revealing a secret maliciously or carelessly is, to some degree, sinful. The seriousness of the revelation depends on your awareness of what you are doing, the importance of the information, and the damage done as a result. If you unintentionally reveal secret information, you are not morally guilty, but if you can you should try to repair the damage that results.

The obligation to keep secrets and promises is a serious one, but it can cease under certain circumstances:

- *if the person to whom the promise was made or who entrusted the secret removes the obligation;*

17. *Share an instance when you revealed a secret and it caused no damage at all.*

18. *Give an example of revealing a secret to get revenge.*

19. *When might you be justified in breaking a promise or in revealing a secret?*

Protecting a Reputation

Your reputation is one of your most precious possessions. Even though a reputation does not always reveal your inner character, it will affect how others think of you. Reputation is what others think of you. It determines the trust people place in you. It affects your ability to make friends, to acquire and hold down a job, to advance in your career, or to lead a happy adult life. A good reputation is easy to lose and, once lost, is very difficult to regain.

Reputations can be lost by doing something that society judges to be bad or by rumors of something considered bad. For some reason, people are more inclined to believe a bad report about someone than a good one. Even after proof of innocence has been shown, a little suspicion seems to linger in the minds of some people.

Detraction and slander are both sinful by their nature because they are intended to hurt another. The seriousness depends on the degree of harm done to his or her good name. We have an obligation to try to repair the damage done by our statements.

Protecting Friends

Loyalty to family, friends, and business colleagues calls for protecting them from harm which can come from sources outside the family or the group. Loyalty in intimate relationships is considered so essential for daily life that it is protected by civil law—a person does not need to testify in court against his or her spouse.

Detraction: taking away from, tearing someone down.

Slander: lying about someone intentionally in an effort to ruin his or her good name.

If you expect your privacy to be respected, you must also learn to respect others' privacy as well.

But loyalty is not the highest value. It may not be used as a cover behind which family or friends abuse others. For example, a child should call the police if his or her parents are endangering each other by physical violence. The values of a good name, of justice, and of emotional or moral well-being are higher than that of blind loyalty. The same principles that justify lying, breaking a promise, or revealing a secret may force a person to choose loyalty to the greater good over loyalty to a friend who is involved in an immoral activity.

Living a Moral Life: Gifted and Growing

Truthfulness in the Bible

Mutual trust is so essential that honesty is one of the basic moral laws found in the Bible. The eighth commandment, "You shall not bear false witness against your neighbor," is aimed at the most critical truth-telling situation the Israelites faced, that of being a legal witness.

The Israelites had no lawyers or juries. The only way someone could get restitution for damage or punish an evildoer was to produce two eyewitnesses who saw the accused person commit the crime. The testimony of these two was enough for conviction, which could mean death. Therefore, it was a serious violation against a fellow Israelite to give false witness. It was considered so serious that if someone were caught lying, he or she received the same punishment the innocent neighbor would have received.

Bearing false witness was not the only lying prohibited by God's law. All forms of trickery and deception aimed at self-advancement or harm were also condemned. The story of Jacob and Esau in Genesis 27 is an example of a condemnation of such trickery. Although Jacob stole Esau's inheritance through deception, Jacob is shown to have suffered doubt and fear all of his life. The Bible traces the enmity between the Jews and the other peoples living in Palestine back to the deception of Jacob.

The prophets spoke out clearly against deception and hypocrisy. They called people back to faithfulness to God and truthfulness toward one another. John the Baptizer is one of the strongest voices to demand honesty calling the Pharisees a "brood of vipers" for their deceptive practices (see Luke 3:7-14). John challenged people to be honest to the roots of their beings.

Restitution: payment for damage done.

Chapter 11   Honesty

Personal privacy is comparable to confidentiality. A person has an inner life that is delicate, vulnerable, and needs protection. That is the underlying need supporting the right to privacy. In general, a person's intimate relationships, conscience, mail, personal possessions, and telephone conversations are as sacred as the person. No one has the right to investigate them through force or deception. Parents should not read their children's mail merely out of curiosity, but they may have an obligation to do so to uncover foul play. Nor should children open mail addressed to parents, even when they know the letter concerns them. The trust that our privacy will be respected and that we will respect others' privacy is so important in our relationships with others that only a very serious reason can justify tampering with it.

A Case in Point

Jocelyn, a reporter on the school's newspaper staff, was jealous of a classmate's success as a cheerleader. In both her Sophomore and Junior years, Jocelyn tried out for the cheerleading squad, and each year she failed. Her classmate, Deana, made the squad each of those years. "It's so unfair that Deana made the team two years in a row," Jocelyn would tell friends. "Nobody thinks she's any good."

Later that year, Jocelyn was writing a story on the cheerleading squad. She interviewed each member of the team about their life goals and ambitions. When it was Deana's turn to be interviewed, Jocelyn decided to ask some really personal questions about Deana's friendship with members of the football team. Deana answered honestly, "I'm not dating anyone on the team. I'm still seeing Zach."

When the school paper was distributed later that week, Deana was quite surprised to read the piece on the cheerleaders. Jocelyn quoted Deana as saying that she was dating the star player, and leading "scorer" on the team. Rumors began to spread among the students, as well as among the school faculty. The cheerleading moderator called Deana in to her office, asking her to explain her involvement with members of the football team. Surprised, she replied that the article was mistaken and that she was

Living a Moral Life: Gifted and Growing

not dating a football player. The moderator, however, publicly suspended her from the squad for violating one of the dating rules of the school.

Other students, especially friends, began teasing her about her involvement with the "star player." Even her boyfriend, Zach, confronted her and demanded that she explain how she could say such things without telling him first. In each case, she told them that she had been misquoted in the newspaper, but many refused to believe her.

Finally, Deana approached the faculty moderator for the school newspaper and explained the incident. The moderator agreed that the action taken by the cheerleading moderator was unfair, and that the story was a defamation of her character. Jocelyn was called to the newspaper moderator's office and asked about the story. She agreed that the comments she wrote were in jest and that she meant no harm by them.

In the next edition of the paper, a public apology was printed. However, Deana still faced the snide remarks and cruel comments of her classmates. Zach broke up with Deana, not sure that he could ever believe or trust her again. Deana was reinstated on the cheerleading squad, but she felt that people viewed her differently. How she wished that article had never been written.

Petty jealousy often leads to cruel gossip. In this case, Deana's whole life was directly affected by Jocelyn's intentional lies. What responsibility does Jocelyn have for Deana's problems? What obligation does Jocelyn have to correct the situation and restore Deana's good name?

Jesus' Honesty

Jesus was the perfect example of an honest person. He never pretended to be more or less than he was. He spoke with authority, but was not boastful. He demanded sincerity from his followers and directly attacked phoniness. He taught his followers to be ready for deception but never to use it. "Behold, I am sending you like sheep in the midst of wolves; so be shrewd as serpents and simple as doves" (Matthew 10:16). He advised them to be simple and clear

Defamation: an attack on a person's good name.

and to avoid exaggeration in their speech. "Let your 'Yes' mean 'Yes' and your 'No' mean 'No.' Anything more is from the evil one" (Matthew 5:37). Saint Paul develops these ideas of Jesus, condemning lying among members of the same Christian family (see Ephesians 4:25, Colossians 3:9, and James 5:19).

---

20. *What does it mean to be loyal to a friend? What would be some examples of when loyalty might conflict with honesty?*

21. *How is privacy essential to the trust shared between parents and children? between friends?*

22. *Give a modern day example of where you need to "be shrewed as serpents and as innocent as doves."*

Summary

- Keep promises and secrets except when keeping them would harm life or a higher value.

- Protect a reputation as carefully as you would a life.

■ Review

1. When may you talk about secret information?

2. When must you reveal a secret?

3. Why is reporting evil doing an essential element of justice?

4. Why is slander a more serious sin than detraction?

5. What was the original meaning of the eighth commandment?

6. Words to Know: slander, detraction, retraction, defamation, restitution.

■ In Your World

Share a situation where gossip hurt a person's reputation. What was the rumor? How did people view this person after hearing the rumor? How did the gossip defame the person's character? What, if anything, was done to make restitution?

■ Cases

Ellen, Toni's closest friend, is the only one who knows Toni is pregnant. She has promised not to tell anyone else. Toni has said that she cannot tell her parents because they love her too much and would be too hurt. She plans to have an abortion very soon. Ellen knows Toni's parents would support her through her pregnancy and has urged Toni to confide in them. Toni says she can't.

■ What are Ellen's alternatives?

■ Is she bound by her promise to Toni? Give reasons.

■ What course of action do you think will achieve the best for Toni?

■ Do you think Ellen would be justified in telling Toni's parents about the pregnancy? Why or why not? In doing so, what would be the risks?

11 Review

■ Study

1. What is the worst form of deception? Why?

2. What is a lie? In what ways does it spread?

3. What are the most common excuses for the use of deceptive speech?

4. How can a relationship with Christ help you to be honest with yourself?

5. Give an example of greed being used as an excuse for lying.

6. Give an example of the justified use of veiled speech. Support your example with reasons.

7. Why is John the Baptizer a good model for us in this competitive, success-seeking society?

8. Give some ways to confront public dishonesty. Use an example.

9. What are the Twelve Steps towards growth?

10. List six alternatives to lying. Explain each.

11. Give an example of where discretion could be used in telling someone a difficult truth.

12. How do counter-questions help avoid telling lies?

13. Under what conditions may you reveal secret information?

14. What is the difference between slander and detraction? Explain.

15. Give an example of when you would be obligated to reveal a secret?

16. What was Jesus' advice concerning the eighth commandment?

17. Why is silence a positive alternative to lying?

◼ Action

1. Use your creativity to write a speech entitled "How to succeed without lying."

2. Debate this statement: "Defamation of character is a worse assault than stealing a person's car or robbing a house."

3. Research types of deception aimed at, or participated in, by teenagers.

4. For a week, do a survey of deception in entertainment. Record how many TV plots revolve around deception. Take note if lies are necessary for the hero's success. Share your findings with the class. Do you think TV deception has an effect on people's dedication to honesty in real life? Explain.

◼ Prayer

1. Apply the Twelve Steps to Spiritual Recovery to a problem you are currently facing. Keep a journal to record your struggles and progress. Share that journal with a trusted friend.

2. Meditate on the words of the "Serenity Prayer." Reflect on some areas in your own life that need healing and might require "Letting go and Letting God."

Serenity Prayer
God,
Grant me the serenity
To accept the things I cannot change,
The courage to change the things I can,
And the Wisdom to know the difference.

True Wisdom

Property, the more common it is, the more holy it is.
—Saint Gertrude

The Purpose of Things

God created everything with a purpose. Our purpose is to use our talents and gifts to praise God and promote the goodness of creation. With the gift of life comes certain responsibilities to humanity. These responsibilities are linked to our mission in life. This mission involves affirming our relationships with nature, with friends and family, with society, and with God. Both the seventh and the tenth commandments address this important mission. To truly succeed in life it is crucial that we learn not to take or even want what belongs to others—whether it's a personal possession, or a resource of the world.

The Winner

Rich took a last sip of cola as Jake, the quiz show announcer, flashed his huge grin on the screen. "Laverne, will you take the $50,000 you've won, or risk it to win the $1 million?"

"Risk it! Risk it!" Rich yelled. "It's so easy!"

"Jake," Laverne answered, "I think I'll take the money now."

"What a dummy!" Rich muttered as he turned off the set. He settled back on the sofa and fell asleep.

"And here's Rich," Jake announced, "back to claim his $1 million prize or risk it for—the all-time jackpot—the entire world! Well, Rich, what's your answer?"

Rich stood nervously on the bright stage. He had a million dollars. His wife and three children would be set for life! He could quit teaching electronics. Suddenly, he

Making A Moral World

The obligation to give is found in all of the major religions of the world. Devout Muslims practice Zakat—giving a certain percentage of their wealth directly to the poor. Buddhists and Hindus alike emphasize the importance of giving to the poor. In the fourth century, Saint Augustine also advised people to be charitable. He writes, "Find out how much God has given you, and from it take what you need; the remainder which you do not require is needed by others. The superfluities of the rich are the necessities of the poor. Those who retain what is superfluous possess the goods of others" (*Peace and Nonviolence* by Dorothy Day). Sharing possessions shows in a tangible way just how much we care for our neighbor. This is a powerful example of Christian living—following Jesus' commandment to love others.

remembered what his wife, Tina, had said: "Rich, you love teaching. You're a great father, and our boys miss you since you've been so involved with this quiz show. Please stop!"

"Rich, we're waiting." Jake had a note of impatience in his voice. "I'll go for it," Rich answered, relieved that the decision was over. The audience roared with delight. "Your task," Jake said, "is to study the wisdom of the world. After a month, I'll ask you one final question." Rich hid himself from everyone, including his wife and family to prepare for this question. He became so nervous that he could not eat or sleep. At the end of the month, Rich was so weak he could hardly drag himself to the television studio.

"Well, folks, here's Rich back tonight to win the world! Do you know how famous you are, Rich?" Rich didn't care. He didn't want fame, fortune, or anything else. He just wanted the question. "And here's the question: What is the most important thing in the world?" Rich felt faint. "It's so easy, too easy. I wouldn't have had to study at all. Of course the answer is: to win—to win!" He whispered the answer and then fell to the floor.

"No! No! I'm not dead! I don't want it!" Rich screamed as Tina shook him by the shoulders to wake him from his nightmare.

---

1. *What events in Rich's dream struck you as being true? Did you sympathize with Rich at any time?*

2. *What were Rich's priorities? List in order the things he really valued.*

3. *Is there a winner in the story? Who and why?*

Inner Value

The first purpose of creation is to give glory to God by celebrating life and goodness. God doesn't need the world, nor is God greedy for praise. But God's goodness wants to overflow, so God made the angels, the world, and human beings to share the divine life and beauty. The very existence of all these creatures honors and celebrates God.

Living a Moral Life: Gifted and Growing

This purpose may not seem very practical to bargain-conscious Americans, but practicality is simply not the most important value. The most important value is love which witnesses to goodness.

Another purpose of created things is to reveal God. Every work of art expresses the personality and uniqueness of the artist. So, too, everything in the world can tell you something about the mystery of God. In fact, it is through the created world that God speaks to us most of the time. A third purpose of the world is to offer us God's gifts. Besides telling us about God, things are gifts—wonderful treasures that money can't buy. A mirror, for example, holds God's gifts of truth and humor. A pillow offers God's comfort.

Since the world is full of God, everything in it is sacred. The sacredness of all things requires that you respect them and use them reverently, avoiding waste and neglect. You will only find these hidden gifts if you are gentle, generous, patient, and willing to be surprised. If you see only the price tag on things, you will miss God's best gifts.

Material things do not insure happiness.

Using your gifts can help to reveal God's mystery.

Praise of God the Creator

Bless the Lord, O my soul!

In wisdom you have wrought them all—the earth is full of your creatures; The sea also, great and wide, in which are schools without number of living things both small and great, And where ships move about with Leviathan, which you formed to make sport of it.

They all look to you to give them food in due time.

When you give it to them, they gather it; when you open your hand, they are filled with good things. If you hide your face, they are dismayed; if you take away their breath, they perish and return to their dust. When you send forth your spirit, they are created, and you renew the face of the earth.

May the glory of the Lord endure forever; may the Lord be glad in his works! He who looks upon the earth, and it trembles; who touches the mountains, and they smoke! I will sing to the Lord all my life; I will sing praise to my God while I live.

Pleasing to him be my theme; I will be glad in the Lord.

May sinners cease from the earth, and may the wicked be no more.

Bless the Lord, O my soul. Alleluia (Psalm 104:1-4, 24-35).

The Practical Side

The world also has many practical purposes. You depend on the earth for food, clothing, shelter, and air. These are nature's useful gifts. Further, being a creature of intelligence, curiosity, and creativity, you develop your talents by properly using the earth's natural resources. Arts such as sculpture or painting are a combination of human creativity

Living a Moral Life: Gifted and Growing

and nature. Human scientific genius applied to practical problems produces such technological wonders as electrical generators, freeways, power tools, and computers.

Setting Priorities

You need things for your physical, emotional, intellectual, spiritual, and social well-being. But it is important that the things you need are placed in their proper places in your life. Wisdom is the virtue that helps you put first things first. Wisdom will guide you to love good things in the right order. It will prevent a good thing from becoming so important to you that it controls your life. You can gain wisdom by praying for it, by studying Jesus' wise choices, and by observing wise people you know.

Technology is a gift which allows humans to be more productive and creative.

---

4. *Jesus used and spoke about things as signs of God. How do created things reflect God?*

5. *Give an example from Jesus' life showing his enjoyment of material things.*

Summary

■ Respect material things because they are gifts of God for your use and pleasure.

■ Use things wisely and don't let them become substitutes for God in your life.

Leviathan: either a mythological sea monster or some living sea creature, such as a dolphin.

SECTION 1
Checkpoint!

◼ Review

1. What is the purpose of material things in human life?

2. Why is the whole earth sacred?

3. Why is wisdom needed in the use of material things?

4. How do you go about setting priorities with respect to material goods? Explain.

5. Words to Know: priority, wisdom.

◼ In Your World

1. Give one practical example of someone you know making a wise choice in the use of possessions or money.
   Why is their use wise? Contrast it with an example showing how things were substituted for God in a person's life.

2. Rank these items in order of preference for your future life: financial success ＿＿; attractive spouse ＿＿; inner peace ＿＿; travel and excitement ＿＿; career success ＿＿; respect of friends ＿＿; physical attractiveness ＿＿; opportunity to serve humanity ＿＿. Compare your answers in class.

◼ Cases

Discuss the purpose behind each of the following uses of resources. Identify the resource and how its use may or may not reflect God's purpose. Support your opinions with reasons.

1. A botanist discovers a unique type of mold that can be grown more efficiently than that used for penicillin, yet accomplish the same effect.

2. A scientist in New Mexico invents a more efficient way of fashioning plutonium into atomic weapons.

3. A rancher razes 5,000 acres of redwoods to make room for his cattle.

4. A wealthy investor uses her profits to support research in ways to develop arid lands for food production.

Living a Moral Life: Gifted and Growing

SECTION 2
Sharing the Earth

Who actually owns the earth? Each nation? The United Nations? Each person who has a legal title to a plot of ground? The group with the strongest military might? The people who have lived in one place the longest? The question of land ownership is both a legal and a moral one. American law provides one answer: The person who holds legal title to the land owns the land and can do with it what he or she wishes. Native American beliefs offer a second answer: The land belongs to the creator. We only live upon the land and use it because of the goodness of the creator. Scripture teaches a third answer similar to that of the Native Americans: We are stewards of this land. It belongs to God who has left it for us to use and improve. It is not ours to do with as we wish.

God's Creation

Christians believe the earth belongs to God, but also to the human family. Furthermore, some of the earth's gifts can be claimed by individuals as personal property. All these competing rights of ownership must be balanced with justice.

God created the earth from nothing and continues to be with it as it grows and changes. God has placed the world in the care of human beings. Outside forces such as demons or fate do not control the earth. That is one of the meanings of this Biblical command: "Have dominion over the fish of the sea, the birds of the air, and all the living things that move on the earth" (Genesis 1:28). The command also means that the human family should use intelligence, guided by wisdom, to develop the earth's potential. The earth's purpose, as well as the basic rights of all human beings, must be respected. This includes the right to private ownership of property.

What can you do to respect the earth?

Some rights that have to be balanced with the right to private ownership are these: the right of every person to have food and medical care; the right to education and dignified work; the right to worship freely; the right to live in a healthy environment; the right to a fair share of the earth's natural resources; the right to enough freedom to develop one's talents as one sees fit; the right to pass on to one's children a safe and healthy earth as a home.

The Need to Share

God is not a corporate president who hires certain executives to run the world for their profit. God is a father who expects every son and daughter to care for one another and to interact intelligently and compassionately. Since God gives everything as a gift, not as a deserved reward, God expects us to share the earth's riches with one another.

The Gospel is clear. To be a follower of Jesus, we must share the material goods that we possess beyond what we need for a decent life. If we have more than what we need, we must share with those who have less. This is not, according to Jesus, an optional act of charity, but a point of justice, a necessity, a duty.

By collecting money from others through taxes, the civil government tries to help people who can't support themselves. The reality is that no individual enjoys paying taxes. Some avoid paying taxes by finding legal loopholes, while others try to cheat. By not paying the taxes we legally owe, we cheat the person who depends upon the government for support. Many people feel that tax laws, as written, unfairly favor the wealthy. This may or may not be the case, but justice seems to oblige the well-to-do to give much in return.

Even if you do not yet pay taxes, you are called by Jesus to help others live more human lives by sharing what you have. This doesn't mean making yourself destitute in the process. What it does require is that you be concerned about others, sharing even if you have only a little. Exactly how much to give depends on many things, and you and your family need to make the decision. Some basic human needs are these: food, adequate shelter, decent clothes,

Living a Moral Life: Gifted and Growing

medical care, education, means of transportation, means of recreation and celebration, possessions that have personal value because of relationships, such as photographs, hand-made gifts and family heirlooms, works of art.

One way that Christians give to the poor is through their local church communities. Collections are taken up regularly for the support of the parish, for national and international needs, for the poor, the hungry, and those who need a special hand. In this way the collective effort of the Church goes much farther than individual efforts ever could.

In the first centuries of Christianity, bishops of the Church preached the duty of sharing. Their words are very strong:

- *"You are not making a gift of your possessions to the poor person. You are handing over to him what is his. The rich are in the possession of the goods of the poor, even if they have acquired them honestly or inherited them legally"* (Saint Ambrose—fourth century).

- *"Do not say, 'I am using what belongs to me.' You are using what belongs to others. All the wealth of the world belongs to everyone in common, as do the sun, air, earth, and all the rest...Don't neglect your brother and sister in their distress while you decorate God's house. Your brother and sister are more truly God's temple than any church building"* (Saint John Chrysostom—fourth century).

- *"You must not try to distinguish between the deserving and the undeserving...It is better to benefit the undeserving than, in avoiding this, to miss the good"* (Sheperd of Hermas, an unknown early Christian writer—second century).

How does your local church community respond to the homeless people in your neighborhood?

Christian Principles

Christian principles governing the use of material things hold true for everyone, but their application must be made individually. People need not apply principles in the same way. Neither should someone adapt another's application of principles, nor neglect them altogether. The principles are these:

- *Put first things first: Seek God's will before worrying about material things.*

- *Don't hurt people to save money. Let money make people happy (see John 12:3-8).*

- *The more we have, the more we must share (see Luke 12:48).*

- *Distinguish between needs and luxuries. Don't pile up luxuries (see Matthew 19:23-26).*

- *Respect and care for possessions as if they were God's property.*

- *Use possessions for your personal benefit. Don't let possessions own you. Don't waste or neglect them.*

- *Don't depend on possessions for happiness (see Matthew 5:3).*

6. *What practical applications do these words, addressed to wealthy adults centuries ago, have for you today?*

7. *How does each principle for the use of possessions relate to your life? How did Rich, in the story of "The Winner," neglect these principles?*

Living a Moral Life: Gifted and Growing

8. *What are some of the benefits, besides the knowledge that they are doing God's will, that come to generous people?*

9. *America has often been accused of being a "throw-away society." Explain why someone might say this.*

Questions Teens Ask

■ **Q.** *Do you have a responsibility to give to poor people when you know their poverty is their own fault?*

A. Christian charity is not determined by fault, but by need. If someone has more than he or she needs and others, for whatever reason, don't have enough, yes, we have a responsibility to that person.

■ **Q.** *Is it morally wrong to see someone steal and not report it?*

A. We have a double moral obligation: to protect ourselves and to try to correct injustice to the extent of our power. If the thief is a friend, our silence may seem like approval for his or her actions. We do have an obligation, for his or her sake, to speak to the friend or to let someone in authority know of the problem. If reporting the theft would directly endanger an innocent person, then use extreme care. But remember, the police are very careful to protect the anonymity of criminal witnesses.

■ **Q.** *Is it acceptable to keep something that someone gave you if it is stolen?*

A. We become an accessory to the crime if we accept stolen property. If the property is known to be stolen, then it should be reported. Accepting stolen property knowingly is certainly an immoral act.

■ ***Q.*** *Why do I have a responsibility for the poor if I have no involvement with them?*

A. Jesus said that every person is a brother or a sister to him. Since that makes us a brother or sister to each other, we are responsible to the extent of our power to help. A good example of this principal in action involves an eleven-year-old boy who saw a television report about homeless people sleeping on downtown streets. He asked his father if he could take some blankets to them. The boy took some old blankets and cups of soup and gave these to the people he and his dad found on the street. No civil laws will force us to take action for those in need. Jesus, however, invites us as his followers to do so.

PRAYER FOCUS

Jesus said, "For where two or three are gathered together in my name, there I am in the midst of them" (Matthew 18:20). Jesus requested that we share with the poor and that we work for peace and justice in the world. Jesus assured us that we would not be alone in these efforts, especially when we come together in his name. This is the power of group prayer. We have the strength and guidance of Jesus' presence within the community.

One way we can respond with Christian charity is to give of our time in soup kitchens or other community projects.

Living a Moral Life: Gifted and Growing

■ **Q.** *Sometimes I wonder if giving things to poor people is wrong because it hurts their pride and makes them feel degraded. Is it better not to give?*

A. The dignity and self-respect of every person is of utmost importance. We must respect that dignity and not humiliate others by our charity. If there is a way to help another maintain and preserve his or her dignity, then we must do so. One of the best ways to respect others' dignity is to ask them for their help, thus enabling them to pay for the services rendered. By acting in this way we preserve the dignity of others.

---

10. *When might you have an obligation not to share your personal talents or material possessions with others? Give an example.*

11. *How could a person morally justify taking material goods from wealthy individuals who refuse to share with the poor? Explain.*

Summary

■ Things necessary for life belong to everyone: air, food, and water. These items must be protected by all and shared with all.

■ You must share with others what you have over and above what you truly need.

S E C T I O N 2
Checkpoint!

■ Review

1. What rights must be considered when you defend the right to own property?

2. Explain: "Sharing one's abundance is a duty, not an option."

3. How can you determine how much of your property you should personally share with those in greater need?

4. List the seven Christian principles that should be applied to the use of material things.

5. Words to Know: destitute, luxury, rights, necessity.

■ In Your World

Make two columns. Head one "Simple Recreations" and head the other "Luxury Recreation." In groups, list as many items under each as possible. Simple recreations focus on the creativity of people having fun together, while luxury recreations demand expensive objects, clothes and settings. An example of simple recreation would be playing charades and eating popcorn. Luxury recreation would be season tickets to a professional sports team. Then, as a class, discuss types of recreation that combine elements of simplicity and luxury.

■ Cases

Advertising promotes many objects as if they were necessary for life. Look at the following list and decide which of these things are optional and which are essential to your life. Be prepared to share your reasons with the class:

■ a 4-Wheel drive vehicle;

■ a speedboat;

■ a television set for every family member;

■ a VCR;

■ a luxury car;

■ a second home or condominium;

■ clothes with designer labels;

■ a horse or pet.

Living a Moral Life: Gifted and Growing

SECTION 3
Abuses that Hurt Everyone

A Chinese curse goes, "May you get all that you wish for." Wouldn't getting everything you ever wanted be more like an answer to a prayer than a curse? The answer, of course is "No." Part of being human is that we wish for more than we can possibly ever use. Even when we have more than we need, we tend to want more, especially if someone else has something we don't. Humans are affected by the sins of greed and envy.

Many of the evils in the world result from greed and envy. These passions promote actions that disrupt our moral life. They harm our relationship with others and God by promoting our own selfish interests.

Envy

Envy is the desire that another will lose a possession or an honor that you do not have. Envious people reason illogically that they should have what someone else has and be considered equal with the other person in every way. They refuse to accept their uniqueness and tend to judge themselves as inferior to others. They judge others to be somehow at fault in having more or in being better. They feel the need to cut down to size those with greater possessions by taking away those possessions.

The sin of envy is not in wishing to have something more. In fact, the desire for a better life may urge us to work harder. Rivalry and a competitive spirit can be good things when they are balanced by a sense of one's own mission and respect for others. The sin of envy occurs when people fail to recognize the many good things they already possess and the valuable persons they are. Envious people can't enjoy their own treasures.

Jealousy is not the same as envy, although the two ideas are often used synonymously. Jealousy is a strong protectiveness of what one already possesses. Jealousy can be a good thing. The Bible calls God "jealous" of our love. Jealousy may become sinful if it grows into an excessive, unreasonable fear that others will steal what belongs to us. It breeds suspicion and hate. It makes life unbearable for one's family, especially if a spouse is a "jealous lover." Many crimes of violence are committed out of jealousy.

Here are a few suggestions to help combat feelings of envy or jealousy:

- *Thank God for your unique talents and gifts.*

- *Tell God why you sincerely like yourself.*

- *Talk to God about any person you hate or would like to see have bad luck. Ask God to bless that person.*

- *Think about the only success that matters, that of doing God's will for you. That will bring you a unique reward that no one can take from you.*

Greed

Greed, avarice, and covetousness are the exaggerated desires to possess things, not so much to enjoy them, but to control them. When greedy people are not using their energy to acquire things, they are worrying about losing what has already been acquired.

Greed is evil because it makes the greedy one a slave to his or her possessions, raising material things to the status of a god. Greedy people spend their time, energy, and affection on things rather than on God and other people. They are no longer free even to love themselves for who they are, only for what they have. They neglect caring for the poor, since they can think only about protecting their own property.

Jesus tells us that "No one can serve two masters. He will either hate one and love the other, or be devoted to one and despise the other. You cannot serve God and mammon" (Matthew 6:24). Not surprisingly, greedy people fail

Living a Moral Life: Gifted and Growing

Greed makes people slaves to their possessions.

to use their precious possessions reasonably. They see their possessions only as status symbols, objects that make them more important in others' eyes. Greed reduces every-thing—whether it is a spouse, an athletic skill, a musical talent, or the gift for making people laugh—to its monetary value. "For the love of money is the root of all evils, and some people in their desire for it have strayed from the faith and have pierced themselves with many pains" (1 Timothy 6:10).

The basic message of the tenth commandment is that greed or covetousness is evil. "You shall not covet your neighbor's wife, nor his male or female slave, nor his ox or ass, nor anything that belongs to him" (Exodus 20:17). God is making it clear to us that there is evil not only in taking that which belongs to another, but even in desiring it so strongly. The prophets of the Hebrew Scriptures—Old Testament—were very strong in their condemnation of greedy people, especially because they were the ones most capable of caring for the helpless and the poor (see Isaiah 5:8; Jeremiah 5:27; and Amos 2:6, 3:15, 4:1, 8:4-6).

Jesus, too, condemned greed, and insisted that his people have an active concern for their neighbors. He said that the nearest person in need is your neighbor. The two parables of the Rich Man and Lazarus (Luke 16:19-31) and

Greed: the excessive need to own things.

Avarice: insatiable desire for things.

Covetousness: wanting someone else's property.

Mammon: an Aramaic word for wealth or property.

the Good Samaritan (Luke 10:29-37) show clearly Jesus' teaching on generosity. Recall that the rich man seems to have committed no sin in getting his wealth. He simply remained unconcerned about his poor brother. Notice, too, that the Good Samaritan was very personally concerned with the wounded man, as if they were blood relatives.

Theft

According to the FBI, most of the crimes reported in the United States are property crimes. Over half the rest of the crimes involve attacks on persons with the intent to rob.

Theft (stealing) is taking people's property against their will by force (burglary and robbery) or by deception (fraud). Usury, another form of theft, refers to lending money at unjust interest rates.

All forms of stealing are immoral. However, in cases where a person's life is at stake, the right to life comes before the right of ownership. For example, you would be justified in taking food if you or another is starving, there is no other way to obtain food, and the person with the food is not also in grave need. Or, if someone desperately needed transportation to obtain emergency medical aid, you could use a car without permission, provided you returned the car after the emergency.

Shoplifting is a crime affecting all areas of society. You pay more because of other people's thievery.

Living a Moral Life: Gifted and Growing

The Seventh Commandment

The seventh commandment, "You shall not steal" (Exodus 20:15), originally meant "You shall not kidnap a fellow Israelite and make him or her as a slave." It was easy in the life style of the Jewish people to kidnap a person and sell him or her to a caravan passing through on its way to another country. This act would deprive a member of the community his or her freedom to live and to worship the Lord God. Death was the penalty for kidnapping (see Exodus 21:16; Deuteronomy 24:7).

New Testament writers extended the meaning of this commandment to prohibit theft of anyone's personal property. What you own is, in a way, a part of yourself and gives you freedom. Stealing attacks human dignity. It also breaks down trust among people. It may deprive persons of their means of livelihood and of significant personal possessions.

◆

The seriousness of the theft is determined by the value of the stolen property, as well as the need of the victim. That means that while it is morally wrong to steal from a wealthy person (except in cases where a life is in danger), it is doubly wrong to steal from a poor person.

There are many excuses for stealing. "The owner has so many, one won't be missed." "I get ripped off, so I'm just getting even." "I get a thrill out of being clever enough not to get caught." "I want something for nothing." "I'm not paid enough, the company owes it to me." The underlying motive for such excuses is usually greed or selfishness. No excuse, except to save a life, ever justifies stealing.

Many people think that stealing is mostly done by the poor. In reality, most of the money stolen in this country is taken by respectable—well-dressed, hard-working, intelligent—citizens. "White collar" criminals embezzle money

Embezzle: to steal money through fraudulent bookkeeping or accounting practices.

from their companies, cheat on their income tax returns, pad expense accounts, pay unjust wages, and deceive customers. Only wealthy thieves can afford to buy stolen art objects or gems. The Savings and Loans fiasco of the 1980s and 90s, which is costing each U.S. citizen thousands of dollars, is a contemporary example of "white collar" crime. Many shoplifters carry credit cards or enough cash to pay for the items taken, and statistics tell us that clerks and employees steal more than four times as much as customers. Once again, stereotypes are misleading. Theft, either by poor junkies, multi-millionaires, or teenagers on a lark, is immoral and almost never justifiable.

Fraud

Fraud is stealing someone's goods under the pretense of legality, usually by promising one thing and delivering something else, or nothing at all. An example would be someone offering to sell you an expensive watch well below the regular price. You think you're getting a steal. The watch falls apart soon after you buy it because it really is cheaply made—not the original at all. Now you recognize which end of the steal you were on. Home "improvement" companies sometimes travel from city to city, collect deposits for their services, and then never return to do the job. False advertising, check forgery, and unjust insurance collections are all forms of fraud. All are legally and morally wrong.

How can you prevent yourself from becoming a victim of fraud? Here are some suggestions.

- *Never expect something for nothing.*
- *Never pay for a service or an item until you have received it and are satisfied.*
- *Report any suspicious person to the police or some other authority.*

Values for Life

"Blessed are they who hunger and thirst for righteousness, for they will be satisfied" (Matthew 5:6). The social implications of the Sermon on the Mount are obvious. As Christians we have a responsibility to work for justice in our society. Those who hunger and thirst for justice are those who passionately feel the needs of others. The opportunity to work, earn a living, find food and shelter, and be treated with human dignity are the issues that should concern every devout Christian.

Living a Moral Life: Gifted and Growing

12. *What are other excuses for stealing? What are the flaws in each of these reasons?*

13. *How can you tell when a "good deal" is really stolen property?*

Respecting Other's Property

Respecting another person's property is a way of showing respect for that person as well. There are ways of not respecting someone's right to property other than stealing it. These ways include acts of vandalism, borrowing someone else's belongings without permission, and not attempting to find the owner of lost property. A more common problem is borrowing something with permission, and then, because of accident or carelessness, the object is ruined.

Martin owns a couple of "old" records, some of the Beatles' original LPs. The records are in good shape with little buzz or hum, and no scratches. Kim asks to borrow them to play at her party. Martin agrees on the condition that the records be treated with care, and that they be handled only by Kim. When Martin arrived at the party he saw someone other than Kim mistreating his prized possessions. Before he could stop the record-mauler, the needle was jerked across the disk and the record, sans cover, was thrown on the floor. Martin was heart-sick. He vowed never to let anyone use anything of his again.

Martin's story is all too common. People borrow things and then treat the other person's property as if it were trash. A rule of thumb to follow when borrowing property is to treat it as if it were priceless. Consider what the cost would be if you had to repair or replace the borrowed object. Treat what you borrow with the same respect that you would show the thing's owner.

Vandalism may seem like a lark, but it causes millions of dollars in damage to property each year.

Damage to Property

Violence can be done to public or private property by vandalism, carelessness, or neglect. The seriousness of the moral guilt depends on the damage done to the property, the need of the owner, and the deliberateness of the action. If the damage is the result of an accident, there is no moral guilt, but there is still a moral obligation to attempt to repair the damage.

Vandalism, the deliberate destruction of property, is not only a crime causing millions of dollars of damage annually, it is also the cry of frustrated people in need of constructive channels for their creative energies. Angry people inflict destruction more readily than others.

All forms of theft, fraud, and deliberate damage require restitution before the sin can be forgiven (see Exodus 21:37 and 22:3, 6-8; Numbers 5:5-8). Restitution means to return property that was stolen, to pay for any damage that was done to it, and to reimburse the owner for any loss he or she suffered while it was in the possession of the thief.

Lost and Found

People sometimes justify keeping someone else's property because they found it or they were given it as a result

Living a Moral Life: Gifted and Growing

of an error. But neither finding an item nor receiving it in error justifies keeping it. Both actions are legally and morally wrong.

If the value of the article warrants it, the finder of an article must take reasonable efforts to locate the owner. George Catanolos found a briefcase containing $20,000 in jewelry in a parking garage. When he returned it to the jewelers, he received a $500 reward. His father had done a similar thing after finding a bag of cash that had fallen out of an armored truck. "I trained my children to learn that honesty is the best policy. What's ours is ours. What belongs to somebody else, belongs to somebody else."

A finder does not become the legal owner of a lost article. He or she may keep it, though, after seriously attempting to find the owner. If a person can prove that he or she owned the property, even after a period of time has passed, the item must be returned. Abandoned goods, such as trash, become the property of the finder immediately.

---

14. *Within three minutes, list as many examples as you can of damage, waste, and destruction done to public or private property for whatever reason. Share your list with the class.*

15. *If you caught some neighborhood children puncturing car tires in a parking lot, what would you do?*

Pulling It All Together

As you have seen in this text, living a moral life is a process that continues throughout your life. Learning Catholic moral teachings is the first step, but it must be followed by a lifetime of practice if you are to be a moral person. And that, of course, is the challenge for all Christians, to live as Christ lived—with the true dignity of a human man, with honesty and integrity, concerned for the welfare and dignity of everyone he met.

You can live your life gifted for mission through the wonderful generosity of God, both in your person and in the body of your faith community. Because of the covenant of God with the Hebrew people you have the the gift of the commandments—laws which offer you the experience of the ancients. Through the life and teaching of Jesus you have the Beatitudes and the virtues which you require to live his life. Finally, through God's love, you are given what you need to live as a child of God and, through your living, bring forth new life in the kingdom of God. The gift of your life and what you need to live it are freely given to you by God. Living a moral life is your responsibility.

Summary

- Greed can make a person a slave to material things.

- Envious people often do not feel good about themselves.

- Stealing and fraud are morally wrong.

- Restitution for stolen or damaged property must be made (to the owner of the property) to the best of a person's ability.

- The gifts you need to live a moral life are freely given by God. It is your responsibility to use these gifts wisely.

■ Review

1. What is the difference between envy and jealousy?

2. What social evils flow from greed?

3. When is stealing justified? Use an example to illustrate your answer.

4. Give an original example of fraud.

5. Under what conditions may you keep lost property?

6. Why is restitution a moral duty?

7. Words to Know: restitution, envy, fraud, greed, avarice, covetousness, gluttony, jealousy.

■ In Your World

1. Give some examples of recent vandalism in your area. What may have been some of the reason for the vandalism? What are some creative ways to stop vandalism?

2. What would be a reasonable effort in locating the owner of these items?

   ■ A purebred dog without a collar, found near your yard.

   ■ A wristwatch found in a shopping mall.

   ■ A twenty-dollar bill found in your school hallway.

   ■ A new sweater found in a shopping bag on a bus.

■ Cases

Compare and contrast the morality of each of these pairs. In each set, discuss whether the moral gravity of "A" is the same as "B". Why or why not?

1A. Bert meets a friend who is very poor. This friend tells him that he has had no dinner that day because there was nothing to eat in his home. Bert goes into a baker's shop, and since he has no money, he waits until the baker's back is turned and steals a roll. Then he runs out and gives the roll to his friend.

1B. Patricia goes into a shop. She sees a pretty blouse on a "thrift" table and thinks to herself that it would match her skirt perfectly. So, while the salesperson's back is turned, she steals the blouse and runs away at once.

2A. Gloria had a friend who kept a bird in a cage. Gloria thought the bird was very unhappy. She was always asking her friend to let the bird out, but the friend wouldn't. So, one day when the friend wasn't there, Gloria let the bird fly away.

2B. Juliette took some pain-killing drugs from her sick mom to give to her friends. She later denied taking them.

C H A P T E R

12 Review

■ Study

1. List the various purposes for God's gift of creation.

2. How does wisdom help a person set priorities? Explain.

3. What do the Gospels say about owning an abundant supply of material goods?

4. List the basic human rights that must be upheld when considering the use of private property.

5. What are some basic human needs? In what way are we obligated to meet those needs?

6. How can you determine how much you should give others?

7. How do real needs differ from luxuries? How do you know whether or not a need is in fact a luxury? Explain.

8. Give seven Christian principles for the use of material goods and how they should be applied.

9. How do greedy people view their possessions? How does greed affect one's relationships? Explain.

10. How can envy become sinful?

11. Give an example of justified stealing.

12. How is fraud a form of stealing? How is fraud a form of deception?

13. What must be done before the sin of stealing can be forgiven?

14. What was the original meaning of the seventh commandment? How did that meaning expand in the New Testament?

15. What is your moral obligation when you find lost property?

■ Action

1. Do research on teen shoplifting. Give reasons for it and state possibilities for restitution. Report your findings to the class.

2. Interview two or three elderly people with these questions: How did you learn to regard material things wisely? What monetary decisions that you made in the past are you happiest with now? What are your favorite charities? Why?

3. Debate this statement: "A university which offers a sports scholarship to an athlete and then prohibits him or her from taking more than two classes at a time is guilty of fraud because the athlete never gets a complete education."

■ Prayer

1. As a class, compose a short prayer after giving some thought to what each of these things tells you about God: air, electricity, fire, bees, glass, bricks, windows.

2. Reflect on Jesus' words below. How do they relate to the message of this chapter?

"If you belonged to the world, the world would love its own; but because you do not belong to the world, and I have chosen you out of the world, the world hates you" (John 15:19).

"I do not ask that you take them out of the world but that you keep them from the evil one...As you sent me into the world, so I sent them into the world. And I consecrate myself for them, so that they may be consecrated in truth" (John 17:15, 18-19).

Index